ALAN
TURING
DECODED

ALAN TURING DECODED

The Man They Called Prof

DERMOT TURING

First published 2021

The History Press
97 St George's Place, Cheltenham,
Gloucestershire, GL50 3QB
www.thehistorypress.co.uk

First published in 2015 as 'Prof: Alan Turing Decoded'
This revised and updated edition first published in 2021

British Library Cataloguing in Publication Data.
A catalogue record for this book is available from the British Library.

ISBN 978 0 7509 9867 3

Typesetting and origination by The History Press
Printed and bound in Great Britain by TJ Books Limited, Padstow, Cornwall.

MIX
Paper from
responsible sources
FSC® C013056
www.fsc.org

Trees for LYfe

CONTENTS

INTRODUCTION

Alan Turing is now a household name, and in Britain he is a national hero. There are several biographies, a handful of documentaries, one Hollywood feature film, countless articles, plays, poems, statues and other tributes, and a blue plaque in almost every town where he lived or worked. One place which has no blue plaque is Bletchley Park, but there is an entire museum exhibition devoted to him there.

We all have our personal image of Alan Turing, and it is easy to imagine him as a solitary, asocial genius who periodically presented the world with stunning new ideas, which sprang unaided and fully formed from his brain. The secrecy which surrounded the story of Bletchley Park after World War Two may in part be responsible for the commonly held view of Alan Turing. For many years the codebreakers were permitted only to discuss the goings-on there in general, anecdotal terms, without revealing any of the technicalities of their work. So the easiest things to discuss were the personalities, and this made good copy: eccentric boffins busted the Nazi machine. Alan may have been among the more eccentric, but this now outdated approach to studying Bletchley's achievement belittles the organisation which became GCHQ, and distracts attention from the ideas which Alan, among others, regarded as far more important than curious behaviour.

I am sceptical about that solitary genius picture of Alan Turing. It doesn't fit well with what little was said about him at home during my childhood, and it doesn't fit with the personal recollections of those work colleagues of his with whom I have had opportunities, over the years, to talk. A man called 'Prof' by his friends – who knew he wasn't a professor and so were teasing him, gently – wasn't shut away from intellectual or social interaction. Who, in fact, was Alan Turing, and where did his ideas come from?

Of course, these questions have been explored before and from a variety of angles. Yet some of the people who influenced and mentored Alan have perhaps received less attention than their due: notably, M.H.A. (Max) Newman, who was not only an intellectual equal but also provided a compass to help steer Alan's career and a social anchorage in a less rarefied family setting. There is a temptation to portray Alan as a victim of his childhood and schooling; I don't think that is accurate or fair. There is also a tendency to zoom in on the last tragic years of his life, to view the whole of his existence through that Shakespearian lens, and then to define Alan Turing by reference to his sexuality or suicide. Again, I think that is an error. To complement my personal viewpoint I have had access to new documents and sources which were not available even to Alan's most recent biographer. Moreover, a wealth of material has been made available to me in the form of first-hand recollections of those who lived and worked alongside Alan; I wanted to allow those voices to be heard again.

I have been constantly surprised and delighted by the enthusiasm with which each enquiry I made relating to this project was received. So many people I contacted were willing to volunteer additional information and suggestions, going far beyond any ordinary duty in the help offered to me. I had the privilege of interviewing Donald Bayley and Bernard Richards who were able to share their personal recollections with me and answer my foolish questions – a big thank you for letting me intrude into their lives. I was also allowed to preview documents scheduled for release to The National Archives, not available to previous biographers, and for that I am grateful to the

Director of GCHQ. I should also like to acknowledge in particular the varied contributions of Shaun Armstrong, Jennifer Beamish, Claire Butterfield, Tony Comer, Barry Cooper, Daniela Derbyshire, Helen Devery, Juliet Floyd, Rainer Glaschick, Joel Greenberg, Sue Gregory, Kelsey Griffin, John Harper, David Hartley, Rachel Hassall, Cassandra Hatton, Kerry Howard, Paul Kellar, Miriam Lewis, Barbara Maher, Gillian Mason, Patricia McGuire, Christopher Morcom QC, Charlotte Mozley, Harriet Nowell-Smith, Brian Oakley, James Peters, Brian Randell, Hélène Rasse, David Ridgway, Rachel Roberts, Isobel Robinson, Sir John Scarlett, Lindsay Sedgley, Susan Swalwell, Turings past and present, Cate Watson and Abbie Wood. Nor would I have been able to succeed without the friendly and useful assistance from the staffs of the British Library, Chester Records Office and various local libraries in Cheshire, The National Archives, and the Science Museum; and, in the US, the Library of Congress, the Mudd Manuscript Library at Princeton and the National Archives Records Administration. In none of these places was anyone anything other than welcoming, helpful and informative.

However, I have to pay tribute in particular to Andrew Hodges's masterly biography *Alan Turing: The Enigma*. I bought my copy in February 1984 as soon as it came out. It is a big book and it covers the ground with majesty as well as rigour. Nothing – certainly not what follows between these covers – can possibly stand up to it. It has been my constant reference source. It has stood thirty years without need of fundamental correction. Sure, there are materials available now which were not open to Andrew when he did his research, but these colour in points of detail, and affirm his conclusions where there was limited evidence available to him. My perspective is of course different, otherwise this book would not have been worth writing, but I commend it to the reader whose appetite I have managed to stimulate. Errors are to be blamed on me, not others.

Dermot Turing
St Albans, UK

1

UNRELIABLE
ANCESTORS

It is May 1790. Major-General Medows, the officer commanding Fort St George (later called Madras), has been in office for three months. His governing council is not behaving in the manner which suits him, and the war with Tipu Sultan – stirred up by the French, of course, notwithstanding their own domestic upheavals – has reached a critical phase. The General needs to go on campaign, and he needs to leave a sound man, or ideally some sound men, in charge of the council in his absence. There is nothing for it. John Turing, who was put onto the council by the General in February, and has shown he can be depended upon, will take over as Acting President.

John Turing has a long and respectable history in Fort St George. Indeed, the Turing family has been a pillar of the community since anyone can remember. Dr Robert Turing arrived in Fort St George in 1729 and was a surgeon in the district until the early 1760s; he even treated Sir Robert Clive in 1753. Dr Robert Turing's daughter Mary is married to John – they are second cousins. Mary knows everybody: 'by the marriages of her family and relatives [she is] connected with half the settlement'.[1] Dr Turing's house is being talked about, now that war has flared up again: in the Siege of Madras in 1758 the French approached the town through his garden, of all things. Mary isn't going to let the citizens of Fort St George forget this. Another Robert Turing, another cousin, is serving in the Madras Army; in full time he will retire grandly to Banff Castle in Scotland and pick up the family baronetcy. John and Mary's son William is serving as Paymaster too, and in 1813 he will be killed in Spain at the battle of Vitoria. The Turings are an Empire family, sound but not famous.

In 1790 the Turings are also reading the *Madras Courier*, which has over the years carried the gossip from home. One scandal concerns another ancestor of Alan Turing, and this particular one is both unsound and infamous. One might expect that the main influences on a child born to Edwardian parents, in the Indian Empire, out of the house and lineage of the Turing family rooted in the Indian Empire, would be from the father's side. But, while the influence of old-fashioned patriotic service is relevant to Alan's upbringing and early years, greater direction on his life was given from Alan's mother's side, the Stoney family. And of all of Alan Turing's ancestors, the best-known and most scandalous is Andrew Robinson Bowes, born Andrew Robinson Stoney in 1747.

A close shave in heredity

Thomas Stoney immigrated to Ireland in the 1690s, when William III encouraged Protestants to settle there. His grandson Andrew entered the Army, married Hannah Newton in 1768 for her money, and is said to have 'locked his wife in a closet that would barely contain her, for three days, in her *chemise* (some say without it), and fed her with an egg a day'.[2] To establish his right to a life interest in Hannah's fortune after her death, Andrew Stoney had to prove that a child had been born alive; unfortunately all were stillborn, though that did not stop Stoney from ordering the church bells rung in order to rig the evidence. Being nurtured on an egg a day, and required to produce live children notwithstanding, meant Hannah died in 1775. But this merely opened the field for Stoney to try for the biggest fortune in Europe. Mary Eleanor Bowes was worth over a million pounds.

Her father's will obliged any man who married her to take the name of Bowes; when her husband, the Earl of Strathmore, died in 1776 she was in the market. Everyone was after her, and the hot favourite was a Mr George Gray, who had held some office in India under Sir Robert Clive. Indeed, the noble Countess had been carrying on for some time with Mr Gray. Stoney was not going to be put off by any of this. Acting in cahoots with the newspaper editor, an article was run in the *Morning Post* which alluded offensively to Lady Strathmore. Stoney took it upon himself to defend the Countess's honour and call out the editor; the two of them staged an encounter at the Adelphi, at which Stoney appeared to have been mortally wounded. The Countess took pity on the one lover who had defended her honour and − a low-risk stratagem, given his imminent demise − agreed to marry him. Four days later, Stoney was carried into St James's Church, Westminster, where the ceremony took place.

Unfortunately for the Countess, Stoney did not do the considerate thing, and remained obstinately alive. Unfortunately for Stoney, the Countess had already become pregnant by Mr Gray − a state of affairs which, with every passing day, more urgently demanded to be covered up with a marriage to somebody, perhaps anybody − so with all that in mind she had settled all her estate on trust in such a way that it was out of reach of any convenient, or, as the case might be, inconvenient, husband. But Stoney was equal to this challenge. He recovered from his fatal wound with alacrity, assumed the name Bowes, coerced his wife into making a new Deed to revoke her trust settlement, locked her up wherever there was an available closet, felled her trees, sold her estates, gambled away her money, got the wet-nurse pregnant, raped the nursery maid, and told everyone who enquired that the Countess was a little mad. After some years of this treatment she was, with the aid of her lady's maid, able to escape, and she started legal proceedings in the labyrinthine complexity of the Georgian courts, to have Stoney Bowes bound over to keep the peace, to have the Deed of Revocation annulled, and to obtain the unthinkable: a divorce. As usual Stoney Bowes was unfazed. As insurance against such unwifely behaviour, he had directed the Countess to write a lengthy account of her own wild behaviour, her extramarital affairs, and the true parenthood of her children. The Confessions were brandished in various courtrooms, but they merely served to prolong the litigation and ensure that the case received the maximum attention in the press, such as the *Madras Courier*. Stoney Bowes was confined to prison – but in those days he could buy (with his wife's money) the plushest suite and days out on licence, and he had sufficient liberty to sire two children with the daughter of a fellow inmate. In the words of Dr Foot, the surgeon who had patched up Stoney Bowes's fake wounds after the fake duel back

How odd, or not, it is that Andrew Robinson Stoney, Thomas Stoney's eldest son, has not been mentioned on the Stoney family monument? (Author)

in 1777, Stoney Bowes was 'cowardly, insidious, hypocritical, tyrannic, mean, violent, selfish, jealous, revengeful, inhuman and savage, without a single countervailing quality'.

Alan Turing was descended from the Stoneys on his mother's side. John Turing, Alan's brother, noted thankfully that Stoney Bowes 'was a collateral, but it was a close shave in heredity'.[3] Despite the high risks arising from being nearly descended from Stoney Bowes, it was the Stoney family inheritance which shaped Alan's ideas and laid the foundation for his breakthroughs in mathematics, engineering and science. Stoney Bowes was the exception: the rest of the Stoneys were not schemers, womanisers, gamblers and deceivers. In fact, by the end of the Victorian era the Stoneys had piled up an immense portfolio of achievements.

The descendants of Stoney Bowes's two brothers were glittering:

- George Johnstone Stoney FRS (1821–1911). This extraordinary scientist published 75 papers during his career, on subjects including optics, gas theory and cosmic physics. He is probably best known for coining the word 'electron' when he was arguing for units of measurement to be based on real physical things – in the case of electricity, the unit of electrical charge which flows when a single chemical bond is ruptured. But to a Victorian eye, one of his most astonishing decisions was to ensure his brainy daughters Edith and Florence were given a head-start in life equal to their brothers.
- Edith Anne Stoney (1869–1938). George Johnstone Stoney's eldest daughter was sent to Cambridge to study mathematics, where she achieved 17th place in the formidable final exams. After lecturing in physics at three universities and teaching at Cheltenham Ladies' College, Edith became President of the Association of Science Teachers, and served in the Great War as a radiologist in France, Serbia and Greece, being awarded the *Croix de Guerre*.
- Florence Ada Stoney OBE (1870–1932). Florence was a consultant radiologist. In addition to her various hospital appointments, like her sister she served in the Great War, notably during the bombardment of Antwerp in 1914, in France, and in London,

using her skills to locate foreign bodies embedded in the flesh of the wounded. She was awarded the Admiralty Star as well as becoming an OBE.

- Bindon Blood Stoney FRS (1828–1909). Bindon was George Johnstone Stoney's brother. He was a railway engineer, wrote a treatise on strains in girders, and reconstructed the port of Dublin to accommodate deep-water ships, which involved inventing a method for placing huge concrete blocks weighing 350 tons apiece. For these and other achievements he is known, without irony, as 'the father of Irish concrete'.

- George Gerald Stoney FRS (1863–1942). George worked as chief designer in the Steam Turbine Department of Sir Charles Parsons's company. In this capacity George enjoyed a moment of triumph aboard *Turbinia*, the experimental steam-turbine yacht part-designed by him. The yacht caused consternation by disobeying all the rules at the Queen's Diamond Jubilee Review in 1897. By weaving in and out of the other craft at 34 knots and outpacing the Admiralty police vessels, it showed that bulky, slow, old-fashioned reciprocating engines were no longer appropriate for the propulsion of dreadnoughts. Later, George became Professor of Mechanical Engineering at the Manchester College of Technology, as well as serving on the panel of the Admiralty Board of Invention and Research.

- Francis Goold Morony Stoney (1837–97). Francis was also an engineer. After a stint in India, working on the Madras Railway, he designed and patented a series of sluices, used in places such as the Manchester Ship Canal, the Rhône, the Clyde, and posthumously the old Aswan Dam.

- Edward Waller Stoney CIE (1844–1931). Edward went to India in 1866 and served as a railway engineer in Madras for many years, becoming Chief Engineer in 1899 and being decorated as a Companion of the Order of the Indian Empire in 1904. He wrote numerous technical papers on bridges, flooding and other railway topics, and was a fellow of Madras University. It was in his house in Coonoor, Madras province, that E. W. Stoney's daughter Ethel Sara lived with her husband Julius Turing.

And this is just to mention those Stoney descendants who carried the name Stoney. In *Who Was Who 1929–1940*, there are three entries for Stoneys but none for Turings. With this array of Stoney achievements, nothing the undistinguished Turings had done was going to measure up. Since the early days of Empire, the Turings had been soldiers and vicars and merchants; they had been established in England, the Netherlands, and Indonesia as well as India; they had been conventional, upper middle class, impoverished, occasionally snobbish and always unexceptional. It was, however, the Empire that brought the Turings into contact with the Stoneys; although the laws of symmetry suggest that the contact should have come about through the province of Madras, in fact it arose from the state of poverty.

The importance of being poor

According to the parish council website, in 1334 the Vicar of Edwinstowe was convicted of venison trespasses. The vicars holding the living of Edwinstowe in the nineteenth century were more law-abiding, but correspondingly hungry. On 8 October 1879, the incumbent celebrated the birth of a healthy boy, bringing to eight the number of children (not counting the two who died in infancy) that had to be fed and clothed from his stipend. The parish council website also suggests that parishioners had the privilege of letting their pigs root for acorns in Sherwood Forest, but rooting for acorns might be unbecoming for a vicar. So the System was introduced: on Sundays, there was a 'great spread' of roast beef or similar; on Mondays, there were leftovers; and on Tuesdays to Saturdays inclusive, there was bread, dripping and cocoa. In 1883, aged only 58, the vicar suffered a stroke and had to resign even this insufficient living, and the family moved to Bedford. Shortly afterwards he died. Julius Mathison Turing, the fifth of the eight children, was ten.

The Turings did not speak of how they managed to ride this terrible storm. The eldest girl, then aged 21 and known to posterity as Aunt Jean, took over the management of the house. Aunt Jean was

The senior generation – Grandpa Stoney and Aunt Jean. (Author)

a formidable character – allegedly the only person of whom Alan Turing's mother Ethel Sara was truly afraid. Later in life Aunt Jean married (and ruled over) Sir Herbert Trustram Eve, and served as a councillor for 12 years after the Great War, representing the Municipal Reform Party on the London County Council. Her training was in the Turing household of the 1880s. Aunt Jean and the other two eldest children, also girls, also resourceful, earned money through teaching, enough to keep the boys at school: Arthur and Julius at Bedford, and in due course the younger ones Harvey and Alec at Christ's Hospital in London. Sybil, the girl between Julius and Harvey, went to Cheltenham Ladies' College, and became a missionary in India when she was old enough to fly the nest; India was the destiny for Arthur and Julius as well. Bedford School was a feeder for the services, military as well as civil, in India, and these were genteel, but more importantly well-paid, occupations. Arthur headed for the remunerative staff corps in the Indian Army, until aged 27 he lost his life fighting for the 36th Sikhs in a skirmish on the North-West Frontier in 1898. Julius was bound for the Indian Civil Service.

The legacy of childhood for Julius was a lifelong obsession with accounts. Alan's brother John wrote:

> When I first left school and was articled to a firm of solicitors in London, I was allowed £5 a month for my expenses, including the midday meal, and a separate allowance for clothes. This was not ungenerous but there was one fly in the ointment: I was bidden to submit a monthly balanced account. Great was my father's chagrin when he discovered that 'umbrella repairs' figured in three monthly accounts out of four and that a mistake in casting showed 2/9d in his favour for which I had failed to give him credit! The maddening thing was that I *did* spend the money in umbrella repairs but, being a Turing, I never thought to add verisimilitude to truth by making it something else.

And again:

> On one occasion when we were on holiday in Wales, there arrived a bill from a Harley Street specialist for a consultation to which my mother had taken my brother and myself for advice on our hay-fever. The fee was ten guineas – a large sum in those days. There was considerable dudgeon and my father cried out loudly from the breakfast table that he was ruined. This sticks in my memory as one of the deeper dudgeons.

But, in India, Julius met his match. On completion of his studies at Bedford School, Julius Turing won a scholarship to read history at Corpus Christi College, Oxford. And there he sat the Indian Civil Service exam, passing high in the list. (Julius had to borrow a hundred pounds from a family friend to pay for his passage, his tropical outfit, an English saddle and an Indian pony. The lender asked that Julius insure his life for the amount of the loan and charge it as security.

Julius faithfully paid premiums on the policy until his death, when John collected on the policy as his father's executor. It had never occurred to Julius to discontinue it when the loan was paid off, which he had punctually done within six months.) In India, and having secured his decent salary, Julius was posted to Madras, as befitted a Turing. Madras was also where his future father-in-law was to be found, and E. W. Stoney could outsmart any Turing in the matter of book-keeping. This became apparent as soon as Alan's parents got married. As was the custom, a red carpet was laid from pavement to porch, which the happy couple trod. John reports:

> No sooner was the honeymoon over than my grandfather sent the bill for the carpet to my father. My father deemed it to be part of the wedding expense traditionally at the charge of the bride's father. My grandfather thought otherwise. After much fuming my father paid the bill but the incident rankled for upwards of forty years.

In later days, Grandpa Stoney would bring to an end any family argument with a statement of ultimate finality: 'I am off to King & Partridge to alter my will.' But that is to get ahead of ourselves. Despite the Madras connection, it was entirely a matter of chance that Alan's parents met, let alone got married. Really, they should not have met at all.

An Irish upbringing

Unlike Julius Turing, Ethel Stoney was born and spent her early childhood in India, where E. W. Stoney was working his way up the Engineering Department of the Madras Railway Company, having been appointed fourth-class engineer in 1866. He married Sarah Crawford, a suitable Irish girl, in 1875; there were four children, of whom Ethel was the third. Expatriate families all have the difficult problem of what to do with the children. In the case of the Stoneys, the answer, they concluded, was to deposit all four with Sarah's brother William Crawford, who was a bank manager working in County Clare. The Crawfords already had a full house, with six children, two of whom belonged to William's previous marriage. Late in her life Ethel complained that Aunt Lizzie, William's wife and thus Ethel's foster mother, showed her no affection – doubtless the fostering arrangement was a trial for all involved. And the Crawfords were not the Stoneys – respectable, middle class, and wholly lacking in connections to the Bowes family, certainly, but not engineers or fellows of the Royal Society either.

In 1891, when Ethel was ten, the Crawfords moved to Dublin, and after a spell at school there both Ethel and her elder sister Evie were sent to board at Cheltenham Ladies' College, Evie joining aged 14 in 1892 and Ethel, aged nearly 17, in 1898. This was in the days of the pioneering and dynamic principal Miss Beale, who was offering advanced courses for young women which prepared them for university exams as well as the kind of secondary education more commonly expected of boarding schools. Her philosophy was expressed in 1898 as follows:[4]

> How can girls be prepared for such work as falls to them as heads of great schools, and hospitals, and settlements, as doctors in foreign lands, if their education was, as I found it, minus mathematics and science, and concluded at seventeen or earlier?

It was also the family school. Edith Stoney had been on the mathematics staff during Evie's time as a student, although she left the term Ethel arrived, and another cousin, Anne, the daughter of Bindon Blood Stoney FRS, joined Ethel a year later. Yet, despite the influences of family and school, Ethel was led not in the Stoney tradition of science and engineering, but in a more conventionally ladylike direction to study art and music. The norm for the Edwardian era was for girls to be educated with a view to social, not academic, achievement: a good marriage was more important than any sort of technical career. So Ethel spent six months at the Sorbonne, mastering French, and perfecting her skills as a draftswoman and watercolourist.

Julius Turing, Alan's father, in 1907. (Author)

The days of the Raj. Ethel Turing in 1909 with a very young John perched on the Ranee Sahib's pony, and a syce (groom). (Author)

Ethel's portrait of Sarah, her own mother, looks at me as I write this; she has captured the benignity of the older lady together with a hint of something sharper – the need to keep an eye on her daughter who might at any moment get up to no good. Aged 19, Ethel left the Sorbonne and went back to India with Evie – 'thrown,' as John puts it, 'on the Indian marriage market – that is to say, she went out to India to live with her parents and her sister Evie at Coonoor. My mother and aunt seem to have led a life of singular futility, driving out in the carriage with their mother to drop visiting cards, doing little water-colour sketches of the Indian scene, appearing in amateur theatricals and occasionally attending dinners and balls.'

Although this picture of the apogee of the Raj is perhaps characteristic of the period, it is not clear that it suited Ethel. For Ethel was a strikingly beautiful girl, and was not going to wait long for suitable, or even unsuitable, offers, occasionally vetoed by E. W. Stoney on the grounds of inadequate financial resources. And Julius Turing was not offering, or even in the offing. On the one hand, the over-nice late Victorian social stratifications put the covenanted Indian Civil Service – the so-called 'heaven born' – two notches above mere professionals like railway engineers. Engineers were people of whom you might be aware, but there were other people whom you might *meet*. But, in truth, the reason they did not mix socially was more mundane. Julius was not bidding in the marriage market because he was constantly on the move, and just too busy. The duties of an early twentieth-century subdivisional Indian Civil Service officer typically included being excise officer and collector of land revenue, issuer of stamps, land registrar, inspector of schools, minister of roads and irrigation, planning inspector, magistrate and district judge, food-and-drugs controller and inspector of distilleries, receiver of petitions, and preserver of the peace.

So it was by chance that they met: on a homeward-bound ship, in 1907, going by the long Pacific route, almost five years after Ethel's return to India. On reaching Japan, Julius took Ethel to dinner, and ordered the waiter to 'bring beer and go on bringing beer until I tell you to stop'. Ethel was bowled over, and on announcing their engagement to E.W. Stoney, who was on board as well, Julius was deemed just sufficiently solvent to be allowed to wed his daughter when they reached Dublin. Provided, of course, that the red carpet was for Mr Turing's account.

2

DISMAL CHILDHOODS

Alan Turing was born in Maida Vale on 23 June 1912. Despite all the indications, Alan would never visit India during his lifetime, even though Julius continued in the Indian Civil Service until Alan was 13.

John Turing's unpublished autobiography has chapters headed 'Dismal childhood of my father', 'Dismal childhood of my mother' and 'Dismal childhood of myself', which sums up the story of young children wrenched, in each case, away from a nuclear family. Alan, John's younger brother, never experienced such a wrench; from the very outset he was brought up away from his parents, and on that account has been thought by some to have had the most dismal childhood of all. So much for the psychology. In the context of the times, and in the factual analysis, that easy conclusion, so readily reached from a twenty-first-century perspective, might need further scrutiny.

Fairy princess

The early childhoods of John and Alan Turing were, to all appearances, quite different. There are photographs of John, born in India in 1908, watched in his pram by a benign E.W. Stoney, being cuddled by his ayah, playing in the garden of the bungalow at Coonoor, and generally being made a firstborn fuss-of. John's memories, given that he was sent away to England before his fourth birthday, were fuzzy but fond:[1]

I *seem* to remember the elephants and the fireflies – the largest and the smallest of my Indian acquaintances. Certainly I saw much of the elephants, for they were wont to wash themselves with great drenchings and slurpings from their trunks outside my father's bungalow, so that I was soon in trouble with my ayah for attempting the elephant trick. In 1942 I returned to India by courtesy of the Army. In Deolali transit camp I was at once transported back to my wicker chair and little charpoy cot by the smell of burning cow-dung and the chitter of crickets in the hot Indian night.

And again, in a piece written in 1964:

I prefer to think of [my mother] as she was when I was a little boy and (as it seemed to me) a sort of fairy princess when she came to kiss me goodnight in her flouncy dinner-gown.

But John had given his parents a scare:

My mother incessantly inspected pots and pans and the habits and hands of her platoon of Indian servants but despite this rigorous watch on hygiene I contracted dysentery from infected cow's milk and became dangerously ill. In despair my mother resolved to remove me from the heat of the plains where my father was stationed and risk the long train journey to the nearest hill station. In the middle of the night I was fluttering away but she revived me with a mammoth swig of brandy.

So Alan was born, and the boys would stay, in England. John described the trip to London as a halcyon time:

My father, perforce, had to look after me for the one and only time in his life. His solution of the problem could not have been bettered: we visited the White City, went on round-abouts, sat in restaurants and travelled around the metropolis on the tops of buses with the tickets stuck in our hat-bands. So it did not seem to me at all a bad thing that my mother should be taking a nice long 'rest'. I was not a little astonished and put out when I was taken to the nursing home one day and found that I had a new baby brother. The decision to leave the boys in England was not easy.

Probably it was the right decision for me, for I had given my parents a bad fright with my dysentery in India and by the time my father was due for long leave again I should be seven and a half. But it was a harsh decision for my mother to have to leave both her children in England, one of them still an infant in arms. This was the beginning of the long sequence of separations from our parents, so painful to all of us and most of all to my mother.

Alan did not have a fairy princess, and his relationship with his mother would forever be asymmetrical: from her side, Alan was the baby she had left at home; for him, Ethel was, if not a princess, something not dissimilar to the queen, or, to express it differently, Mother. But that is not to say that Alan had no family when he was growing up. Quite the contrary. He had the Wards, and the Wards were, certainly, a family.

Wardship

There are two resolves that the Anglo-Indian mother will do well to make and keep so far as in her lies. In the first place, she should at least go home with her children, and see them safely launched upon their new path in life; in the second, she should register a vow, and keep it – Fate permitting – never to desert either husband or children for more than three or four years at a stretch.[2]

Maud Diver, novelist and Anglo-Indian, was writing guidance for women in 1909. It is implicit in her advice that sending the children home to Britain was an inevitability, part of the sacrifice implicit in the Service. And so, for the upper echelons of the expatriate community, it was. Keeping children in India was, according to one contemporary writer,[3] likely to leave them puny, pallid, skinny and fretful, whereas, remarkable as it may seem to us, British food and British meteorology would convert them into fat and happy English children. Schooling in India, while theoretically available for some children of the Raj, was unlikely to be the pukka experience of a school at home, or to open the doors to a good and lucrative career. Leaving the children in Britain meant that a home had to be found for them. The historian Vyvyen Brendon explains:[4]

> The dearth of suitable relations was a common problem for Raj families in the twentieth century. Since many [Indian Civil Service] men and army officers now came from quite ordinary backgrounds, their British relations lived in smaller houses which could not easily accommodate several extra children. To respond to the need there grew up a network of holiday homes which took in strangers' children. Relations, whom expatriate parents did not always know very well, could turn out to be unkind or negligent while paid guardians could offer kindness and understanding to lonely children.

Rudyard Kipling had had a miserable time with his foster family, and Rudyard Kipling was a famous author, so it is all too easily assumed that all foster families were awful. Mostly the ICS families accepted the separations as their lot: an unavoidable experience about which it was not the done thing to moan, whether now or later, whether you were the parents or the children. (They also devoured Rudyard Kipling's Anglo-Indian children's literature: my copy of the *Just So Stories* has the classic drawings, and is inscribed 'John Ferrier Turing – Prize for learning to read. from Mother. June 7 1915'.) The question for the Turings was not whether separation would happen, but who would be the boys' foster family. Ethel Turing spent months in Britain following the birth of Alan, and she left nothing to chance.

The Wards were numerous. Colonel Ward was a veteran of the Boer War, 'spare, gruff and taciturn, with eyes of the palest blue. His military bearing and manner concealed a warm heart.' Mrs Ward – known to the children as 'Grannie' – was from another military family, the Haigs. She was 'dumpy, resolute, outspoken, full of zest for life, sometimes severe but always meting out justice with a faintly perceptible twinkle. We both loved her very much.' Grannie would hand out a smart biff to a child whose back was not as ramrod straight as hers. The Wards had four daughters of their own, 'an assortment of Mrs Ward's powerful Haig nieces', and an incumbent boarder called Nevill Marryat, who was slightly older than John. The daughters were Nerina, Hazel, Kay – all significantly older than the boys – and Joan. John wrote acidly about Joan, but significantly said, 'twelve years younger than Kay …, she was dreadfully spoilt and deserves no blame for making the most of it. She was half-way in age between Alan and myself and honesty compels me to admit that we both cordially detested her though not in the same way: I thought her a pest but my brother rated her a tyrant.'

The family, with a suitable retinue of servants, lived at Baston Lodge, in St Leonards-on-Sea near Brighton. The house is still there, with the requisite blue plaque. It was Victorian, Italianate and slightly rambling, situated in the lee of the church and just up the hill from the house of the African-adventure novelist Sir Henry Rider Haggard. John recalled, with a touch of envy, that Alan found a diamond and sapphire ring belonging to Lady Rider Haggard in the gutter ('he always preferred the gutter to the pavement'). He was sent with it to the front door of the great man's house, and was rewarded with a florin. What everyone wanted to know was what it was like inside, but on this question, alas, history is silent.

Alan's nursery experience was longer than John's, and different. The nursery was vigorously ruled according to old-school standards by Nanny Thompson, assisted by an under-nurse, who had her hands full with Nevill's practical jokes (Wellington boots filled with water and so forth) as well as Joan's tantrums. Alan was just the baby. John remembered the pre-war smells of nappies – and bacon fat, part of Alan's diet, which for some reason was prescribed as a cure for rickets.

There was a delicious sniff of release when, leaving Julius in India, Ethel braved the menace of the U-boats to spend the spring and summer of 1915 with her boys, taking rented rooms in St Leonards.

Baston Lodge in about 1905. (East Sussex County Council Library & Information Service)

'Nothing in the whole range of the cussedness of inanimate objects competes with a sailor suit' – Alan Turing in 1917. (Author)

Her next visit to England would be in the spring of 1916 – again the U-boats failed to find their mark – with Julius, and this time with a holiday in Scotland into the bargain.

> My mother [wrote John, commenting on Ethel's biography of Alan] does not think fit to mention that it was by no means amusing or safe to do these long sea voyages in wartime during the submarine menace, nor that a close friend of hers had been pitched into the sea when the *Egypt* sank and had swum around for hours before she was rescued. Forewarned, my mother carried about her person on these voyages a mass of emergency equipment for the fatal plunge. If I remember rightly it included a whistle (to attract the attention of passing ships, whales, etc.), a small Meta stove, tabloid provisions, sea-proof matches and improving literature in waterproof bindings. Happily she was never obliged to put these aids to survival to the test.

In all this, Alan's childhood was not really different from that of other Empire children. The household was typical for an Edwardian Army family, and the horrors experienced by Rudyard Kipling at the hands of his foster mother were certainly absent. Ethel Turing had chosen well. Yet, notwithstanding the large household, the benevolent oversight of Grannie Ward, and the brisk attentions of Nanny Thompson, one is left with the sense that Alan was often left to his own devices. John, four years older, preferred to keep his nose in a book than engage with his little brother. In any case, in May 1917 John was despatched to board at prep school, and about this time Nevill also left the custody of the Wards.

Sampled snapshots

In John's absence there was no one left to record the days of Alan's infancy except in the endless series of sailor-suit photos. In the Christmas holidays the Turing boys were allowed to stay with the formidable Aunt Jean, Julius's older sister:

The house, known as 'Rushmoor' (all their houses were called Rushmoor) was number 42, Bramham Gardens. It was one of those up and down houses of the Victorian era – a more inconvenient version of Baston Lodge but on a grander scale and with more storeys. All might have been well at Rushmoor but for that wretched brother of mine. At Baston Lodge he was not my responsibility. At Rushmoor I was held accountable for his clothes, deportment, hygiene and punctual appearance at meals. To make matters worse, he was dressed in sailor suits, according to the convention of the day (they suited him well); I know nothing in the whole range of the cussedness of inanimate objects to compete with a sailor suit. Out of the boxes there erupted collars and ties and neckerchiefs and cummerbunds and oblong pieces of flannel with lengthy tapes attached; but how one put these pieces together, and in what order, was beyond the wit of man. Not that my brother cared a button – an apt phrase, many seemed to be off – for it was all the same to him which shoe was on which foot or that it was only three minutes to the fatal breakfast gong. Somehow or another I managed by skimping such trumpery details as Alan's teeth, ears, etc. but I was exhausted by these nursery attentions and it was only when we were taken off to the pantomime that I was able to forget my fraternal cares.

Apart from John's account, most of which was written about his own childhood experience and (because of their difference in age) features Alan only incidentally, there are few sources on which to draw. Until Alan was four, his mother was keeping oversight remotely, through correspondence with Grannie Ward. Then, for a period, Ethel managed to get a good deal of time with Alan, since she took rooms in St Leonards when Julius returned to India in late 1916 and, saving her a further round of cat-and-mouse with the U-boats, stayed there until the end of the war.

Alan's Kirwan cousins might from time to time invade the household – these were Ethel's sister Evie's children, all older than Alan. He was not one of the boisterous crowd, with their multi-bike pile-ups at the bottom of the steep hill in St Leonards and pillow fights versus the Baston Lodge maids. As with most children, Alan found his own way of dealing with all of this: if the occasion demanded it, he could put on his sailor suit smile and let the waves flow past. In 1919 and 1922 there were more Scottish trips when the Turing parents came home again on long leave. Alan went fishing with his father and on mountain walks with Mother. Ethel noticed a change in Alan when she came home in 1921: 'From having been extremely vivacious – even mercurial – making friends with everyone, he had become unsociable and dreamy. I decided to take him away from his pre-preparatory school, where he was not learning much anyway, and teach him myself for a term and by attention and companionship get him back to his former self.'[5]

Before long, in early 1922 it was time to join John at boarding school. Hazelhurst had that inestimable quality of the small British preparatory school of the twentieth century. It had only 45 boys aged 8 to 13, giving everyone a chance to achieve in something, in particular sport. The Turing parents were not sporty:

My father [continues John] was considerably indulged by his mother, so that she contrived to have him excused from all games and athletics at Bedford. One direct result of this mollycoddling was that he could never summon up the faintest interest in games. My modest prep-school achievements – such as the magnificent 21 against Crowborough Grange which saved the side! – were wholly ignored. My brother's even more artful and singular feats of non-gamesmanship were totally ignored in like manner: it would be a distortion to suggest that they were tacitly discouraged, certainly not – they were ignored.

Only such past masters of the art of passive resistance as my brother Alan could fail to count themselves athletes [in the small school]. When he in turn outdistanced us all and became a marathon runner of Olympic standard, he attributed his success to his running away from the ball at Hazelhurst. 'He believed that it was at his preparatory school that he learnt to run fast, for he was always so anxious to get away from the ball': so wrote my mother. But it isn't true: he propped himself on his hockey stick and studied the daisies.

John might have been over-harsh about his parents' attitude to sports: the *Hazelhurst Gazette* reports that on Saturday 11 March 1922, the hockey season had opened with the fixture School *v* The Staff. 'J. F. Turing (inside right) – rather slow, but combines well: a very poor shot' – was playing for School. Both Mr and Mrs Turing had been co-opted to play for the Staff. The Staff won 6–1. The *Hazelhurst Gazette* prudently did not offer commentary on the performance of individual members of the Staff team.

Perhaps Hazelhurst's greatest asset was its headmaster, W.S. Darlington. Mr Darlington wrote up the school magazine every term, and this gives us a wry insight into Alan's time at prep school. For the first term all was not easy, since John (due to go to Marlborough imminently) was head boy and Alan was the youngest in the school. The *Hazelhurst Gazette* hinted at Alan having made his mark immediately. First he started an origami craze: 'not just darts and paper boats which all of us knew how to make, but paper frogs, paper kettles, paper donkeys, paper hats of all sizes and shapes. Seemingly you could boil water in a paper kettle over a naked flame – so Alan assured all the lower echelons, who were now industriously acquiring his skills and dropping paper all over the place.'

Practical skills were honoured at Hazelhurst. Naturally, there was scouting: Mr Darlington commented, in his benignly sardonic way, on the deterioration in fire-lighting technique in his report for May 1922. But more importantly, there was carpentry. From time to time the excitement of carpentry got the better of Mr Darlington:[6]

As we sit down to write, we can only think of doors, doors, dovetails and bookshelves! As we think of the first of these our memories go back a term or two when we mentioned a door as being still unfinished. Oh! just as it was receiving the final touches before being put together, one of those final touches was too much for one of the tenons and it broke off; our present belief is that the door of happy memory is not yet finished, but we are quite sure the maker has learnt much more in the way of joinery than one who only puts together about six pieces of wood, more or less decently planed up, and then calls the article a book-case.

Hockey

or

Watching the Daisies

Grow

Photostat copy of Caricature by his mother of Alan at hockey: sent to Miss Dunwell, matron at Hazelhurst. Date. Spring term 1923.

The sporting life. Alan is fully devoted to something on the hockey field. (© The Estate of P.N. Furbank and reproduced by kind permission of the Provost and Scholars of King's College, Cambridge)

And there was also the triumph of the geography exam, to which all the school were subjected. Alan had been poring over maps, both at Baston Lodge and at school, and this habit had caught Mr Darlington's eye. 'We departed somewhat from our usual custom,' writes Mr Darlington on the subject of end-of-term exams: there was an 'innovation [which] took the form of three prizes, one for each division of the school, for filling in blank maps with given names. The experiment was popular and successful.' Successful for some, but not so popular with everyone. Turing II distinguished himself with 77 marks, beating by a wide margin all the other boys in his division and all but five in the whole school; Turing I, despite being top of Form I, mustered only 59 marks. The end-of-term song celebrating the forthcoming holidays included the shameful line: 'and no Map will make an Elder Brother take a lower place'.

Another perspective on Alan's time at Hazelhurst is provided by Alan himself, in his letters home, of which 16 survive. Most of the letters are dated, and all but two bear Sunday dates. Like many prep schools, it seems that Hazelhurst obliged its pupils to write a letter home as part of the regular Sunday routine. Children at prep school have no idea what to write about to their parents; the weekly letter can be an ordeal for all involved, particularly given that even in the 1920s it would take at least a month for a letter to get to India from Sussex. It seems that Ethel kept these 16 – and then gave them to King's College, Cambridge, in 1960 – because they actually have something of interest in them. No tales of magnificent 21s against Crowborough Grange can be found in this collection, then. The ones that remain, though, have more than something of interest; here are some from the sample:[7]

- (1 April 1923): 'Guess what I am writing with it is an invention of my own it is a fountain pen like this:– [diagram follows]'
- (undated, summer 1923): 'This week I thought of how I might make a Typewriter like this [uninterpretable partly crossed-out diagram follows] you see the the funny little rounds are letters cut out on one side slide along to the round (A) and along an ink pad and stamp down and make the letter, thats not nearly all though'

- (8 June 1924): 'I do not know whether I told you last week but once when I said how much I hated tapioco pudding and you said that all Turings hated tapioco pudding and mint-sauce and something else I had never tried mint-sauce but a few days ago we had it and I found out very much that your statement was true.'
- (21 September 1924): 'in Natural wonders every child should know it says that the Carbon dioxide is changed to cooking soda in the blood and back to carbon dioxide in the lungs. If you can will you send me the chemical name of cooking soda or the formula better still so that I can see how it does it.'

Many of the letters contain meticulous accounting in accordance with Julius's standing requirements, and an inordinate proportion go on about Alan's handwriting, which appears to have been an obsession with Ethel. And perhaps of greatest interest is that, from the very earliest, the letters all begin with the startling salutation 'Dear Mother and Daddy'. Here is fertile ground for psychologists, so perhaps it is not necessary to add any commentary. John corroborates the conclusion, easily reached from these letters, that Alan was already showing a bent towards mathematics and sciences

Alan Turing as THE WIDOW in the Hazelhurst School play in 1925. (Author)

at Hazelhurst, and this early indication was to influence the choice of Alan's public (secondary) school.

Natural Wonders, by E.T. Brewster, does deserve some particular commentary. Ethel gave Alan's copy to the Sherborne School Archive, and inside it she wrote: '*Natural Wonders Every Child should know* was given to Alan Turing aged 10½. This book greatly stimulated his interest in science and was valued by him all his life.' Alan had, however, developed an interest in the sciences (as well as geography) at an earlier age: Ethel mentions in her own biography of Alan how he was trawling gutters with a magnet to pick up the iron filings left by iron-tyred cartwheels, and asking questions about the bonding of hydrogen to oxygen in water in 1921; he had been reading other nature-study materials aged seven; and at the age of eight he had written 'a book entitled *About a Microscope* – the shortest scientific work on record for it began and ended with the sentence, "First you must see that the lite is rite"'.

Hazelhurst followed the traditional preparatory school curriculum. The 'preparation' offered by the school was for the Common Entrance examination to public schools, which was introduced in 1904, with papers in Latin, French, English, and Mathematics, plus a General Paper (Scripture, History and Geography). Greek could also be taken; so could Latin Verse. Science did not make it onto the core curriculum until 1969. Science at Hazelhurst was covered through occasional lectures on Natural History. It was fun, but it was not mainstream. To indulge his interests, Alan was having to make his own way; but that was fine, it was the way that suited him.

Science in the cellar

In the summer holidays of 1923 there was a short stay in Rouen at the house of a Madame Godier. John had been to the Godiers' once before. Getting solo to France was no mean feat:

Mother left nothing to chance and I was armed with her travel notes which Alan and I always called 'moral maxims'. We were constantly

bidden to chant 'tickets, money, passport, keys'; many travellers have
come to grief for want of this useful piece of advice. Admittedly my
brother soon developed his own methods of travel and always tended to
pay little attention to mother's moral maxims. There was one occasion
when they were travelling to Switzerland and somewhere en route
to Dover mother requested Alan to throw some rubbish out of the
window. Thereupon he picked up a bundle comprising tickets, money,
passport and keys and made for the window, remarking that he hoped it
would not injure any workmen on the line. Mother made a frantic grab
and averted disaster by inches.

On the first trip to Rouen John had taken his bicycle, giving rise to
a troublesome encounter with the French customs – a contingency
not provided for in Mother's moral maxims. 'I flatly declined to take
my bicycle to Rouen on the second occasion. This was not because
I feared another encounter with the customs but because my brother
Alan had just learned to ride a bicycle and would have to bring his
along as well. I was greatly alarmed at the prospect which opened before
me of navigating wobbly Alan through French traffic and over greasy
cobblestones.' John soon realised this was a mistake, since there was now
no means of escape with Madame Godier to the countryside, and to
make matters worse for him, Madame Godier took a shine to Alan:

> It did make things awkward for I was neatly impaled upon Morton's
> fork. If Alan did not wash his ears (and he never did, save under
> threat), it was my fault for not supervising him; and if by chance he
> did, 'comme il est charmant'. But I must give Alan his due and declare
> that his loyalty to me was unwavering. This in no way helped to soften
> Madame Godier and much did I deplore my folly in leaving our bikes
> behind in England.

In 1923 John had asked for a change from the Wards. It had been ten
years, more or less, and Ethel agreed, finding a new foster family for
the summer holidays and then on. The destination to which the boys
were bound after their three weeks in Rouen was the Hertfordshire

vicarage of the Meyers, a Church of England parson and his family, whose house was much more relaxed than the military Baston Lodge.

> What was it going to be like? [wrote John.] Had I made a dreadful mistake in urging mother to remove us from the Wards? On arrival I knew it was no mistake. The sun shone upon rose-beds and tennis-court. I was never happier than at the Meyers; even Alan – games-hater and non-conformist that he was – fitted in there. Alan's stock rose several points when a gipsy revealed to Mrs Meyer at the Church fete that her younger charge was a genius. All credit to her that she half believed it!

The secret of the Meyers was, according to John, that 'given minimum standards of hygiene and punctuality for meals and passable table-manners you could do more or less what you liked'. Ethel said that John and Alan 'fitted very happily into the family life there and Alan enjoyed bicycling round the country and carrying out various experiments in a neighbouring wood. Letters tell of his coming in black all over and of his singeing his eyelashes as he fired the clay pipe he had made. Mrs Meyer wrote later that he was always doing dangerous things.'

Alas, the sunny days at the Meyers were only brief. While all this liberty, science and self-directed experimentation had been fine and good, in order to move beyond Hazelhurst it would be necessary for Alan actually to *pass* Common Entrance.

In 1924 Julius Turing resigned in a huff from the ICS, and the Turing parents returned to Europe for good. And so, from Easter 1924, holidays were under a stricter regime. There was the serious matter of the handwriting to be tackled. Ethel said '[Alan's] hand-writing was so appalling that in the Easter holidays of 1924 when he was nearly twelve he and I settled down together to reform it, and for a time he took great pains and improved his handwriting beyond recognition, but by the end of the year it was reported to be "as bad as ever"'. Later in 1924 the Turings took up residence for the winter and spring months in a villa called *Ker Sammy* at Dinard, a coastal town in northern France, to 'avoid the ruinous British income tax, lately raised to 4/3d in the pound'. Dinard had a well-established retirement community with all suitable facilities for the less-well-off former ICS, including a golf course, a bracing outdoor seawater swimming bath and a Church of England church. At *Ker Sammy*, while John went off hopefully with his tennis racket in search of girls, Alan was allowed to indulge in chemistry experiments in the cellar, with equipment given to him for Christmas, and to have some coaching in science from Mr Rolf, a schoolmaster from Shrewsbury. And Mother pushed ahead with her own lessons in French. She need not have worried: 'in 1925 he took the Common Entrance examination for Marlborough and with his usual aptitude for examinations he demolished the papers.' Alan was all set now to make his way at public school.

3

DIRECTION OF TRAVEL

The coal-miners had had enough. It was bad enough that their pay had been cut by about a third since the end of the war. The mine owners had threatened a further cut, which the Baldwin government fended off with the time-honoured ploy of a Royal Commission. On 10 March 1926 the Commission reported, recommending a new settlement, which included a further reduction in miners' pay and a longer working day. The mine owners gave their workers an ultimatum: accept these terms or be locked out of the workplace after 1 May. The Trades Union Congress was not impressed.

On Sunday 2 May 1926 Alan Turing caught the ferry from St-Malo, the port town just a stone's throw across the River Rance from Dinard. Alan was due to join his new school at Sherborne the following day. Mother's moral maxims were clear: ferry to Southampton; Southern Railway to Salisbury; change for the Exeter service; alight at Sherborne; remember to check tickets, money, passport and keys at each point; hire porters as necessary to assist with trunk, bicycle and other impedimenta.

Unfortunately Ethel wasn't negotiating with the TUC. The TUC brought out the printers, dockers, ironworkers and steelworkers in a strike in sympathy with the miners, together with the railwaymen and other transport workers. The General Strike was timed to begin on Monday 3 May. Alan's ferry docked in Southampton just hours after the country had been shut down.

May 5th Wednesday

Westcott House
Sherborne
Dorset

Dear Mother & Daddy

On ship found that <u>all</u> railway services were cancelled except for milk. [Porter 6d. Breakfast 1/6. Registration 4/-. Berth 1/-. Ticket 14/-.]* Funnily enough heard someone say in Dinard that they would have to go to London in an empty milk can. Good crossing and sleep. Buses to Salisbury but noone knew about farther on from there here. Would not take my bycycle so could not supplement one with other & could not walk with all that lugge far so I cycled as programme left luggage with baggage master started out of docks about 11 oclock got map for 3/- including Southampton missing Sherborne by about 3 miles. Noted where Sherborne was just outside. With an awful strive found General Post Office sent wire O'Hanlon 1/-. Found cycle shop had things done 6d left 12 o'clock had lunch 7 miles out ¼ loaf 3/6 went on to Lyndhurst 3 miles got apple 2d went on to Burley 8 miles pedal a bit wrong had it done 6d went on Ringwood 4 miles.

The streets in Southampton were full of people who had struck. Had a lovely ride through the New Forest and then over a sort of moor into Ringwood & quite flat again to Wimborne. Just near Blandford some nice downs & suddenly merely undulating near all the way here but the last mile was all downhill. The people at Blandford were very amused. Its an awful nuisance here without any of my clothes or anything. Mr O'Hanlon is v. nice. Fancy being called 'teacher' though. It's rather hard getting settled down. Do write soon. There was no work on Wednesday except for 'Hall' or prep. And then its a business finding my classrooms what books to get but I will be more or less settled down after a week or so. The matron's name is Miss Crawley & she talks good brogue.

*   Interlineated by Alan.

I do not need any eggs for tea or anything of that sort. Anyhow if ~~I did need it I would~~ have to order ~~the~~ jam. [[??] do you mean me to]* We will begin early Hall work on Monday. We go to bed at 9 or 9.30 & will get up at 6.30 only having 9 hrs sleep.

Yr loving son Alan.

Please find Kitty's address & send it to me. No mastiffs seen yet. I am in a choir of sorts. Sending back £1-0-1 in £ note & penny stamp[1]

Alan had arrived. Late, untidy, in his own unorthodox yet practical way, and without assistance from Mother's moral maxims. His exploit even made it to the local paper. Sherborne was going to be a turning point in Alan's life.

The decision that Alan should go to Sherborne, rather than follow John to Marlborough, was significant: both John and Mother wanted to claim credit for the choice of school; both recognised that it was Sherborne that enabled Alan to develop in the way that he wanted, rather than force him onto the traditional public-school path leading to a career in the Army, the Indian Civil Service or the professions. Of the 242 pages of John's unpublished autobiography, 33 or so are devoted to the trauma of his time at Marlborough. John was the more adaptable of the boys: if Marlborough could not suit him, how much more difficult it would be for Alan. Nevertheless, Alan had been put down for Marlborough and satisfied their requirements for the Common Entrance. But he had been allowed another go in the Lent term of 1926, and satisfied Sherborne's (higher) requirements, and so it was to Sherborne that Alan had headed on that bicycle ride.

*   Interlineated above the crossed-out passage.

Alan in Dinard, shortly before the bicycle ride. (Author)

Three Rs

Sherborne was not an 'Empire' school, like Bedford: only 6 per cent of the boarders' families were serving in colonies overseas in 1905. Nor was Sherborne at the forefront of intellectualism; boys' schools were of longer establishment and more conservative, and had had more time to develop traditions than newcomers like Cheltenham Ladies' College. The school had been deservedly criticised in a Board of Education Report by HM Inspectors in 1905. At that stage, Sherborne had only reluctantly and partially moved into line with the Taunton Commission's recommendations, the purpose of which was to move the public schools away from a curriculum providing a 'largely "ornamental" education that, at best, rendered their sons "good cricketers" and "indifferent classicists"'.[2] Canon Westcott's Sherborne was solid on the three Rs: rugby, religion, and relentless Latin. The Board of Education said: 'The bias of the School is predominantly classical and, although Mathematics, Science, and Modern languages are by no means neglected, the best work is classical and other subjects suffer from being regarded as of secondary importance. The cleverer boys almost always find their way to the classical side and, in consequence, on the modern side, work of the 6th Form type which should foster intellectual ambition may be said scarcely to exist.'[3]

But things had changed since then. In 1908 Westcott had retired and, after a brief interval, Nowell Charles Smith was appointed in his place in September 1909. He was the first layman to be appointed in 250 years, and while firmly anchored in the classical tradition, Nowell Smith's agenda was to modernise. His first report to the governors announced: 'I have provided that all boys, whether Classical or Modern, should pass through a course of Elementary Physics and Chemistry, when they have reached the middle part of the School. In our present stage of civilization, some acquaintance with the elements of natural science must be regarded as one of the most obviously desirable parts of a liberal education.'[4] Nowell Smith wanted his boys to be rounded out, practical, and well equipped for a variety of careers. By 1926, towards the end of Nowell Smith's tenure, this culture was well established, encouraging teachers of quality in the mathematics and science departments. New science teaching facilities were built in 1910 to supplement the 'old silk mill' which the 1905 inspectors had sniffed at. (These buildings were still in use for physics and chemistry teaching when I attended Sherborne in the 1970s; they were perfectly all right then despite the historic – and interesting – use of the chemistry building as a silk mill. Only recently has Sherborne's science teaching moved to a shiny, modern, purpose-built laboratory.)

Ethel Turing had taken the measure of the Nowell Smith regime. While Alan was trying to get his Latin into shape for the Common Entrance exam, Ethel was visiting Sherborne:

> Before Alan went to Sherborne I had met Mrs Nowell Smith and given some hints about what to expect. She contrasted my description with the more favourable accounts given by other parents of their boys. Though he had been loved and understood in the narrower homely circle of his preparatory school, it was because I foresaw the possible difficulties for the staff and himself at a public school that I was at such pains to find the right one for him, lest if he failed in adaptation to public school life he might become a mere intellectual crank. It will be seen later how Sherborne School justified Mr. Nowell Smith's hopes and mine.[5]

Alan seemed to fit in, just about. Enough of Canon Westcott's sportive regime survived to ensure that rugby was compulsory, as were inter-house Swedish drill competitions. Alan participated in these, of course, but from the start (when he showed the chemistry master his home-brewed iodine, cooked up from Dinard seaweed in the *Ker Sammy* basement) he was pleased to be in a place where science and maths counted as much as Ovid and Virgil.

Initially all seemed to be going well, or at least not badly. Alan seemed to cope with the initiation ceremonies (such as singing a song, giving the older boys plenty to laugh at), fagging duties, and other heartinesses of senior boarding-school life.

Alan Turing aged 16. (Courtesy of Sherborne School)

Fagging starts for us next Tuesday. It is run on the same principle as the Gallic councils that tortured & killed the last man to arrive; here one fagmaster calls & all his fags run, the last to arrive getting the job. You have to have cold showers in the morning here, like cold baths at Marlborough.

After-dinner speeches

The business with the bicycle ride had built up a store of credibility on which Alan drew for the first few terms. His school reports were all right, particularly if you focused on the maths:[6]

- Summer Term, 1926: '*House Report*. Quite a good start. He appears self-contained & is apt to be solitary. This is not due to moroseness: but simply I think to a shy disposition. GOH.' 'Very good promising work. I am glad to promote him. Nowell Smith, Headmaster.' On the back, in GOH's handwriting, is the following, probably added after the front page was completed: 'I am quite pleased with his start; He's a very grubby person at times. I hope Ireland will de-ink him.'
- Michaelmas Term, 1926: '*Mathematics*. Works well. He is still very untidy. He must try to improve in this respect. MBE.' '*House Report*. Slightly less dirty and untidy in his habits: & rather more conscious of a duty to mend his ways. He has his own furrow to plough, & may not meet with general sympathy: he seems cheerful, though I'm not always certain he really is so. GOH.'
- Lent Term, 1927: '*Mathematics*. Very good. He has considerable powers of reasoning and should do well if he can quicken up a little and improve his style. JHR.' '*House Report*. He is frankly not one who fits comfortably for himself into the ordinary life of the place – on the whole I think he is tidier. GOH.' 'He should do very well when he finds his *metier*: but meantime he would do much better if he would try to do *his* best as a member of this school – he should have more *esprit de corps*. Nowell Smith, Headmaster.'

By late 1927 the picture emerging from the reports was rather less tolerant. The well of credibility was drying up, and the exasperation sometimes boiled over into rage:

- Summer Term, 1927: '*Mathematics*. Not very good. He spends a good deal of time apparently in investigations in advanced mathematics to the neglect of his elementary work. A sound ground work is essential in any subject. His work is dirty. JHR.' '*House Report*. No doubt he is a strange mixture: trying to build a roof before he has laid the foundations. He is mistaken in acting as if idleness and indifference will procure release from uncongenial subjects. GOH.' 'I hope he will not fall between two stools. If he is to stay at a Public School he must aim at becoming *educated*. If he is to be *solely a scientific specialist*, he is wasting time at a Public School. Nowell Smith, Headmaster.'

- Michaelmas Term, 1927: '*English Subjects*. I append one sheet of a recent History Paper, as it probably says more eloquently than I can where his weakness lies. AHT-R.' '*House Report*. I have seen cleaner productions than this specimen, even from him. No doubt he is very aggravating: & he should know by now that I don't care to find him boiling heaven knows what witches' brew by the aid of two guttering candles on a naked wooden window sill. However, he has borne his afflictions very cheerfully: & undoubtedly has taken more trouble, e.g. with physical training. I am far from hopeless. GOH.' 'He is the kind of boy who is bound to be rather a problem in any school or community, being in some respects definitely anti-social. But I think in our community he has a good chance of developing his special gifts & at the same time learning some of the art of living. Nowell Smith, Headmaster.'

- Michaelmas Term, 1927: '*English Subjects*. I can forgive his writing, though it is the worst I have ever seen, & I try to view tolerantly his unswerving inexactitude and slipshod, dirty work, inconsistent though such inexactitude is in a utilitarian; but I cannot forgive the stupidity of his attitude towards sane discussion on the New Testament. AHT-R. *Latin*. He ought not to be in this form of course as far as form subjects go. He is ludicrously behind. AHT-R.'

This outburst, from Mr Trelawny-Ross, is explained in a note added by Ethel Turing to the report: Alan had been caught doing algebra during a divinity lesson. Not surprisingly, the arrival of a report from Sherborne might bring on a dudgeon in Dinard. John Turing again:[7]

> Mother was constrained to suppress every report until my father had been fortified by breakfast and a couple of pipes. Alan would then be given a lecture in my father's study. His only recorded comments were 'Daddy should see some of the other boys' reports' and 'Daddy expects school reports to read like after dinner speeches.' Personally I found it a good time to be out of the house.

Setting aside the exasperation of schoolmasters like Trelawny-Ross, what shines through the reports is the perceptiveness of Nowell Smith's remarks, and indeed those of Geoffrey O'Hanlon, the housemaster to whom Alan had sent his telegram from Southampton in May 1926 – a pen-portrait which would remain more or less accurate for the whole of Alan's adult life. John was wrong when he said that 'the only person who was forever exasperated with Alan, constantly nagging him about his dirty habits, his slovenliness, his clothes and his offhand manners (and much else, most of it with good reason) was my mother'. Ethel was not fighting alone. Back in England the establishment was also trying to get Alan to conform, and exasperation was not the only remedy available. The problem and the solution were in the hands of O'Hanlon, who had to choose another boy to share a study with Alan when he graduated from the day room in which junior boys lived. O'Hanlon roped in Matthew Blamey, hoping that the mild and well-organised Blamey might be able to instil order, discipline, punctuality, and an appreciation of things other than maths and science into the wayward Turing. For more than a year Blamey endured Turing's untidiness and witches' brews and attempted fruitlessly to get Alan to turn up to chapel on time. He even took Alan along to the Gramophone Society. Eighty years later, Blamey doubted that he had made any difference.

Geoffrey O'Hanlon's house was a model boarding house, attracting glowing praise in a 1930 Board of Education inspection report. After the usual intensely all-male classical education at Rugby and Oxford, O'Hanlon had dedicated his life to Sherborne School. He was appointed just before the end of Canon Westcott's regime, acquiring the nickname 'Teacher' as perpetual form-master for Form 4a – the brighter boys in middle school. Having a role in the school's Officer Training Corps, O'Hanlon served in France from 1914 to 1917, leading a mixed group of men, and winning the MC. An apparently confirmed bachelor (like so many schoolmasters at Sherborne at that time), he returned to teaching in 1919, and bought a house.[8] In those days, housemasters typically owned their own houses (so the boys would ask '*whose* house are you in?' rather than '*which* house are you in?') and were responsible for all the appointments. The inspectors didn't much care for this state of affairs, even though the housemasters took on the financial burden of improvements – in O'Hanlon's case, extending the premises substantially. The house he built was not beautiful: 'probably the best in the school, but somewhat gaunt. It is a fact that in the recent war an American soldier in all good faith asked a delighted occupant whether this was the town penitentiary.'[9] In 1925 O'Hanlon gifted the house, now renamed Westcott House after the ex-headmaster, to the school, subject to the school taking over his £5,000 mortgage. From then on, O'Hanlon paid rent, and was put at risk of being ejected in favour of a younger man. This was dedication beyond any usual measure.

O'Hanlon's was a house of tolerance as well as discipline. Although literature and classics were O'Hanlon's passion, he had the largeness of soul to recognise other enthusiasms. Boarding schools are normalising, as well as rough, places, and his aim was to ensure that boys outside the mainstream could be coaxed into just enough conformity to survive, and ideally to thrive. Thus Alan found a survivable balance between conformity and indulging his more solitary passions for experimentation and mathematics. Alan became known as Old Turog. This was, in the 1920s, a loaf, rival to the longer-lasting Hovis brand. It may have been marketed as 'the bread of health' but as a nickname

The stairwell at Westcott House where Alan set up a Foucault's pendulum. (© David Ridgway, Sherborne School)

Westcott House. Alan's study was on the ground floor – the window nearest the tree. In my final term at Westcott I had the study on the opposite side of the corridor (window nearest the road). (Courtesy of Sherborne School)

its inelegance fitted a mis-spelled Alan Turing rather well – and a nickname implied a degree of social acceptance. Westcott House did not cure Alan of untidiness, unpunctuality, or smelly experimentation; it did not convert him into a socialite, though it ensured he was never wholly alone; it did not require him to excel at games; best of all, it did not force him to devote his surplus time to mastery of the classics.

Michaelmas 1927 was Nowell Smith's last term at Sherborne. A new headmaster, who 'had tried (unsuccessfully)' to teach Latin to John at Marlborough, was to replace him. And, under the new regime, the difficult issue arose as to whether Alan could be entered for the School Certificate examination – the 1920s predecessor of GCSEs. The Common Room boiled over, according to Alan's mother:[10]

> There was considerable tension in the common room between the literary and the scientific members of staff; the former maintained that Alan was quite unqualified for the examination, the latter protested that he should not be held back. The Headmaster, Mr. C.L.F. Boughey, gave the casting vote to permit him to have a try at a term's notice. But Mr. Bensly, who had a special form – called by him the 'Vermisorium' – for School Leaving Certificate candidates, promised to give a billion pounds to any charity named by Alan should he so much as pass in Latin.

Members of Mr Bensly's Vermisorium – the wormery – were encouraged in their endeavours by means of a stick, in the form of an unappealing brush called Bonzo, and a carrot, or rather a weekly circular called the *Weakly Worm*, of which a few examples survive. The unfortunate Bensly had had to try to teach Alan French and 'English subjects' (Scripture, English, History and Geography), as well as Latin; his misfortune was compounded by Alan unthinkably passing his School Certificate. On Alan's Summer 1928 report, O'Hanlon's comment was: 'I only hope he will dish his form-master's [Bensly's] expectations'. At a later date Ethel gleefully reported, 'He did so with 7 credits in school certificate including English, French, *Latin*.' Of these events, John remarked, 'There is no evidence that Mr Bensly paid up the billion pounds.'

The teaching of Latin requires the administration of mercy.

Above: Birching, according to a mercy-seat in the choir at Sherborne Abbey.
Right: Bonzo, as applied by Mr Bensly. (© David Ridgway, Sherborne School; and courtesy of Sherborne School)

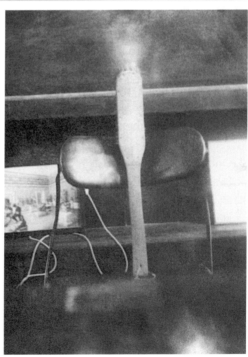

Interplanetary gravitation and a supernova

The Dinard days were over for the Turings. Now they had moved to Guildford, living in suburban obscurity, with Julius ever more bored and Ethel continuing to strain for something to do with her surplus energy. With School Certificate behind him, the way was clear for Alan to specialise and Ethel was thirsty for information; Alan obliged in his Sunday letters with stuff about Schrödinger's theory. From here on, the school reports, covering chemistry, mathematics and physics as principal subjects, improved – with, of course, the now-customary comments about untidiness and slovenliness, and the expected grumbles from teachers of 'subsidiary subjects': French, English and German ('He does not seem to have any aptitude for languages'). He was also 'sociable & makes friends: & he seems unselfish in temper'. One such friend, in the year above Alan, was the stellar Christopher Morcom. In September 1928, Turing and Morcom came into the same orbit when they were put in the same form.

It was easy to hero-worship Chris Morcom. He had blond, boyish good looks and he was wholly free of ink stains. His contemporary and companion at Lyon House, Victor Brookes, described his intellect, his smile, his artistic nature and his sympathy for those in adversity. And his practical jokes:

> One term he made a star chart of the most intricate design; another he bought numbers of balloons, which he filled with gas and named after his favourite goats! These would be fitted with a fuse of waxed string, lighted and despatched over the girls school, often, I fear, complete with messages from the Upper Studies! The excitement was terrific when they exploded high in the air.[11]

Goats? Chris Morcom's mother bred goats, and Chris defended this eccentricity with passion. It was just one of his charming traits. Masters like Trelawny-Ross were inclined to be dismissive, if not hostile, when boys preferred sciences to arts, fearing they would turn into 'soulless specialists'. Trelawny-Ross was Morcom's housemaster, and having noted mournfully 'he could have done very well if he had stayed on the Classical side', he acknowledged that Morcom had many redeeming features. First and foremost, games: despite his size and the handicap of illness, Chris played as a rugby forward, and he counted among his house friends the Captain of (rugby) Football. Then, he had charm, ability, modesty, kindness and loyalty. He folded up his clothes at night. He had made a positive impression in Trelawny-Ross's Confirmation class. And, not least of all for Trelawny-Ross:[12]

> Possibly other boys in the House did not realize it fully, for it would have been quite consistent with his unselfishness and modesty to hide the fact, but the Jazz type of 'music' certainly was more than a little distasteful to him and he must have spent some uncomfortable hours with it in other boys' Studies.

Despite their obvious differences, in deportment, tidiness and compliance with the rules and conventions, Alan Turing and Chris Morcom found each other to be kindred intellects:

> A question about the orbits of planets brought them together, and keen though Chris was upon his games it was actually during half-time at a game of football that the discussion was resumed. They soon found much common ground and worked side by side in the Science laboratories. Chris seems to have delighted in enlarging upon the technical beauties and value of apparatus and there was hardly a subject open to Scientific investigation which did not grip him. So talk ranged from an analysis of the iodised salt prescribed for a boy in another House to the age of the stars with every imaginable sort of subject in between. Everything connected with his work, however trivial, fascinated him. He was for instance as Turing tells me, delighted to find some fungi growing in a beaker and at once took them to Mr H. Davis for a thorough investigation.

Trelawny-Ross sent his senior students off to the school library on Wednesday afternoons for a stint of essay-writing, whereas O'Hanlon expected his own students to stay at Westcott House. Having mislaid a book one day in 1929, Alan went over to the main school buildings to the library 'to share with someone from Ross' [house]. I so enjoyed Chris's company that ever since I always used to go to the library instead of my study.'[13] In the summer and Christmas holidays in 1929 Alan and Chris wrote each other haphazard letters on astronomy and chemistry and friction and whatever other technical topic came to mind. Morcom and Turing travelled together to Cambridge in December 1929 to try for a maths scholarship at Trinity College – Chris succeeded, Alan did not, but Alan could have another go next year.

And then, tragically, it came to a sudden end. There was a reason that Chris was underweight for his age: he was suffering from a form of tuberculosis, which flared up on 6 February 1930. The tuberculosis had been attributed to cow's milk, and the Morcoms' goats were kept to provide a source of safe milk for Chris. He was whisked off to hospital, then removed to London, but on 13 February Christopher Morcom died.

It is perhaps rather easy to conclude that Alan was knocked sideways, and that the death of his best friend was bound to exert an influence over the rest of his life. Certainly Alan felt the loss, and keenly. Within a day, guided by Mother, Alan had written a letter of condolence to Chris's mother, whom he'd met briefly en route to Cambridge two months before.

But Chris was not Alan's only friend, and not the only Sherborne student who was in his intellectual peer group. Alan's maths teacher from the autumn of 1928 was Canon D.B. Eperson, who had been teaching Morcom for a year already. In January 1929 another boy, Pat Mermagen, joined the set; he already had a Cambridge scholarship under his belt. They all sat their Higher School Certificate (HSC) exam in July 1929; the results were Morcom 1436, Mermagen 1365, Turing 1033, 'and some also-rans'. Mermagen stayed on for another year to be Captain of the School, Captain of Rugby and Captain of Cricket.

Alan with Pat Mermagen, another maths student at Sherborne, in June 1930. (Author)

Chris Morcom's death did, however, have significant consequences. First and foremost, in the absence of the one person with whom he could collaborate, Alan Turing's preferred approach to problem-solving – to tackle it on his own – was left unchallenged in his peer group. From now on, Alan would always do things his way. Eperson summed it up:[14]

In July [1930] his H.S.C. marks reached only 1079; these figures show that Turing, though potentially a gifted mathematician, never did really well in the conventional H.S.C. topics. In one sense he was difficult to teach, as he preferred to make his own independent investigations. He was reputed to have 'discovered' Gregory's series, $\pi/4 = 1 - 1/3 + 1/5 - 1/7$ + ad inf., without using any calculus during his early school days. He was less interested in studying text books and developing a good style.

His HSC examiner made similar comments:[15]

A.M. Turing showed an unusual aptitude for noticing the less obvious points to be discussed or avoided in certain questions and for discovering methods which would at once shorten or illumine the solutions. But he appeared to lack the patience necessary for careful computation or algebraic verification and his handwriting was so bad that he lost marks frequently – sometimes because his work was definitely illegible and sometimes because his misreading his own handwriting led him into mistakes.

Oh dear. But Alan was not moping; rather the contrary: Old Turog was succeeding. A photograph with Mermagen shows Alan in June 1930 happy and relaxed (and with typically ghastly unpressed trousers) in the Sherborne School courts, just outside the classrooms where maths was taught. That summer he set up a Foucault's Pendulum at Westcott House in the 'black-and-white' – the boys' entrance hall, named for its floor tiles, which had a broad, open stairwell going all the way up to the second floor. This gave him awed, if uncomprehending, credibility among the junior boys. He surprised his Head of House with a useful performance on the rugby field. He became a school prefect. He was a participant in holiday trips with other senior boys, some hosted by Mr O'Hanlon – a convenient way to escape the strictures and tensions of Guildford, now that John had qualified as a solicitor and was working in London. He even wrote, with the confidence of a past master, to the Editor of the *Weakly Worm*, the unforgotten Mr Bensly:[16]

To the Editor of the *Weakly Worm*. Dear Sir,

We hope that the following will be of use to those who intend taking the School Certificate this term. It is the result of the careful work of A.M.T....g O.W., Fellow of Group III, sometime member of the Vermisorium.

The formula is designed to discover the number of credits which will be obtained in the Certificate Examination.

$$C = \frac{L\pi}{M} \left[\frac{ma - v\sin\theta}{R - r} \right]$$

where:–

C = no: of credits which will be obtained.

m = weight of boy in lbs.

M = momentum of Bonzo on impact with hind-quarters of boy, at last application of same.

a = day of month on which Exam: is taken.

v = capacity for work of boy in 'Greek Prose Hours' (1 G.P.H. = 550 ft. lbs. of work).

θ = angle of inclination of body at last application of Bonzo.
R = no. of ice-buns eaten per week in break.
r = quantity of food consumed during working hours, in Cho-hones.*
L = no. of impositions done per week, on average.

From this we see that:–
        C is greatest when $R = r$.
Therefore, eat as many ice-buns as possible, and consume in Form at
every available opportunity.
        $C = 0$ if $ma = v \sin \theta$, or if M is very large.
Therefore:–
    (1)   Put on weight (see ice-buns), and avoid Bonzo.
    (2)   Humour your master so that he will not beat you hard.
Trusting this may prove useful,
        we are
            yours truly
                VERMES DUO EMERITI.

Veritably, Turing's first formula. Although Chris was gone, he was
not wholly absent from Alan's life. Chris's parents endowed a prize
for science, which Alan won in 1930 and again in 1931. And, as Alan
matured from the Sherborne environment, he found he was accepted,
on his own terms, in the wider Morcom family.

---

*   A variety of milk chocolate.

4

KINGSMAN

In December 1930 Alan Turing won a scholarship to study mathematics at King's College, Cambridge, and his first term there began in the autumn of 1931. Alan occupied the spring and summer terms at Sherborne – in those days staying on was usual practice, as it wouldn't do to seek a temporary job, and institutional culture was deeply embedded. John was amazed:[1]

> Rumours of these matters reaching me, I began to realise that my brother was becoming a power in the land. He outdistanced his mathematics master and for the rest of his time at Sherborne he was borne upon his own pinions; he had out-soared the shadow of Sherborne's night. Since nursery days I had often pondered the story of the goose which turned into a swan. In the Brown, Yellow, Green, Blue and Red Fairy Books it was an unwritten rule that the younger (usually, one must concede, the third) son should make good. Now, suddenly, all was coming true as in the Fairy Books. Alan was making good. My father and I suffered successive phases of disbelief, scepticism and recognition as Alan's scholastic achievements smote us in rapid succession after the manner of Samson's jaw-bone of an ass.

To the parsimonious delight of Julius Turing, Alan's scholarship was worth £80 a year, and on top of that Sherborne made him a grant of £50 a year. In 1931 this was more than enough to live on, particularly for an undergraduate, and it contrasted agreeably with the payment Julius had had to make to buy John into articles of clerkship with a London firm of solicitors.

Chip off a new block

Alan indeed had become a swan, and in more than one sense. Generations of children have been taught that the light-bulb was invented by a Mr Edison in the United States. There is, however, another story. In 1845, a 20-year-old man began experiments using coiled strips of paper to make a carbon filament, which could incandesce under the influence of electricity if placed in a vacuum. The man carried on his experiments for some years, the principal challenge being the vacuum.

By 1878 the difficulties had been overcome, and he demonstrated an incandescent carbon-filament lamp at a meeting of the Newcastle Chemical Society. That man was Joseph Swan, and he was Chris Morcom's grandfather. (Edison also announced his separate achievement in 1878.)

Not Alan's mother. Isobel Morcom, sculptor and foster mother of science, by Walter Paget RA. (© Shaun Armstrong/Mubsta. com and by kind permission of Christopher Morcom)

The Turings might, dimly across a family tree, claim kinship with George Johnstone Stoney, godfather to the electron, but this hardly held a candle to Sir Joseph Swan, FRS, inventor of the electric light-bulb.

Sir Joseph's inventions were manifold:[2]

> Amongst these are to be reckoned, for example, the *carbon process*, better known in this country as the 'Autotype' process; *bromide printing paper*, familiar to all photographers; the *incandescent carbon filament electric lamp*; the *cellular lead plate electrical storage battery*, and perhaps most important of all, *artificial cellulose thread*, the prototype of artificial silk.

Hardly surprising, then, that Alan Turing was fascinated by the Morcom family. In 1929, on his first trip to Cambridge, Alan had accompanied Christopher Morcom and been introduced to Chris's mother in her flat and studio in London. Mrs Morcom wrote in her diary:[3]

> Friday 6 December, 1929. Chris travelled from Sherborne to Cambridge today, via Town. He is going to try for a Scholarship at Trinity. Went to Waterloo to meet him 11.15, but found train came in earlier & he had left. Came straight back to flat & Chris & his friend Allan Turing came next minute. Took them to studio & they tried marble chipping.

Marble chipping under the guidance of someone's mother was a new experience for Alan. Indeed, Isobel Morcom was a new experience. For Alan's own mother, the conventions of India were still ingrained, and art could go as far as watercolour but no further. The dangers and physicality of marble were quite out of bounds.

Alan Turing's relationship with Isobel Morcom began when Chris died. Alan's house tutor was worried about how he would take the unexpected news, and broke it to him as gently as possible; it was suggested Alan might write in condolence to Mrs Morcom, and Ethel Turing agreed when Alan told her the news. Ethel also wrote, despite not having been properly introduced:

Dear Mrs Morcom,

Our boys were such great friends that I want to tell you how much I feel for you, as one mother for another. It must be terribly lonely for you, & so hard not to see here the fulfilment, that I am sure there will be, of all the promise of Christopher's exceptional brains & loveable character. Alan told me one couldn't help liking Morcom & he was himself so devoted to him that I too shared in his devotion & admiration: during exams he always reported Christopher's successes.

He was feeling vy desolate when he wrote asking me to send flowers on his behalf & in case he feels he cannot write to you himself I know he would wish me to send his sympathy with mine.

Yours sincerely,

Ethel S. Turing

But Alan had written, and it was Alan, rather than Ethel, who could help Isobel Morcom in her grief. Almost immediately, the Morcoms offered Alan Chris's berth on their Easter trip to Gibraltar. A Sherborne schoolmaster – Mr Gervis, who taught chemistry – was going as well. Ethel visited Isobel Morcom in her London flat in early April 1930 and they had a long conversation about Chris; and a few days later Alan was aboard the *Kaisar-i-Hind* sharing a cabin with Chris's older brother Rupert. The Morcoms took to Alan, and Alan took to the Morcoms. He even had interesting conversations with Rupert, which wouldn't have happened with John back in Guildford. When the ship docked at Southampton eleven days later, Alan didn't go home to Guildford. He went to Bromsgrove, where the Morcoms lived, and spent a few days 'helping' Isobel with Chris's books and papers.

Escaping the stifling boredom of Guildford during the holidays by retreating to Bromsgrove became a routine for Alan – even if Mother wanted to come too. In August 1930 they both spent a week with the Morcoms, and Alan was prevailed upon to write his impressions of Chris, as well as an unsafe piece on the 'Nature of Spirit', appeasing the Christianity of both mothers without compromising his own (church-going – not that there was much choice) agnosticism. An invitation was issued for summer 1931, when Alan left Sherborne, but for whatever reason Alan went to Sark with O'Hanlon and the senior Westcott boys instead. Further visits followed, in 1932, 1933 and 1936; by 1932 Alan was in control and able to go to Bromsgrove alone.

On the water

Alan Turing didn't want to go to King's, but as will be seen, this choice of college could not have had better consequences for his country. Mathematicians are, or were, supposed to go to Trinity, the college of Newton (and the college which had offered Chris Morcom a scholarship). But Trinity had filled all their scholarships, and their arrangement was to pass on near-miss candidates to King's. King's offered Alan his scholarship, and so to King's he went. Just as Sherborne had struggled to modernise itself in the Victorian era, so had King's. To start with, King's was a sister foundation to Eton, and the college was barred to non-Etonians until 1861. Back then, it was not much of a place for academic glory. King's had had a tradition of ignoring university exams, and had only conceded that its scholars sit such things in 1851; nobody at King's got the top maths classification of 'senior wrangler' until 1885. Then there was the absurdity of the chapel: the college was founded for a provost and seventy scholars, yet the building is the size of a cathedral, with fan-vaulting, misericords and stunning stained-glass windows to match. The rest of the architecture at King's became a muddle: an exuberant pseudo-Palladian white marble oddity by James Gibbs, quite out of place next to the chapel; and a gloomy range of institutional stone buildings by William Wilkins which give the college a passably grand dining hall.

By 1888 it was time for a serious change, and the fellows elected Augustus Austen Leigh as provost. As well as building an attractive court of residential buildings adjacent to the river (in which Alan would eventually have rooms), Leigh set out to make teaching and academic excellence the purpose of the college, and began to attract some brains to the place. We will meet some of them later. By the time Alan arrived in 1931, King's was at the top of the academic tables, and, unlike many other colleges, King's required all its students to sit the 'tripos' exams for an honours degree. If you wanted to study at King's, you now had to study.

Sixty-four other young men went up to King's at the same time as Alan Turing in 1931. Only six were Etonians – more than from any other school bar Winchester – and two others were from Sherborne. One of the Shirburnians was from Ross's House, but he had left to go to the Royal Military Academy at Woolwich in 1928, so missed the shock of Christopher Morcom's sudden death. The other Shirburnian was John Patterson, a bit younger than Alan and from another house; Patterson would go on to become Captain of the King's College Boat Club, of which Alan himself was to be a member for the next few years.

As a novice rower, Alan did rather well, winning the first of several tankards for a performance in trial eights in his first term. Rowing provided a social life to counterbalance the academic side of things, and he participated enthusiastically and with occasional distinction until, and beyond, his graduation. The highlight of the rowing season was the 'bumps', in which boats line up behind one another and try to bump the one in front. In the May 1934 bumps Alan was juggling difficult and conflicting duties: not only did the races coincide with his final exams, but Julius Turing was in hospital and Alan was trying to fit in a visit to his father. Patterson recorded in the Boat Club log that it was:

> unfortunate to lose A M Turing who, owing to his father's illness had been sleeping at home and returning each day to race, but was unable to get back for the last night. He rowed consistently well, and under the circumstances, he had our admiration and sympathy.[4]

There was more rowing drama the following year, when Alan was still at King's preparing for 'Part III', the supplementary post-honours course for scholar mathematicians. By this stage Alan had, in theory, retired from rowing, but the second May boat had trouble:

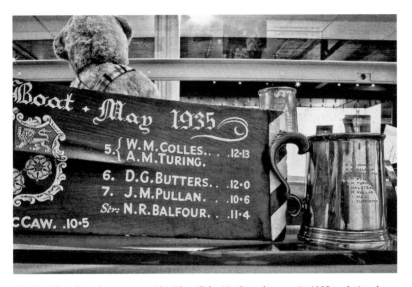

Alan's trophies from the water war. Alan 'shared' the No. 5 seat honours in 1935, replacing the injured William Colles on the last day of the races. (© Bletchley Park Trust)

Third day. Colles was unfortunately injured in a brawl. Turing took his place, the change making but little difference. An excellent start, and made their bump in the gut (St Catherine's IV). Fourth day. Made short work of Peterhouse III just before the ditch.

The outcome was excellent: King's II had made a bump every day, earning the honour of a set of ornamental oars. One of these is now on display in the museum at Bletchley Park.

King's, then, was not just about academic excellence. There were 'hearties' and 'highbrows'. There was the Chetwynd Society ('a somewhat noisy drinking club for popular athletes'), there were dunkings in the fountain of the front court for those who offended too grossly against institutional norms, there were musical performances in the chapel complete with risqué costumes, and Vive-las[5] were sung at smoke-filled gatherings such as took place after the annual Founder's Feast. For the highbrows there were various intellectual debating clubs. Alan didn't fit into any of the clubs, but at King's just being highbrow was perfectly in order. It was a bit like Sherborne, only bigger and better.

Alan had friends beyond the boat club. David Champernowne and James Atkins were also maths scholars. For a while, Atkins was rather more than a friend; and Champernowne became a life-long ally with whom Alan would write a chess-playing computer program in 1948 (the 'TuroChamp') and one of the four men to inherit under his will. Champernowne was remarkable: he was the discoverer of the 'Champernowne constant' $C_{10} = 0.123456789101112\ldots$, which is said to have important properties. It's not everyone who has a constant named after them – and Champ's achievement was to have his discovery and analysis published in the *Journal of the London Mathematical Society* in 1933, when he was still in his second undergraduate year. There was also Fred Clayton, a classicist, who would go on to become a fellow of King's and have a wartime career in intelligence.

Alan fitted in at King's. In part this was because homosexuality was part of the establishment, almost suffused into the stonework. Back before the Great War, men studying classics in all-male schools and colleges were constantly admiring each other, falling in love with each other, and occasionally going further still. With some of them, the object was 'sensual pursuit of beautiful young men', involving Kingsmen such as John Maynard Keynes, Goldsworthy Lowes Dickinson, E.M. Forster and John Sheppard, and other members – most famously, Lytton Strachey – of the Conversazione Society, more familiar to us as 'the Apostles'.

Dear Boy. Provost Sheppard's avuncular approach to governance ensured Alan's early election to a fellowship. (By kind permission of the Provost and Scholars of King's College, Cambridge)

The Apostles formed another link between King's and Trinity, from where the members were drawn, provided they had the requisite qualifications, which seem to have included intellectual arrogance, aesthetic priggishness and yellow hair. In theory the Apostles met to debate topical and intellectual issues with complete candour and freedom of speech: 'people and books reinforced one another, intelligence joined hands with affection, speculation became a passion, and discussion was made profound by love.'[6] What is more, those men could find classical justification in the culture of ancient Greece, as explained by the scholar Julie Anne Tadeo:[7]

> In an 1896 publication Dickinson promoted the 'Greek View of Life'. In particular, Dickinson admired the Greek's gendered system of work and love. He praised the women of Ancient Greece who nurtured the state's future soldiers and citizens but noted their shortcomings as emotional and intellectual companions of men. As objects of romantic love, women merely complemented men, while in male-male love, the superior male self was duplicated. The Greek View of Life was also Dickinson's response to the recent Wilde trials. Passionate friendships between Greek men, he argued, were an 'institution', particularly pederastic ties between youths and adults, and should be emulated, not condemned. Dickinson and the other Apostles evoked the friendships of Achilles and Patroclus, Solon and Peisistratus, and Socrates and Alcibiades.

The Apostles would later become notorious for including Anthony Blunt and Guy Burgess, near-contemporaries of Alan Turing as well as Russian spies, among its members. Unlike David Champernowne, Alan was neither elegant nor outspoken enough to be admitted to the elite and secretive Apostles. His hair was not yellow: it was dark and lanky and not in the least bit aesthetic. After the Great War, a more sombre spirit had reined in the Edwardian outpouring of pseudo-classicism; in any case, much of the Greek view of life had been merely posturing, because even at Cambridge it was dangerous for men to indulge too openly in homosexual relations. Nonetheless, there were still vestiges of the classical culture at King's College in the early 1930s.

Keynes was still very much in evidence, Dickinson was still around, and Sheppard was vice-provost.

In February 1932, towards the end of Alan's second term at King's, Isobel Morcom came to Cambridge. It was in the middle of the Lent bumps.

My dear Mrs Morcom,

Thank you for your post-card & for asking me to dinner on Friday. I can certainly manage it, thank you very much. I have just been round to Brookes. He says he will be able to come. His college is Trinity Hall & his rooms are at 2 Round Church street. Fortunately I was able to get you rooms at the Bull for Friday. I thought possibly they would be full because of the Lents. I shall be rowing, so will have to be rather abstinent on Friday evening. First day of Lents is to-morrow. Am quite excited about them already. Was Chris going to row ~~when~~ if he had come up?

I shall have to go down to the river now. Looking forward very much to seeing you on Friday.

Yours

Alan

I have just one lecture on Saturday morning 9–10.

The Bull Hotel was right next door to King's. After dinner, Isobel Morcom recorded that Victor Brookes took the Morcoms 'round to see his rooms (not in College). He is at Trinity Hall. He had Chris' portrait over his writing table & the smiling photo on his dressing table. He loved Chris.' The next day 'Alan came round at 10 & took us to see his rooms in King's then we went into Chapel & then on to Trinity. Alan showed us where Chris' and his rooms were when they came for their Scholarship exam, then we went into Trinity Chapel & I imagined where Chris would have sat. (Alan's rooms were very untidy in contrast to Victor's).'

The domination of the Germans

Perhaps the distractions and relative liberties of university life led Alan away from the path of study in his first year. For whatever reason, he under-achieved in his first-year maths exams, being ranked only in the second class. He was heartily ashamed:

> My dear Mrs Morcom
>
> I am up here for the 'long' so that your letter has just reached me from home. I remembered Chris' birthday & would have written to you but for the fact that I found myself quite unable to express what I wanted to say. [...]
>
> I suppose you saw that I had only got a 2nd in 1st part of Maths. I can hardly look anyone in the face after it. I won't try to offer an explanation. I shall just have to get a 1st in Mays to show I'm not really so bad as that.
>
> Yours affectionately,
>
> Alan M. Turing[8]

In 1933 Adolf Hitler came to power in Germany. The league of Nations had already decided not to punish Japan for the invasion of Manchuria, and 'collective security' was proved to be a chimera. At King's, as elsewhere, there was much debate about the future, and many predicted that the country would be entangled in another war. In May 1933 Alan wrote to his mother, with a further round of excuses for avoiding holidays at home:

> Dear Mother
>
> Thank you for socks etc. No hurry for map. Daddy tells me you are shutting up house on June 6. I shall probably stay here till about 16th. I go for walking tour on 21st to 28th. Am thinking of going to Russia some time in vac but have not yet quite made up my mind.
>
> I have joined an organisation called the 'Anti-War Council'. Politically rather communist. Its programme is principally to organise strikes amongst munitions and chemical workers when government

intends to go to war. It gets up a guarantee fund to support the workers who strike. [...]

> Yours,
>> Alan

Beyond the façade of the Wilkins screen along the front court of King's, there was a world recovering from the Great Depression. One of the fellows wrote later:[9]

> Even the most complacent student could not be blind to the plight of the working class. There was (so far as I know) no don in King's who actively recruited members for the Communist Party; but Communists did their best to infiltrate any College society they could, whatever its aim.

It was fashionable to be leftish at Cambridge in the 1930s, and most of the country was dismayed by sabre-rattling; in 1933 the full horror of the Nazi and Stalin regimes had yet to be revealed. Only if you were in the Apostles did Russian trips and being rather communist turn into something more sinister, though it seems unlikely that Ethel Turing would have approved of politically motivated strikes. Nothing more appears about communism in Alan's letters, but later in 1933 he reports to Mother the successful protest against a showing of *Our Fighting Navy* at the Tivoli Cinema ('blatant militarist propaganda'). It does not seem that Alan was greatly attracted by activism; and he formed his own views about Nazism during a couple of holidays to Austria and Germany in 1934. In 1933, though, he spent a week on retreat with the Morcoms; in that year he had begun to study again.

Alan was getting interested in the logical aspects of mathematics. One of the prize books awarded to Alan by Sherborne was *Mathematische Grundlagen der Quantenmechanik* (Mathematical Foundations of Quantum Mechanics) by John von Neumann, whom we will encounter again. (Sherborne was sniffy about prize books. Writing to Isobel Morcom in December 1932 about his choices for the Christopher Morcom prize, Alan had explained, 'in 1930 they were bound in the same way as other school prizes, but in 1931

The Morcom Prize for Science. *Robinson Crusoe* is not a science book and is still in mint condition; John von Neumann's *Mathematische Grundlagen der Quantenmechanik* bears tea stains to prove it has been read. (© Shaun Armstrong/Mubsta. com and by kind permission of the Bletchley Park Trust and the Provost and Scholars of King's College, Cambridge)

Mr Boughey relaxed this condition but said that if I got books not bound in full calf they could not be signed by him.' So the copy of *Robinson Crusoe*, a 1930 prize rich with calf, marbling, gilt, bookplate and signature, and displayed in the museum at Bletchley Park, is wholly untouched. Von Neumann's book, by contrast, was read.) Alan reported that von Neumann was 'very interesting, & not at all too difficult reading, although the applied mathematicians seem to find it rather too strong meat'.

It was strong meat because it was in German, a language in which Alan had demonstrated his lack of aptitude at Sherborne; but if you were serious about maths in the 1930s, you had to be able to get on with mathematical German. Another reason it was strong meat was that it was about the axioms underpinning the oddities of quantum mechanics: that there was a consistent logical system in mathematics, into which the problematic results in quantum physics could neatly fit. Logic, consistency, and truth.

Alan's enthusiasm must have caught the eye of Richard Braithwaite, a young King's mathematics don, who was himself exploring the crossovers between mathematics, logic and philosophy. He was influential in the Moral Sciences Club – 'moral sciences' being Cambridge-speak for philosophy – and Alan was invited to present a paper on mathematics and logic at their meeting, in Alan's rooms, on 1 December 1933. Alan said in a letter home, 'I hope they don't know it all already.'

A positive contribution to mathematical thought

Part of the problem in quantum mechanics is that observations mess things up. It is not surprising, then, to find that Alan chose to attend Professor Sir Arthur Eddington's lectures on the methodology of science. Alan had chosen Eddington's *The Nature of the Physical World* for the Morcom Prize in 1930, and Eddington was now trying to create a fundamental theory to unify quantum theory, gravitation and relativity. Eddington's lectures mentioned that scientific observations tended to be distributed according to a normal, or Gaussian, curve, around the mean value. For Alan, this was a challenge; it was all very well to assert such a thing, but assertions needed to be proved.

So, by early 1934, in his trademark get-it-done-best-on-your-own way, Alan proved Eddington's assertion. Here was a substantive result, one that would probably even surpass Champernowne (who, under the influence of Keynes and the other economic brains at King's, had switched to economics), and might even give grounds for election to a fellowship, and a career in academia. Alas for Alan, the Central Limit Theorem, to give the problem its usual name, had been first posited in 1733 and thought about by many famous mathematicians and scientists, including Laplace and Galton; eventually, in 1922, the Finnish mathematician Jarl Waldemar Lindeberg had published a proof (in German, of course). Alan Turing's first major achievement had been scooped.

So it was back to business, with final exams looming in May and the need to prove himself. The timing was terrible, with Julius Turing's prostate operation right in the middle, as well as the duties of a college oarsman. But all went well, despite the best efforts of *The Times* to print a class-list suggesting Alan had got a B grade.

Dear Mother

I enclose list of Maths Tripos II in case you have been taking 'the Times' too seriously. I hope the aunts won't see it & write congratulatory letters on getting a (b).

It is very kind of you all to send me these telegrams. It seems to me more extravagant than taking a taxi. [...]

Yours

Alan.

Ethel Turing has annotated this letter with the remark 'Reference to taxi is due to his father's belief that to take a taxi was great extravagance'. Alan had in fact passed as a B-star wrangler, the obscure Cambridge maths tripos codeword meaning that he had achieved first-class honours (a 'wrangler') with distinction in additional papers. (The explanation on the class-list says, 'The mark ($b\star$) is attached to the names of those candidates who in the opinion of the Moderators and Examiners deserve special credit in subjects of Schedule B.') There were nine other B-stars, from a total of 37 mathematicians ranked as wranglers in 1934. King's was generous to its B-star wranglers, and allowed Alan a £200 research studentship to stay on and try for a fellowship. Meanwhile, in the summer vacation, Alan stood as best man to his brother John, who was getting married to Joan Humphreys, who was, as you would expect, a daughter of the Indian Civil Service.

Because Alan had not been aware of Lindeberg's proof, his work on the Central Limit Theorem might, with a bit of polishing up, be suitable as a fellowship dissertation.

> I have a horrid recollection [wrote John] of 'The Gaussian Error Function' (whatever that might be), reputedly the subject of this monograph, for Alan had left it to the eleventh hour to sort the sheets, parcel and dispatch them. My mother and I spent a frantic half-hour on hands and knees putting them in order; Mother did up the parcel in record time and Alan sped with it to the [Post Office] on his bike, announcing on his return that there were at least twenty minutes to spare. This is my only positive contribution to mathematical thought.[10]

In 1933 Provost Brooke – the uncle of the poet Rupert Brooke – retired, to be replaced by John Sheppard, who was not the bookies' favourite, but who was nonetheless to hold office for the next 21 years. Sheppard's great characteristic was that he loved the young men of his college, and he possessed in abundance the ability to cross social boundaries to put them at ease. Sometimes this could be disconcerting, as noted in a history of the college:[11]

> His fine head of hair had gone white when he was in his thirties, and he early adopted the pose of a benevolent old gentleman scattering 'blessings'. Many of those who came into residence he got to know, sometimes by the simple method of stopping them in the court and

The bachelor existence. Half out of shot, Alan is a bystander as best man beside his brilliantined brother at John's wedding in August 1934. (Author)

saying, 'Who are you, dear boy?' ('I'm not your dear boy,' one replied, 'I'm at Selwyn.')

To the great good fortune of Alan Turing, Provost Sheppard chaired the fellowship election committee, and Provost Sheppard used his personal knowledge of the candidates to ensure that the right man was elected, even if, on occasion, academic evidence pointed in favour of a different candidate. Turing was making his mark on the college – unusual, maybe, but not invisible. Complaining that he had never had a teddy bear in childhood, Alan asked for one for Christmas in 1934; it was duly provided by a bemused Ethel Turing, and Porgy the bear was installed in Alan's rooms to greet visitors. (Porgy is still receiving visitors in the museum at Bletchley Park.) *Basileon*, the King's College satirical magazine, noted in its 1936 edition a pageful of Sayings of the Year, including two aphorisms of Alan Turing: 'I think the College is going to have more kittens', and 'I *am* prepared to admit that there *are* other people besides myself'.

Porgy, Alan's teddy bear, given to him in adulthood because, as a foster child, nobody had given him one in infancy. (© Bletchley Park Trust)

Those 'other people' had to pronounce on the Gaussian Error Function. On 12 November 1934, a dissertation by A.M. Turing on that subject had been referred by the Electors to Fellowships to Professor R.A. Fisher and Mr A.S. Beskovitch for review.[12]

Mr A.S. Beskovitch's Report:
The dissertation is not to be judged from the point of view of its scientific value, as its main results were established long ago and even the fundamental idea of the method is not new.

Prof. R.A. Fisher's Report:
The subject chosen for the thesis is one which I have thought decidedly unattractive, and which has been worked over, from various points of view, by continental and especially Scandinavian writers to the point of making it positively repellent.

Oh dear. But:

Mr A.S. Beskovitch's Report:
The development of Mr Turing's method is very much different from that of Lindeberg, which makes me completely confident that the work has been done in a genuine ignorance of Lindeberg's work. Mr Turing's proof is somewhat more complicated than the Lindeberg proof, but all the same it is an excellent success and it would be so not only for a beginner but also for a fully developed scientist. If the paper were published fifteen years ago it would be an important event in the mathematical literature of that year. In Mr Turing's case we see a display of very exceptional abilities at the very start of his research work, which makes me to recommend him as a very strong candidate for a Fellowship.

Prof. R.A. Fisher's Further Report:
I have no hesitation in judging Turing's thesis the work of a first-class candidate. He seems to have thought out his own methods. Finally in reading through his paper, I formed a very high opinion of his

taste, virtuosity would not be too strong a term, in the art of framing conclusive mathematical demonstrations.

So the lack of priority on the Central Limit Theorem could be overlooked, and on 16 March 1935, 'at a Meeting of the Electors to Fellowships holden in the Combination Room', presided over by Mr Provost, Alan Turing was elected to a fellowship of King's at the ripe old age of 22. Alan Turing moved from the grimness of his earlier rooms on 'A' and 'Q' staircases to a top-floor set of rooms in the airy Bodley's Court, with a pleasant view of the river, and his friend Fred Clayton downstairs. Fitting for a mathematician, this was on Staircase X, and his rooms would from now on sport the dignified label '*Mr* Turing'. *Basileon* rounded off the achievement with a clerihew:

Turing
must be very alluring
to be made a don
so early on.

5

MACHINERY OF LOGIC

A former pupil of Sherborne School, who achieves a top-class degree in mathematics at Cambridge University, is like as not to be interested in the rules which govern mathematical reasoning. It would be necessary to discuss the subject with philosophy professors who specialise in logic. And a very clever Old Shirburnian might even go so far as to write a world-famous work on the subject.

Alfred North Whitehead went to Sherborne School in 1875. His older brother Henry was also at Sherborne and went on to become Bishop of Madras in 1899, where he was most likely cultivated by Ethel Turing, who had a soft spot for bishops. Unlike Alan Turing, A.N. Whitehead did well on the games field, became head of school, and went to Trinity College, Cambridge to study maths, coming fourth in the list of wranglers. Until Alan came onto the scene, Whitehead was Sherborne's star intellectual alumnus; even when I attended the school in the 1970s his name was spoken with reverence. Whitehead had, with Bertrand Russell as junior author, written the *Principia Mathematica*. To give a book, published over the years 1910–13, a Newtonian title in Latin would seem an act of blazing arrogance were it not for its ambition and achievement. For Whitehead's work set out to do no less than codify the rules of mathematical thought.

Rules, unlike mathematicians, ought to be logical and orderly. They ought to allow for any mathematical proposition to be deduced from a handful of basic precepts, without contradiction or uncertainty. That cleanliness, after all, is what distinguishes maths from metaphysics. And who better to develop notions of tidiness in mathematics than the Germans? In 1920, David Hilbert, a mathematics professor working in Göttingen, posed three objectives about the rules mathematicians need in order to carry out proofs:

1. Completeness. Every proposition which is true, can be proved, using the rules. *Eg: I assert that the angles of a triangle add up to 180 degrees; I can prove this from Euclid's axioms.*

2. Consistency. No contradictions will arise, when applying the rules. *Eg: having proved that the angles of all triangles add up to 180 degrees, I cannot produce from my hat a super-triangle whose angles add up to 200 degrees.*

3. Decidability. There is a method for deciding whether any proposition is true or false. *Eg: you assert that the angles of a square add up to 360 degrees. Neither of us knows whether this is true or false, but we can find out.* Hilbert put it in Latin thus: 'In mathematics there is no ignorabimus'. There should be no unknowable unknowns in maths.

It would all be so neat if these things could be shown to be true. Alas, in 1931 an Austrian mathematician, Kurt Gödel, proved that mathematics was incomplete. There were theorems which could neither be proved nor disproved. Worse, he went on to demonstrate, using a modern rerun of one of Zeno's paradoxes ('this proposition is unprovable'), that a mathematical system cannot be proved to be consistent either, and it absolutely cannot be both complete and consistent.

For students of higher mathematics all this was tremendous fun, and in 1935 Cambridge was running a course of lectures for its advanced students on the foundations of mathematics. The lecturer was M.H.A. Newman, and Alan Turing was one of his students. Newman had done war service in the Army and some teaching

Alan's lifelong mentor, M.H.A. Newman. It was Newman's lecture invoking a 'mechanical process' that set Alan Turing off on a lifetime of work and ideas about machines, logic, computing and shape. (© Godfrey Argent via London Mathematical Society)

before he came to Cambridge. He had taken his degree in 1921 – as a B-star wrangler, needless to say. By 1935 he was 38 years old, newly married, and a fellow of St John's College where he was working up his ideas to write a textbook on topology. He was musical, had an impish dry wit, inspired great loyalty, and was destined to become Alan Turing's lifelong mentor. In 1935 his job was to explain the Hilbert plan, and its partial debunking, to students like Alan. The one piece of Hilbert's architecture which might still be intact was the issue of decidability, in German called the *Entscheidungsproblem*. The *Entscheidungsproblem* captured Alan's imagination. It was tailor-made for his way of thinking, which always, even in relation to the most abstract mathematical ideas, sought links back to the real, practical world. Newman explained:[1]

The point was that Hilbert had announced that he would find really a way of doing mathematics once and for all by putting it into purely symbolic form and analysing the grammar of the propositions of mathematics as put out in symbols, and that he would try to find a decision method, that is to say, a process for finding the answer 'yes' or 'no' to the question 'Can this be proved false, can it be proved …?' And the question, of course, as Turing saw, was what do you mean by 'process'?

Newman had talked of Hilbert's surviving idea as a *mechanical* process:[2]

I believe it all started because he attended a lecture of mine on foundations of mathematics and logic. I think I said in the course of this lecture that what is meant by saying that a process is constructive is that it's purely mechanical, a machine – and I may even have said, a machine can do it. But he took the notion and really tried to follow it right up, and did produce this extraordinary definition of a perfectly general what he called 'computable function', thus giving the first idea, really, of a perfectly general computing machine.

So Alan Turing started thinking about machines. The machine had to be perfectly general, because it had to be able to decide whether any proposition was true or false. It couldn't, therefore, be like regular 1930s mechanical calculating machines, which could do boring adding or subtracting, or – to take the most sophisticated type of machine at the very forefront of technology – solve differential equations. These were single-purpose machines, whereas the 'machine' which Alan Turing needed would be all-purpose. And Alan's all-purpose machine could be put to one special use. It would pull the last keystone out of Hilbert's edifice, and bring the whole thing crashing down.

Mulling over these things took some time. Meanwhile, Alan had been elected to his King's fellowship and produced a short paper taking forward the 'group theory' invented by John von Neumann, the mathematician whose book had inspired Alan's talk to the Moral

Sciences Club. (Von Neumann, who visited Cambridge and lectured briefly in 1935, had also been at Göttingen with Hilbert and was destined to float in and out of Alan's life.) By early 1936 Alan's idea had matured into a draft paper, and by Easter it was ready for review.

Dear Mother, […]

I saw Mr Newman four or five days after I came up. He is very busy with other things just at present and says he will not be able to give his whole attention to my theory for some week or so yet. However, he examined my note for C.R* and approved it after some alterations. I have had no acknowledgment of it, which is rather annoying. I don't think the full text will be ready for a fortnight or more yet. It will probably be about fifty pages. It is rather difficult to decide what to put into the paper now and what to leave over till a later occasion. […]

Yours

Alan[3]

Newman did give his whole attention to Alan's theory, and it was ground-breaking. Alan had demolished Hilbert's plan, and had presented his demolition work with clarity and vision. The centrepiece of Alan's idea was a 'universal' computing machine, a fantastic idea: an imaginary machine which had only a limited range of physical functions, but which could imitate the behaviour of any single-purpose machine. Alan had created a generic description of algorithms.

We may compare a man in the process of computing a real number to a machine which is only capable of a finite number of conditions, which will be called m-configurations. The machine is supplied with a 'tape' running through it, and divided into sections (called 'squares') each capable of bearing a 'symbol'. At any moment there is just one square which is in the 'machine'. We may call this square the 'scanned

---

*   *Comptes Rendus*, a French mathematical journal.

square'. The symbol on the scanned square may be called the 'scanned symbol'. The 'scanned symbol' is the only one of which the machine is, so to speak, 'directly aware'. However, by altering its *m*-configuration the machine can effectively remember some of the symbols which it has 'seen' (scanned) previously. The possible behaviour of the machine at any moment is defined by the *m*-configuration and the scanned symbol. In some of the configurations in which the scanned square is blank (*i.e.* bears no symbol) the machine writes down a new symbol on the scanned square: in other configurations it erases the scanned symbol. The machine may also change the square which is being scanned, but only by shifting it one place right or left. In addition to any of these operations the *m*-configuration may be changed. Some of the symbols written down will form the sequence of figures which is the decimal of the real number which is being computed. The others are just rough notes to 'assist the memory'. It will only be these rough notes which will be liable to erasure.

It is my contention that these operations include all those which are used in the computation of a number.[4]

Using the machine concept, Alan Turing went on to explain how there were various problems which could not be solved by machines. Any given special-purpose machine could have its functionality (its program) rendered into symbols, which could actually be put on the tape as data to be tested by another machine running a different program. By running one program to test another, Alan was able to find some mathematical equivalents to the Epimenides paradox ('Epimenides the Cretan says that all Cretans are liars'). By producing contradictions, certain machines can be shown to be impossible: one example is a program to decide whether any particular program would ever lead to the machine printing the symbol '0'. The 'halting problem' – a program to see if any other program would run forever or halt at some stage – is a similar, more modern example; again, it can be proved by contradiction that such a program cannot be written.

Turing machines - what you need to know

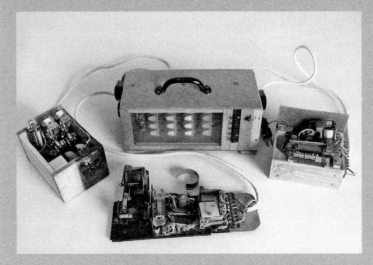

A model 'Turing machine' created in the 1950s by Professor Gisbert Hasenjäger. Without their knowledge, they were to become opponents in the cryptographic war. (Courtesy of Rainer Glaschick and the Heinz Nixdorf Foundation (Paderborn))

Most people have got through life happily and successfully without knowing the first thing about Turing machines, and that's fine. So you probably need to know nothing about them. But it might help a little to have some notion, in order to put the rest of Alan Turing's life – much of which was founded on his greatest mathematical achievement, the paper on *Computable Numbers* – into context.

The machine which Alan Turing conceptualised has a read-write head and a long tape. It also has a set of instructions which tell it what to do when it finds itself in a particular 'state', or as he put it, '*m*-configuration'. So, for example, in State 1, it might view the tape, and if it is blank, print an asterisk, and then go to State 2. In State 2 it might just move the tape one place to the right, and then go to State 1. In State 1, if the tape is not blank, it might just go to State 2. (This might not be a very exciting set of instructions, but no matter.) The point here is that the instructions can all be *coded* into language or numerical form. Kurt Gödel had previously shown that formulae can be re-coded as numbers – and numbers can be handled like data.

Alan Turing's 'universal' machine takes a tape which has the instructions-code for another machine – like the boring machine which just prints an endless set of asterisks wherever it finds a blank space – and by reading the code can mimic the behaviour of the boring machine. Or any machine. The self-referential nature of the universal machine, treating instructions as data, is what enabled him to make his mathematical proof for the *Entscheidungsproblem*.

However, the idea that instructions-code could be put onto a tape, or to express it differently, that a program for a machine could be a simple input (like the numbers you input into a cheap calculator when you want to perform simple addition), was very powerful. Here was the theoretical construct of a stored-program computer for which you could change the program.

Troubles with the post

Alan's first paper on computable numbers went astray in the mail.

> Dear Mother, [...]
>
> I have just got my main paper ready & sent in. I imagine it will appear in October or November. The situation with regard to the note for Comptes Rendus was not so good. It appears that that man who I wrote to, and whom I asked to communicate the paper for me had gone to China, and moreover the letter seems to have been lost in the post, for a second letter reached his daughter.

And then M.H.A. Newman opened his own mail. Working in Princeton, New Jersey, the respected mathematician Alonzo Church had published his own paper, in the first edition of the *Journal of Symbolic Logic* – conveniently enough, the journal of the Association for Symbolic Logic that Church himself had founded in 1935. Church had invented a mathematical grammar, called the lambda-calculus, and while Turing wrote in terms of 'computability' for mathematical functions carried out by his conceptual machine, Church wrote of 'lambda-definability'. But they were basically the same thing, and both concepts were being used to shred the remaining vestiges of Hilbert's plan for tidiness in mathematics. Church thought Newman would be interested; Newman certainly was.

> Dear Professor Church,
>
> An offprint which you kindly sent me recently of your paper in which you define 'calculable numbers', and shew that the Entscheidungsproblem for Hilbert logic is insoluble, had a rather painful interest for a young man, A.M. Turing, here, who was just about to send in for publication a paper in which he had used a definition of 'Computable numbers' for the same purpose. His treatment – which consists in describing a machine which will grind out any computable sequence – is rather different from yours, but seems to be of great merit,

and I think it of great importance that he should come and work with you next year if that is at all possible.

    Yours sincerely,

        M.H.A. Newman[5]

Alan's work had, once again, been scooped. His letter to Mother continues:

Meanwhile a paper has appeared in America, written by Alonzo Church, doing the same things in a different way. Mr Newman and I have decided however that the method is sufficiently different to warrant the publication of my paper too. Alonzo Church lives at Princeton so I have decided quite definitely about going there. […]

    Yours

        Alan

Two could play at the editorial game, and M.H.A. Newman had influence with the London Mathematical Society. Accordingly, Alan Turing's paper on *Computable Numbers* was 'Received 28 May, 1936 – Read 12 November, 1936' and finally published in the *Proceedings* of that Society in early 1937. Alan's paper was different in concept from Church's: the concept of a universal computing machine opened up for exploration a large number of new avenues in logic, and Alan only devoted a couple of pages to the *Entscheidungsproblem*. The wider view he offered meant that Alan's paper became a foundation stone for a whole mathematical discipline, namely computability. And, because it laid down for the first time an account of a programmable computing machine, generations of computer science students have come to curse the name of Alan Turing because *Computable Numbers* appears on undergraduate reading lists: it is long, it uses symbols printed in German Gothic typeface, and, like John von Neumann's German work on quantum mechanics, it is rather strong meat.

Many years later, Alan wrote a different version for more general readers, where the meat was cut up into more digestible pieces. Here is the introductory paragraph:[6]

> If one is given a puzzle to solve one will usually, if it proves to be difficult, ask the owner whether it can be done. Such a question should have a quite definite answer, yes or no, at any rate provided the rules describing what you are allowed to do are perfectly clear. Of course the owner of the puzzle may not know the answer. One might equally ask, 'How can one tell whether a puzzle is solvable?', but this cannot be answered so straightforwardly. The fact of the matter is that there is *no* systematic method of testing puzzles to see whether they are solvable or not. If by this one meant merely that nobody had ever yet found a test which could be applied to any puzzle, there would be nothing at all remarkable in the statement. It would have been a great achievement to have invented such a test, so we can hardly be surprised that it has never been done. But it is not merely that the test has never been found. It has been proved that no such test ever can be found.

He illustrated this new paper with examples of the sliding-square puzzle, where 15 little squares bearing numbers or pictures can be moved within a 4x4 frame using the empty space. Here he uses plenty of pictures, no German Gothic, and far fewer pages, and games take the place of universal computing machines. Games were already occupying Alan's mind back in 1936 as he thought through the implications of *Computable Numbers*. Games were a homely sample of mathematical-logical problems, subject to sets of tidy rules, which could in theory be used to program notional computing machines. Any such program was fanciful, of course, not least because in 1936 there was no practical concept of a programmable computing machine. But Alan was happy to write down systematically the rules for things like the Japanese game with counters called Go.

Autumn leaves

Although Alan's paper was 'read' on 12 November 1936, it was not he that was reading it. By this time he had arrived at Princeton. Through the persistence of Newman, Alonzo Church and John von Neumann – the latter by now a leading light at Princeton's Institute for Advanced Study – had agreed to accommodate Alan Turing for a year at Princeton, and he had left for the United States on 23 September. Meanwhile there had been a round of leave-taking visits: to see Ethel and Julius, of course, though both of them being in the same place at the same time was becoming unusual; and, perhaps more enjoyably, a few days with the Morcoms. By this stage Isobel Morcom was unwell and largely confined to her bed:[7]

SEPTEMBER, 1936.

Wednesday 9

Slept very late & feel much refreshed for first time for ages. Alan Turing came. He arrived in Bromsgrove at an earlier time than he had arranged. He has come for a farewell visit before going out to America for 9 months (Princetown) to study under 3 great authorities on his subject: Gödel (Warsaw) Alonso Church and Kleene. We had talk before dinner & again later to bring us up to date with our news.

Thursday 10

V & Alan tea up here with me. Had long talk with Alan about his work & whether in his subject, some abstruse branch of logic, one would come to 'dead end' etc.

Friday 11

Alan went down alone to church to see Chris' window & the little garden which he hadn't seen before since it was finished only the day he came to the dedication of the window. Alan taught me game called 'go' rather like 'peggoty'.

Saturday 12

Came down dinner first time for 3 weeks.

Too little sleep. Many things to arrange this morning. Rupert & Alan had tea in my room & then I took them all by surprise by coming down to dinner. There were 10 of us – & jolly party. Gramophone concert. Rup's latest cinema photos & the fishing one. Men billiards.

Sunday 13

Alan Rup and 2 girls (Enid & Jean) bathed at Cadbury's pool. Rup & Alan tea with me. Alan tried to explain what he is working at. Had business talk to Enid & then came down while she Jean Rup & Alan were having supper. They went off to catch 7.45 New St.[8]

Passport to Princeton: Alan Turing's passport photograph. (© The Estate of P.N. Furbank and reproduced by kind permission of the Provost and Scholars of King's College, Cambridge)

Princeton was charming in the fall – discreet colonial-style elegance; sunshine and showers; lawns, leaves, trees, and attractive buildings; the greatest assembly of mathematical talent ever collected in one university; a touch of culture-shock for someone with traces of Raj imperiousness, educated at a British boarding school, and not accustomed to the extravagance of taxis.

ON BOARD CUNARD WHITE STAR 'BERENGARIA'
Sept 28

It strikes me that Americans can be the most insufferable and insensitive creatures you could wish. One of them has just been talking to me and telling me of all the worst aspects of America with evident pride. However they may not all be like that.

The Graduate College, Princeton N.J
6 Oct

Passing the immigration officers involved waiting in a queue for over two hours with screaming children round me. Then, after getting through the customs I had to go through the ceremony of initiation to the U.S.A, consisting of being swindled by a taxi driver. I considered his charge perfectly preposterous, but as I had already been charged more than double English prices for sending my baggage, I thought it was possibly right. It seems that some things are ridiculously expensive here, but some definitely cheaper than in England; notably railway travel is very cheap $1 for 50 miles on the single journey. […]

These Americans have various peculiarities in conversation which catch the ear somehow. Whenever you thank them for anything they say 'You're welcome'. I rather liked it at first, thinking that I was welcome, but now I find it comes back like a ball thrown against a wall, and become positively apprehensive. Another habit they have is to make the sound described by authors as 'Aha'. They use it when they have no suitable reply to a remark, but think that silence could be rude.

The Graduate College

Princeton N.J

Oct 14

My dear Mother,

You have often asked me about possible applications of various branches of mathematics. I have just discovered a possible application of the kind of thing I am working on at present. It answers the question 'What is the most general kind of code or cipher possible', and at the same time (rather naturally) enables one to construct a lot of particular and interesting codes. One of them is pretty well impossible to decode without the key and very quick to encode. I expect I could sell them to H. M. Government for quite a substantial sum, but am rather doubtful about the morality of such things. What do you think?

Church had me out to dinner the other night. Considering that the guests were all university people I found the conversation rather disappointing. They seem, from what I can remember of it, to have discussed nothing but the different states that they came from. Description of travel and places bores me intensely.

I had a nasty shock when I got into Church's house. I think I had told you that Church was half blind in one eye. Well I saw his father in the house and he was quite blind (and incidentally very deaf). I should have thought very little of it had it not been for Church being rather blind himself. Any hereditary defects of that kind give me the shudders. […]

Yours

Alan

Looking Glass Zoo

One imagines that the Americans found Alan, and his enthusiasm for mathematical puzzles, just as peculiar. Alonzo Church and his work on symbolic logic were the reasons Alan was in Princeton; most of the other mathematicians whom Alan had hoped to find at Princeton were, for one reason or another, away. It was not obvious that the fastidious Church, whose lectures were so precisely careful as to be

600f340

---

ponderous as well as pedantic, would get along with the untidy and atheistic Turing who would spin off new, partly thought-out ideas as randomly as he dressed. An obituary of Church, written to accompany his collected works, described his style:[9]

> Alonzo Church had the polite manners of a gentleman who had grown up in Virginia. He was never known to be rude, even with people with whom he had strong disagreements. A deeply religious person, he was a lifelong member of the Presbyterian church. In his habits he was careful and deliberate – very careful and very deliberate. The students in his classes would discover this on the first day, when they saw how he would erase a blackboard. The material he wrote out on paper (he did not type) was often done in several colors of ink – sometimes colors made by mixing bottles together – and always done in his distinctive unslanted hand-writing. He was a master at using white-out fluid to eliminate imperfections.

Notwithstanding the shaky start, there was ample hospitality: an invitation to spend Thanksgiving in New York with one of the local Anglo-Catholic clergy; a weekly Sunday social event hosted by the Graduate College Dean, Dr Luther P. Eisenhart; and hockey matches became a regular fixture. By November, Alan was settling in.

GRADUATE COLLEGE
PRINCETON UNIVERSITY

Nov. 11

My dear Mother,

It appears that Dean Underhill[10] has been writing to one of his friends in New York to let him know that I am here. Said friend has written to ask me to stay with him some weekend in the comparatively near future. Certainly these Americans are astoundingly hospitable.

One of the Commonwealth Fellows, Francis Price, arranged a hockey match the other day between the Graduate College and Vassar, a women's college (amer)/university (engl.) some 130 miles away. He got up a team of which only half had ever played before. We had a couple of practice games and went to Vassar in cars on Sunday. It was raining slightly when we arrived, and what was our horror when we were told the ground was not fit for play. However we persuaded them to let us play a pseudo-hockey game in their gymn. at wh. we defeated them 11-3. Francis is trying to arrange a return match, which will certainly take place on a field. [...]

I am told over here that the postage to America from England is only 1½d although it is 5¢ back, so suggest you ask at P.O.

Yours

Alan

Letters home seem to have been more frequent during Alan's time at Princeton. Those that survive are dated more evenly throughout the week, rather than turned out as Sunday duty; certainly more were preserved (27 over two years, compared with 18 for the previous four), and they are longer. It gives a slightly clearer picture of what was happening, though Alan's choice of subject, as always, tended towards the technical and neutral, but perhaps the frequency of letters implies willingness to keep the link to home alive. At Mother's suggestion, Alan kept pace with political and other developments in England and Europe by reading the *New Statesman and Nation* (sent over each week by Mother), which was then fizzing over the abdication crisis. The paper was not completely devoted to politics, though, and had a puzzles section at the back, including a weekly

Alonzo Church, Alan Turing's supervisor at Princeton. (Courtesy of Princeton University (undated; Alonzo Church Papers, Box 60, Folder 3; Manuscripts Division, Department of Rare Books and Special Collections, Princeton University Library))

logic challenge. On 19 December 1936, Problem No. 207 appeared, set by Sir Arthur Eddington, whose lectures had set Alan off on his fellowship dissertation on the Gaussian Error Function. Problem No. 207, 'Looking Glass Zoo', was set in the language of Lewis Carroll, and featured a trip by some boys and girls to the zoo, who had to identify certain animals, and say which were male and female, from an array of apparently nonsensical information. Various solutions were offered in subsequent editions, including one by Alan's mentor M.H.A. Newman, but the prize-winning entry was by 'Champ', whom Alan readily identified as his friend David Champernowne. Conveniently the printed solution came with the Champ's address, so Alan was able to re-establish contact. Champ's solution reads, in part:[11]

> Humpty Dumpty explains. 'There couldn't have been more than three girls,' reflected Humpty Dumpty, 'because a girl is always a square root of minus one, and there are only twelve of those, they taught us that at school.' … 'I suppose so,' said I, 'but what do you mean by saying "a girl is the square root of minus one"?' 'When a girl thinks twice, she thinks contrariwise, but when a boy thinks twice he thinks Truth.'

Square root of minus one? Because the problem could be solved using the calculus of complex numbers, which have a 'real' part (a normal number like 5 or π) plus an 'imaginary' part which is a multiple of $\sqrt{(-1)}$. It seems likely that the ironic and topsy-turvy logic of Alice would have been lost on Alonzo Church. Nor was there much prospect of sharing this sort of fun with the great brains at the Institute for Advanced Study. The Institute was a very new foundation within Princeton, a sort of university within a university, with a Carrollian logic of its own. In 1936 it was still housed in Fine Hall alongside the university's maths faculty; it didn't get its own site until later. The IAS wanted to attract mathematical, and in particular Jewish mathematical, talent from an increasingly hostile Europe. There were large salaries on offer ($16,000 for senior professors), causing some cynics to say the acronym stood for Institute for Advanced Salaries. The idea was that, freed from the burdens of teaching, the world's finest intellects would stand around Institute blackboards and argue together, producing the world's finest ideas. In fact, many stood around and intrigued, and looked for permanent postings at other American universities. New arrivals could find the place isolated and lonely. Excepting John von Neumann, the mathematicians did not, unlike in central Europe, talk to each other much, and when they did it was not about maths. The intrigues along the corridors were not a problem for non-Institute university people like Alonzo Church and Alan Turing, who could comfortably get on with their work alone, but the bubbling pot of excitement that Alan had hoped for had in fact gone rather tepid.

Perhaps therefore it is not surprising that Alan's presentation of his paper on *Computable Numbers*, on 2 December 1936, attracted only 'rather bad attendance', which Alan put down to his lack of reputation: a professor visiting from elsewhere had a good turnout, despite a humdrum presentation, maybe because the audience were trying to catch his eye. Alan was still grumbling about the reception given to his paper, or rather the lack of it, in February. At that stage, there was nobody pushing Alan forward at Princeton. Nevertheless, Alan learned to speak and write in lambda-calculus, turning out a number of papers. He also started working on 'group theory', which was John von Neumann's idea. Catching the notice of von Neumann was important, not just because von Neumann was by many accounts the most brilliant mathematician of the twentieth century, but also because he was urbane and charming and could influence funding for a second year in Princeton, if Alan wanted it.

GRADUATE COLLEGE
PRINCETON UNIVERSITY

22 Feb

My dear Mother,

I went to the Eisenharts regular Sunday tea yesterday and there they took me in relays to try and persuade me to stay another year. The Dean weighed in with hints that the Procter Fellowship was mine for the asking (this is worth $2,000 p.a.). I said I thought King's would probably prefer that I return, but gave vague promise that I would sound them on the matter. Whether I want to stay is another matter. The people I know here will all be leaving, and I don't much care about the idea of spending a long summer in this country. I should like to know if you have any opinions on the subject. I think it is most likely I shall come back to England. […]

      Yours

         Alan

There were three Procter fellowships each year: one each for Oxford, Cambridge, and the Collège de France. Alan had missed out on the Cambridge one for 1936–37 and had subsisted on his King's fellowship stipend, and abstinence from taxis. Alan applied for a lectureship at Cambridge, but by the spring it was clear it wasn't going to be given; a further year at Princeton, with the agreement of King's, seemed a sensible plan. Von Neumann wrote supporting the application, and so it was settled.

Alan took a short American holiday before going back to England for the summer. Terrifyingly, this required mastery of a motor car. Maurice Pryce, a friend of Alan's from Cambridge (who had got a lectureship, and so wasn't coming back), sold Alan the car and took on the job of driving instructor. The holiday included a 400-mile round-trip along the coast to visit a cousin of Ethel Turing on her mother's side: a retired clergyman called Jack Crawford. Cousin Jack rated alongside the much-loved Aunt Sibyl for what Alan called the Relations Merit Diploma: he had studied science in Dublin, had a telescope in a little observatory, and talked about the grinding of mirrors. Fortunately for all concerned, Maurice Pryce came too. Alan reported to his mother rather unconvincingly, 'I am getting rather more competent with the car so should get up there without serious difficulty', but this was a full five months later, when he was planning a second visit to the Crawfords for Thanksgiving.

Alan arrived back in Cambridge for the summer at the end of June 1937. Here there were some new and exciting things. The moral scientists were keen to introduce Alan to Ludwig Wittgenstein, who had been in and out of Cambridge for the previous 20 years or so.

Wittgenstein did not attend meetings of the Moral Sciences Club, allegedly because of complaints that he talked so much that nobody else could get a word in edgeways. Wittgenstein had an engineering background and was a logician, and a meeting of minds between Turing and Wittgenstein seemed a good idea.

Alan was also getting interested in a pure mathematical problem linked to the spacing out of prime numbers, called the Riemann Hypothesis. Alan took delivery of a bundle of papers on the subject, with which he began swotting up. Proving the Riemann Hypothesis was in the list of 23 vital unsolved problems in mathematics put forward by David Hilbert in 1900, and it is still regarded today as the most famous unsolved problem in mathematics. Alan Turing had already had a go at another of Hilbert's designs, and the Riemann problem had been around since 1859. Alan had been thinking about it since, as Alan put it in a letter to Stanley Skewes (another mathematician from King's): 'you made the mistake of talking to me about it from time to time when you were rowing two and I at bow until eventually I thought I had better find out what it was all about'.[12]

What it was all about was the square root of minus one. The Riemann zeta-function is a sum of an infinite series. For any complex number s:

$$\zeta(s) = \sum_{n=1}^{\infty} \frac{1}{n^s}$$

And the interesting question is, for what values of s the sum of the series adds up to exactly zero? Riemann's hypothesis is that whenever the sum is zero, the 'real' part of the complex number s is ½. The Riemann Hypothesis was particularly interesting in 1937, because a Cambridge mathematician called E.C. Titchmarsh had used a mechanical desk calculator to crank through no fewer than 1,041 points and confirmed that they did satisfy the Riemann Hypothesis. To do maths this way was heretical: rather than prove or disprove Riemann by classical analysis, Titchmarsh had been searching for a counter-example by brute-force computing. He had failed, which made the puritans smirk; but Alan

Turing wasn't a puritan, and machine methodology was something which always appealed to him. Soon, though, it was time to go back to Princeton, where there was still more to do. Princeton was suiting Alan rather better in his second year there – 'there is only one feature of American life which I find really tiresome, the impossibility of getting a bath in the ordinary sense'. Alan's mentor M.H.A. Newman was in Princeton as well, having joined the Institute for a year. Alan also made friends with a Canadian physicist called Malcolm MacPhail, who noted that:[13]

> Turing actually designed an electric multiplier and built the first three or four stages to see if it could be made to work. For the purpose he needed relay-operated switches which, not being commercially available at that time, he built himself. The Physics Department at Princeton had a small but well equipped machine shop for its graduate students to use, and my small contribution to the project was to lend Turing my key to the shop, which was probably against all the regulations, and show him how to use the lathe, drill, press etc. without chopping off his fingers. And so, he machined and wound the relays; and to our surprise and delight the calculator worked.

For some reason Alan had also been prompted to think again about codes and ciphers. Malcolm MacPhail again:

> It was probably in the fall of 1937 that Turing first became alarmed about a possible war with Germany. He was at that time supposedly working hard on his famous thesis but nevertheless found time to take up the subject of cryptanalysis with characteristic vigour. On this topic we had *many* discussions. He assumed that words would be replaced by numbers taken from an official code book and messages would be transmitted as numbers in the binary scale. But, to prevent the enemy from deciphering captured messages even if they had the code book, he would multiply the number corresponding to a specific message by a horrendously long but secret number and transmit the product. The length of the secret number was to be determined by the requirement

that it should take 100 Germans working eight hours a day on desk calculators 100 years to discover the secret factor by routine search!

Church-Turing Thesis

The main task, however, was to write a thesis for a PhD degree. This was going to be on the subject of 'ordinal logics', a subject in which John von Neumann had dabbled as a high-school student (and, being von Neumann, on which he had published a precocious paper). Ordinals are a bit like Russian dolls, each one a bit bigger, and including all the preceding ones. In an extension of his work on the *Entscheidungsproblem*, Alan was applying the concept to systems of logic, each one wider and more comprehensive than the last, to explore the boundaries of what might be formally provable, and what might not. Initially Alan thought the thesis would be done by Christmas 1937, but it had an unhappy gestation, not made easier when Professor Church reviewed the draft. Many years later, Alonzo Church was interviewed by William Aspray about his graduate students at Princeton. Initially, Church didn't include Turing in his list of students whom he remembered – this may be because Turing was a rather unusual 'student', given that he was really more in the nature of a visiting professor, albeit one working towards a PhD.

> ASPRAY: Did you have much contact with him [Alan Turing] while he was writing his paper?
> CHURCH: I had a lot of contact with him. I discussed his dissertation with him rather carefully.
> ASPRAY: Can you tell me something about his personality?
> CHURCH: I did not have enough contact with him to know. He had the reputation of being a loner and rather odd.[14]

On 30 March 1938 Alan wrote to a fellow King's mathematics don, Philip Hall: 'I am writing a thesis for a PhD, which is proving rather intractable, and I am always rewriting parts of it.'[15] Seven weeks later, things were not much better, telling Mother: 'my Ph.D. thesis has been delayed a good deal more than I had expected. Church made a number of suggestions which resulted in the thesis being expanded to an appalling length. I hope the length of it won't make it difficult to get it published.' Alan also had problems with the typist, who evidently struggled with Alan's curious Gothic German notations and the horrors of the lambda-calculus. All the rewrites and retypes didn't make the thesis into a straightforward, accessible piece like *Computable Numbers*. Some years later, Dr Robin Gandy wrote to M.H.A. Newman about it. Gandy said: 'Alan considered that his paper on ordinal logics had never received the attention it deserved (He wouldn't admit that it was a stinker to read).'[16] Occasionally Alan conceded that symbolic logic could be heavy-going:

> It has long been recognised that mathematics and logic are virtually the same and that they may be expected to merge imperceptibly into one another. Actually this merging process has not gone at all far, and mathematics has profited very little from researches in symbolic logic. Symbolic logic is a very alarming mouthful for most mathematicians, and the logicians are not very much interested in making it more palatable.

If the mathematicians themselves found this line of work hard to digest, heaven help the rest of us. Yet, holding its head clear of the obscurities, the thesis did contain 'a new idea that was to change the face of the general theory of computation'.[17] This was the concept of the 'oracle', a source of wisdom to which you could go for a solution to the mathematically unsolvable. Human beings depend on their instincts and intuition when they know something is right but cannot prove it logically – Alan, always rooted in the real world, reintroduced this piece of common sense into the arid world of symbolic logic. Without going into it very far in his thesis, Alan's invention of the oracle showed that there were different degrees of solvability, a field of enquiry which proved fruitful for a later generation of mathematical logicians.

Meanwhile Alan was fretting about whether his fellowship at King's would be renewed. The situation was complicated. Usually King's would diligently inform the applicants, but Alan was not in residence and was without access to the high-table grapevine. Gingerly he went to see the Dean at Princeton to ask about a possible job in America, and within a few days John von Neumann had invited Alan to join the Institute for Advanced Study (with a salary of $1,500). So there was a job for Alan either way, but Alan's preference was to return to Britain, 'unless you are actually at war before July'. To find out for certain, Alan indulged in another unthinkable extravagance, and sent a cable to King's. King's had in fact renewed the fellowship – they just hadn't told Alan – and so he declined von Neumann's offer. Eventually, Alan's thesis was accepted on 17 May 1938 and at the end of the month he was examined on it, receiving the doctorate in June. Alan sent a copy in the form he intended it to be published to Philip Hall, saying, 'I also expect to find the back lawn criss-crossed with 8 ft trenches'.

There were no trenches yet across the back lawn when Alan returned to King's in the summer of 1938, but Hitler's 'year of no surprises' had come to an end in December 1937. In 1938 he launched his major programme of expanding the Reich. *Anschluss* with Austria occurred on 11–12 March. The Munich crisis developed in late September, and in November there occurred the notorious *Kristallnacht*, a night of state-sponsored vandalism of all things Jewish. Despite Chamberlain's 'peace with honour' window-dressing, there were tasks to be done. Alan's friend Fred Clayton, who occupied rooms just below him, had helped a Viennese Jewish boy called Karl come to Britain, one of the small number grudgingly allowed in by the British government after *Kristallnacht*. Karl was languishing in a refugee camp in Harwich. Alan went with Fred to visit the camp and this led to Alan sponsoring another refugee boy, Robert Augenfeld, soon anglicised as 'Bob', helping him to get settled at a school and with a foster family. And there was preparation for the war which the dons at King's knew was unavoidable. Shortly after his return to England in July 1938, Alan had been visited by one of those senior dons.

Discomfort before the storm. August 1939: Fred Clayton; boatman; Fred's protégé Karl; and Alan squeezed into the stern with Bob Augenfeld. (Author)

One day in the summer of 1938, after the Nazis had taken over Austria, I was sitting in my rooms at King's when there was a knock on the door. In came F.E. Adcock, accompanied by a small, birdlike man with bright blue eyes whom he introduced as Commander Denniston. He asked whether, in the event of war, I would be willing to do confidential work for the Foreign Office. It sounded interesting, and I said I would. I was thereupon asked to sign the Official Secrets Act form. By now I had guessed what it was all about. It was well known to us that Adcock had been a member of Admiral 'Blinker' Hall's Room 40 at the Admiralty in the First World War, which had done pioneering work on the decoding of enemy messages.[18]

Alas, this isn't Alan's account of his recruitment, but that of L.P. Wilkinson, who was a King's don at the same time. It is tempting to infer, from Alan's conversations about codebreaking with Malcolm McPhail in Princeton the previous year, that he had already been approached informally by Adcock in the summer of 1937.

There is nothing in the files to verify this; what is certain is that in 1938 Denniston was doing his rounds, and Alan signed up formally then. Together with Wilkinson, and another fellow of King's, D.W. Lucas, he attended a cryptology course at the Government Code & Cypher School, then housed in London near St James's Park Underground station. This included an introduction to the fiendish German encipherment machine called Enigma. At some point he was also introduced to A.D. (Dilly) Knox, the veteran codebreaker from the Great War days, who was trying to break it. During the coming months, Alan was allowed to take secret work back to King's, to pit his wits against Enigma, subject always to taking appropriate security precautions. At Cambridge, the older college rooms have two doors, an inner and an outer one: when the outer one (the 'oak') is shut, the occupant is out, or not to be disturbed; if the outer one is open, you can knock on the inner, painted door for admittance. Security for Alan seems to have consisted of 'sporting his oak'; not that any casual spies would have found it easy to decrypt the chaos and clutter in his rooms. For us, Alan's codebreaking activities can wait for another chapter. He had plenty else going on.

For one thing, he had agreed to take over M.H.A. Newman's 'Foundations of Mathematics' lecture series at the university – despite not having a university post to go with his college one. As well as teaching logic, he was also arguing about it. Wittgenstein was also running a series of informal 'lectures' on the foundations of mathematics. Wittgenstein's approach was less esoteric than Newman's, and his discourses were down to earth, amusing and accessible. He would draw a smiley face and ask how this could be a representation of a well-known professor in the audience but not a representation of a mathematical concept. In fact, they weren't so much lectures as facilitated discussions, with Wittgenstein engaging with a member of the audience and carrying on a staged debate, bringing in others as appropriate. During the first six months of 1939 there were 31 lectures, and Alan Turing attended almost all of them. From the very first lecture Wittgenstein used Alan as a foil for debating propositions.[19] By lecture 19 they had got onto negation, contradictions and paradoxes, and a long discussion, spreading over four or five lectures, about the usefulness of contradictions ensued. 'You might want to say,' Wittgenstein suggested, '"logic and mathematics can't reveal any truths if there are contradictions in it."' Of course, that wasn't what Wittgenstein believed, and Alan Turing's proof in *Computable Numbers* depended on contradiction to reveal truth.

While Alan was taking over Newman's course, the Riemann zeta-function had been taking over Alan's rooms. No doubt buoyed by his success in America with the relay multiplier, Alan worked up a design for a computing machine which would tackle the Riemann problem.

It is proposed to make calculations of the Riemann zeta-function on the critical line for $1,450 < t < 6,000$ with a view to discovering whether all the zeros of the function in this range of t lie on the critical line. An investigation for $0 < t < 1,464$ has already been made by Titchmarsh. The most laborious part of such calculations consists in the evaluation of certain trigonometrical sums.[20]

$$\sum_{r=1}^{m} \frac{1}{\sqrt{r}} \cos(t \log r - \theta) \qquad m = \left[\sqrt{\frac{t}{2\pi}} \right]$$

In the present calculation it is intended to evaluate these sums approximately in most cases by the use of apparatus somewhat similar to what is used for tide prediction. I shall be working in collaboration with D. C. MacPhail, a research student who is an engineer. We propose to do most of the machine-shop work ourselves, and are therefore applying only for the cost of materials, and some preliminary computation.

D.C. (Donald) MacPhail was none other than the brother of Malcolm, with whom Alan had been messing about in the Physics Department machine shop at Princeton. Donald appeared at King's in the autumn of 1938 to study for his PhD, and seems to have been adopted promptly by Alan to provide organisation and the dexterity to mill the finely machined pieces which the Riemann zeta-computer would need. Armed with a £40 grant from the Royal Society, and legitimate access

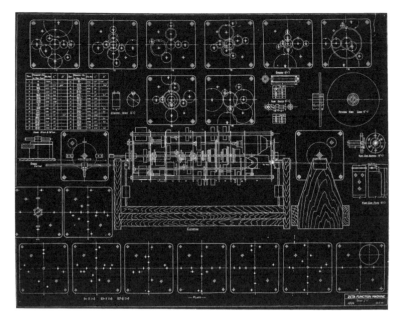

Neatness and order. Donald MacPhail's neatly drawn schematic for the zeta-function machine belies the reality of gear-wheels strewn over Alan's floor at King's. (© The Estate of P.N. Furbank and reproduced by kind permission of the Provost and Scholars of King's College, Cambridge)

to the Cambridge University Engineering Department workshops, Alan and Donald set to work. The concept was extraordinary. The machine would use fractions approximately equal to the logarithms needed in the calculations – Andrew Hodges gives the example of $34 \times 31 / 57 \times 35 \approx \log_8 3$ – and then gear-wheels would be cut with a number of teeth corresponding to the factors in these ratios. Eighty wheels would be needed. If they were foolish enough to call, visitors to Alan's rooms would find an orgy of grown-up Meccano, with the wheels laid out across the floor.

> All I remember [said David Champernowne] is that the machine included a set of gear wheels the numbers of whose teeth were prime numbers, and I liked to fancy that as soon as the machine had found a root of the zeta function its centre of gravity would pass over the edge of a table and it would fall off uttering a swansong.[21]

The intention was that the machine's approximations would – even if they were inexact – show roughly where the zeros of the Riemann zeta-function lay, to enable the mathematicians to follow up more exactly with hand methods. Typical Alan Turing methodology: a combination of machinery, insight, and practical shortcuts. On 1 September 1939 Germany invaded Poland, forcing an indefinite postponement of work on the Riemann machine, but all of the talents Alan was using for the machine would characterise his work in unravelling Enigma at Bletchley Park.

6

PROF

King's College, Cambridge, was a nest of spies. Not Kim Philby or Guy Burgess or Anthony Blunt or John Cairncross: they were at Trinity. Not Donald Maclean: he was at Trinity Hall. In any case, they were all spying for another side. The King's College spies were an altogether subtler group. At least five members of King's had been employed during World War One in a secret establishment forming part of the Naval Intelligence Division. In Room 40 of the Admiralty Old Building in Whitehall, this small elite had read the coded radio messages of the German Imperial Navy, thereby removing the threat of surprise from their sorties into the North Sea. In 1917 they achieved the greatest diplomatic coup to derive from a coded message when the content of the 'Zimmerman telegram' was revealed to the Americans, providing the final push which brought the United States into the war and sealed the fate of Imperial Germany. The members of Room 40 had not retired gracefully to the country in 1919. Some – notably Dilly Knox, a fellow of King's – stayed on to transform Room 40 into the all-service cryptanalytical agency which, by 1939, had renamed itself as the Government Code & Cypher School (GC&CS). Others, like Professor Frank Adcock, went to the country, or rather his elegant set of rooms over the archway in front court at King's, although his was a very active 'retirement'. Prompted by Alastair Denniston, the

Room 40 leader who was now the Director of GC&CS, Professor Adcock was retained to spot talent for the new organisation.

No fewer than 11 fellows of King's (not counting Adcock himself, Dilly Knox and Frank Birch, another Room 40 veteran who had not retired to the country either) were recruited for GC&CS. Another eight alumni of King's were also recruited. One of the fellows was Alan Turing, tapped on the shoulder by Adcock in 1938 in the manner we have seen. GC&CS had been preparing for war for a long time. By November 1938, Commander Denniston was able to write to the Foreign Office, which was responsible for his staffing needs: 'I have been in touch with both Universities and have established direct contact through Dons who worked with us during the war, so that now we have a list of about 50 men earmarked for service under the Foreign Office in the event of war.'[1] On the list of available emergency staff were various 'old members', and over 20 others from Cambridge, of whom seven, including Alan Turing and Patrick Wilkinson, were from King's. One, the literary critic F.L. Lucas, was so well known that his college is not specified and the list just says 'see "Who's Who"'. The Cambridge list also names M.H.A. Newman, but against his name is the word 'no'. Newman was not to go to GC&CS. Not yet.

Monstrous pile

In mid-March 1939 the German Army occupied Bohemia and Moravia, shredding the last scraps of credibility from the Munich settlement. But Denniston had already concluded that 'a sufficient supply of professors is immediately available' and on 2 August he informed the cryptanalysts that they would be moving to their 'war site' on 15 August 1939:

> In order to carry out communication tests the war site will be manned
> a.m. 15th August by those detailed in G.C. & C.S. 1st Wave who are not
> on leave at the time.

All documents required at the war site are to be packed by 5.30 p.m. on 14th August. They will be moved during that night. As many as possible are to be placed in small cupboards and filing cabinets which can be locked. Arrangements for labelling will be promulgated later. Stationery has already been sent down. Sufficient personal luggage should be taken for 15 days. Those going by train should obtain a single ticket of the appropriate class to Bletchley. On arrival they should place their luggage in the cloak room from whence it will be collected after the allocation of billets etc. They should proceed on foot from the station to the war site enquiring if necessary for Bletchley Park, which is on the up (West) side of the railway. On leaving the station turn right up the hill and proceed through the second lodge gates. Suitable trains from Euston are the 8.37 a.m. and the 9.30 a.m. An advance for railway tickets can be obtained from Mr Travis. […]

The address for official correspondence and private letters will be Room 47 Foreign Office and the official telephone No. Whitehall 7947.

The staff are warned against any conversations regarding the work with other members of the staff whilst in their billets. If occasion should arise as to what you are doing the answer should be that you are part of the aerial defence of London. […]

This test is to be treated with the utmost secrecy by all members of this department.

Gas masks are to be taken.

Bletchley Park was not a glamorous place. Its main building was constructed over a 25-year period beginning in 1877, with improvements and innovations stacked one onto another without any concession to coherence or symmetry. It was described by Landis Gores, an American architect who was later stationed at Bletchley as a representative of United States Army Intelligence:[2]

A maudlin and monstrous pile probably unsurpassed, though not for lack of competition, in the architectural gaucherie of the mid-Victorian era, built about 1860 in an undiscriminatingly imitative

Tudor vocabulary out of an endemic dark red brick with beige coadestone trim, quoins, voussoirs and keystones, further hopelessly vulgarised by extensive porches and solaria as well as by batteries of tall casements in intermittent profusion, all of painted wood trim, mingling with what could only be termed incoherent abandon two-centre Gothic, three-centred Tudor, four-centred Perpendicular and ogival Flamboyant arches with English stick and French trefoil tracery. The profusion of top-story gables faced with cottage-style half-timbering, not to mention an overpowering copper-roofed octagonal-walled to onion-topped pleasure dome with finial immediately suggestive of the pseudo-orientalism of the Royal Pavilion at Brighton; oriels, turrets, bay windows and embrasures, all capped by myriad multi-potted chimneys in totally wanton location and configuration; altogether inchoate, unfocused and incomprehensible, not to say indigestible.

A building as exuberant as Mr Gores's prose. Worse, its grounds were going to become a building site, as the GC&CS staff outgrew the mansion house, the outbuildings, the adjacent school, and numerous temporary wooden huts were thrown together quickly to deal with the overspill. The lawns and rose garden were ripped up to provide

A maudlin and monstrous pile: the Mansion at Bletchley Park before the war. The ground-floor room under the dome became Alistair Denniston's office. (© Bletchley Park Trust)

footings for the huts, and eventually the maze went too, when it was decided that brick buildings were needed to house the organisations which had outgrown the huts. By 1943, Bletchley Park had stopped looking like a park and had taken on the appearance of a stolid and functional industrial centre, as indeed it had become. Only the lake and a fraction of the grounds visible from the Director's ground-floor office remained in their pre-war state.

A week after Denniston was installed at Bletchley Park, the German foreign minister Joachim von Ribbentrop concluded his notorious pact with Vyacheslav Molotov, his Russian opposite number. The way was clear for Germany to occupy Poland and recover the territories lost under the Treaty of Versailles. Germans dressed as Poles staged a fake violation of Germany's sovereign rights, and on 1 September Poland was invaded on two fronts. World War Two had begun. Denniston wrote to the Foreign Office:[3]

Ref. No. 767.

3rd September, 1939.

Dear Wilson,

For some days now we have been obliged to recruit from our emergency list men of the Professor type who the Treasury agreed to pay at the rate of £600 a year. I attach herewith a list of these gentlemen already called up together with the dates of their joining.

I will keep you informed at intervals of further recruitment.

Yours sincerely,

A.G. Denniston

Ref. No. 783.

7th September, 1939.

Dear Wilson,

In continuation of my No.767 of 3rd September:–

The following gentlemen have joined subsequently:– [...]

Mr. A.M. Turing   4th September, 1939. [...]

Yours ever,

A.G.D.

The early days. Cottages in the Stableyard where Alan Turing devised techniques for breaking Enigma. (© Bletchley Park Trust)

Although Mr Turing may have arrived on 4 September 1939, his actual mobilisation had taken place considerably earlier. Upon recruitment, he had been earmarked for Dilly Knox's Research Section located in the Stableyard cottages, specifically to work on the breaking of messages encrypted on the German Enigma machine. The workings of the Enigma are now well known: a typewriter-like keyboard had wiring leading to a lampboard, where the enciphered message would appear, joined by wiring which scrambled the message. In the standard Army and Air Force Enigma there were three coding wheels, each of which would substitute one letter for another, and which would rotate with every new letter of the coded message to create a new cipher; and a plugboard which would also switch some letters for others. Further complications were introduced by the rings on the coding wheels, which allowed for the internal wiring of each wheel to be rotated relative to its housing, and the existence of 'turnover' notches on the wheels which meant that more than one wheel might rotate at the same time. In all, the machine had 17,576 positions for the three chosen coding wheels, the same number of ring-settings, and 150 trillion plugboard settings, for a total of 158.9 million million million possible starting configurations, allowing for 10 plugboard cross-pairings and the choice of the three coding wheels for the day from a library of five. If Alan Turing's imagined 100 Germans working eight hours a day on desk calculators were able to get through even a million possible settings every hour, it would take far, far longer than 100 years to pick the right setting by brute force. Even if each codebreaker could crank through 10^{14} permutations per hour it would take nearly 400 years to find the setting. Even allowing for German efficiency, let alone British, something rather cleverer than brute force would be needed to unlock the Enigma.

Alan Turing had been working at Cambridge throughout 1939 on the mysteries of Enigma, and a major breakthrough had happened in July when the Polish *Biuro Szyfrów* shared its hard-won cryptanalytic secrets with Denniston, Dilly Knox, and their opposite numbers from French intelligence. The secrets included the internal wiring used by the German armed forces to connect the Enigma keyboard to the input plate feeding current into the coding wheels of the machine; also particulars of their electro-mechanical devices – a 'cyclometer' and an ominous-sounding '*bomba*' – for finding the settings which gave the Enigma a new *m*-configuration, effectively enabling it to become a completely new cipher machine every day. In mid-August a Polish reconstruction of an Enigma machine was delivered to Colonel Stewart Menzies, the deputy head of the Secret Intelligence Service, at Victoria Station. Marian Rejewski, the chief Polish codebreaker, had used equations as well as machinery to tackle the Enigma. This was the kind of stuff which Alan Turing could get his teeth into. Although the purist Knox was always going to favour hand-based decryption methods, it was obvious to all that using a machine was the way to deal with the millions of permutations presented by the Enigma. Alan Turing went to see Knox at his house to be briefed on the Polish revelations. The questions now were what sort of a machine, how should it be designed, and who could build it.

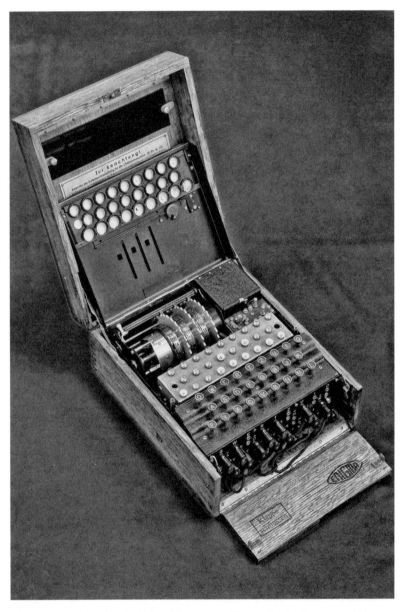

The Enigma machine: the principal encipherment machine used by the Germans could be set up 159 million million million different ways. After February 1942 the German Navy used a version that had 890 million million million permutations. (© Bletchley Park Trust)

Bombe-ish boy

The Poles had described their machinery, and in it lay the foundations of the device which Alan designed to reveal the daily settings of the Enigma machine. The Poles were exploiting a precaution which the Germans were taking in transmitting their messages, and this precaution opened a tiny chink in the Enigma's armour, a chink wide enough to insert the point of a crowbar and prise it wide open. More importantly, the chink was based on a principle which Alan Turing would exploit so as to enable all Army and Air Force Enigma key-nets to be broken open using a combination of mechanical and manual means.

The precaution which the Poles were exploiting was based in the need for a German sender to let his recipient know what 'message setting' he was using. It was all very well for the recipient to have a chart showing which wheels were going to be used, and which ring-settings, and what cross-pluggings, for any given day, but to add further complexity the starting positions of the coding wheels in their slots were to be different for each message. The procedure was for the sender to pick a starting position at random, and to let his opposite number know which three letters he was using by transmitting them at the beginning of the transmission. It would be too obvious, and too helpful to enemy intelligence, to transmit the three starting-position letters 'in clear', so the sender enciphered them. And here was the precaution: Morse code is easily garbled, and without any verbal context there was a danger that the starting position would be incorrectly received and the message would decrypt as gobbledegook, and have to be re-sent. Re-sending messages is very bad security (Bletchley's biggest breakthroughs came when messages were re-sent), so the precaution against garbling was to transmit the enciphered starting position *twice*. Of course, on a small scale, this was making the re-sending error, and the Germans discontinued the practice in 1940. Indeed, the Allies knew they would, sooner or later, do so. But in the meantime, the Poles had used the duplicated transmission to identify which wheels were being used and their relative positions, using giveaways known to the British codebreakers as 'females'. Females happened when the same letter appeared in both versions of the enciphered triplet in the same place – for example, if CIL was transmitted as ABN MRN.

Here was the germ of an idea which let the Poles in and from which the machine designed by Alan Turing grew. The same letter (L in this example, but what it actually was was unknown to eavesdroppers) had somehow got encrypted as N with the coding wheels in, for example, positions 3 and 6. If two Enigma machines were rigged up together, but three positions out of phase, they could test one by one all 17,576 combinations to find one – in fact there would be many – which allowed a letter to be enciphered as N at positions 3 and 6. If there were other females on the same net on the same day, the number of potentially correct combinations could be reduced. And if the relative positions of the coding wheels were found, the Poles were already a long way towards knowing the complete Enigma settings of the day.

The Poles explained the principles behind their *bomba* machine to Dilly Knox in Poland in July 1939, a mere five weeks before the invasion. The simultaneous testing of different enciphered letters at staggered positions in the message was a general principle, even if the Poles had applied it to the special case of 'females'. Yet the principle could be exploited further by the British, to test an intercepted message against guessed-at plain-text (a 'crib'). If replica Enigma machines were wired up together into a loop, the configuration of coding wheels in the German Enigma machine would be open to identification.

That left the problem of the plugboard. Alan Turing's idea was to apply electric voltage to one wire only in the input to the 26-wire cables connecting the replica Enigmas together. Say, for example, that voltage was applied to the wire leading to terminal 'K' on the first wheel of the first replica Enigma in the loop: that would identify which letter the 'K' was cross-plugged to, as well as finding the wheel configuration. The clever part of the idea, which might have amused Wittgenstein, was that it depended so heavily on negative information. Here was a form of halting problem given tangible mechanical form. Alan Turing designed the machine to stop when it had a plausibly good *m*-configuration; it knew when to do so because only in the (rare) case of a good wheel configuration, the voltage would be confined to a single wire in all cables joining the replica Enigmas. If the wheel configuration was bad, one or other of the wheels would be out of alignment, and electricity would reach other wires in the cables. In cases where all 26 wires were live, the machine was to keep on and try the next configuration of the three coding wheels.

The machine would have to be fast, to get through 17,576 possible combinations without taking hundreds of years, and it would have to be designed to stop whenever it found a plausible combination. These were formidable engineering challenges, but the British Tabulating Machine company (an ancestor of the computer company Fujitsu) had a brilliant Chief Engineer called Doc Keen. Keen knew he could build a machine which would rattle through all 17,576 wheel positions in no time (about 12 minutes). He could also deal with the more difficult electrical challenge of having the machine stop – so the operator could read out the plausible combination of settings – whenever only one wire in the input cable was live, but carry on to test the next combination whenever all 26 wires were live. Keen and

Not a computer. The Bombe, designed by Alan Turing and Gordon Welchman, found logically plausible Enigma settings that were worth testing further.

Turing understood each other – or rather, Turing understood Keen easily, and Keen was clever enough to fathom out what Turing wanted – and a prototype machine was designed, turned into blueprints, and built. In homage to the Poles, whose country was now ground under the combined heels of the Nazis and the Soviets, they called their invention the '*Bombe*'.

While the Bombe was being assembled, the codebreakers would have to make do with manual methods. One of the Polish techniques, exploiting the double-encipherment of message settings, used cardboard sheets (called 'Netz' at Bletchley) with alphabets across the top and down the sides, representing all the possible positions of the right-hand and middle coding wheels. One sheet was needed for each possible combination of wheels, making, with five possible wheels to choose from, 60 sheets in all. Small holes were cut into the sheets at each point where the right-hand and middle wheels could create a 'female'. The sheets would be piled on top of each other so that the codebreakers could see whether any holes went right through the stack, and where that happened they could identify the wheels and ring-settings in use. Creating the sheets initially involved cutting out the holes by hand with a razor blade; it was going to take 100 British codebreakers working eight hours a day about 100 years to produce them. Later they were able to punch the holes mechanically, and eventually they were able to share the workload with the French, who were working with the escaped Polish cryptanalysts outside Paris. Alan Turing was sent over in January 1940 with a set of sheets, and had the opportunity to discuss Enigma-breaking with Marian Rejewski as well as the French team. It seems that they didn't discuss his ideas for a Bombe.

In February 1940 Dilly Knox's research group broke the traffic enciphered on the 'blue' *Luftwaffe* Enigma key-net, causing Dilly to burst out into a Carrollian parody:[4]

'Twas HUTSIX, and the WRANGLERCOVES
Did twist and twiddle at the CYC;
All grimset were the JEFFREYBROWS,
And the BABBAGE outschreik.

'Beware the SEVENTHWHEEL, my son,
The pale FULLHOUSE, the NETZ that fail;
Move not the UMKEHRWALZE, and shun
The UNCONFIRMED FEMALE.'

He took the COTTAGECROWD in hand,
Oft times the REGISTRATORS sought;
Then 'midst his CILLIS, SLUGS and SNAKES,
He sat awhile in thought.

And as they over FOSSSHEETS groan,
A REDHOTTIP (with wheels to name)
Came TURING through the telephone.
And DILLIED as it came!

4, 5 and 2! No more ado –
The RINGSTELLUNG. Turn wheels about.
Still doubt appal, but STECKER fall
Uncontradicted out.

'And has thou truly BROKE the BLUE?
Come to the STORE, my BOMBE-ish boy!
Fetch JOSH, KITS, BOLS, AARD, CERA, WALTZ.'
He LUFTGAUED in his joy.

'Twas HUTSIX, and the WRANGLERCOVES
Did twist and twiddle at the CYC;
All grimset were the JEFFREYBROWS,
And the BABBAGE outschreik.

The Bombe prototype was delivered to Bletchley Park on 18 March 1940. They called it *Victory*. There was just one problem. *Victory* wasn't going to win the war, because it couldn't break Enigma. Still, there were other problems for Alan to work on. In particular there was the challenge of naval Enigma. Unlike the land war for Britain and France, the war at sea had begun in 1939. Convoying had begun immediately, but so had U–boat activity. On 14 October, *U-47* crept into Scapa Flow and sank HMS *Royal Oak*. Other sinkings and minelayings indicated where the first front of the war had been established. Secondly, the German Navy used Enigma differently. Instead of enciphering the starting positions for the coding wheels on their Enigma machines and transmitting the three letters for decipherment, the Navy used a different procedure. It was evident that the Germans were using some scheme for enciphering the starting positions, but what was it?

According to the *Cryptographic History of Work on the German Naval Enigma*:[5]

> When the war started probably only two people thought that the Naval Enigma could be broken – Birch, the Head of German Naval Section and Turing, one of the leading Cambridge mathematicians who joined G.C. & C.S. for the duration of the war. Birch thought it could be broken because it had to be broken and Turing thought it could be broken because it would be so interesting to break it. Whether or not these reasons were logically satisfactory they imbued those who held them with a determination that the problem should be solved and it is to the pertinacity and force that, in utterly different ways, both of them showed that success was ultimately due. Turing first got interested in the problem for the quite typical reason that 'no one else was doing anything about it and I could have it to myself'. He started where the Poles left off and set to work to discover how the indicating system worked using the information provided by the 100 or so messages in the period 1–8 May 1937, whose starting positions were known.

Alan Turing needed somewhere to work, and he was established in a loft in the Stableyard. 'He did not want coffee breaks or social meals in the mansion so Claire Harding and Elizabeth Grainger[6] rigged up a pulley to send up coffee and sandwiches to him in a basket.'[7] Fortified by the sandwiches and coffee, Alan observed that the naval Enigma messages used two groups of four letters to encode the three coding wheels' starting positions. He also observed that some repeated two-letter combinations suggested that each starting position was represented by a pair of letters in the eight-letter indicator; if this theory was right, two of the eight letters were padding and the other six were bigrams representing the three starting positions. He built up this theory to unpick the German naval indicator method. Not only that, but on the same night he devised a technique which would allow the whole key to be broken. But to make his technique work, the Allies would need to get hold of a bigram table from the German fleet.

On land, 1 May 1940 was the date on which the Germans dropped double-encipherment of indicator settings and made the Polish decipherment technique obsolete overnight. France was invaded and overrun in a lightning war which shocked and terrified the British. The Battle of Britain began and an invasion of the last opponent of Nazism seemed imminent. In November 1940 a German bomber let loose a stick of bombs on Elmers School, a property adjacent to Bletchley Park which had been commandeered to house GC&CS's traffic analysts. One landed next to Hut 4, where the German Naval Section was housed. Fortunately it failed to explode.

> Crown Inn, Shenley Brook End, Bletchley, Bucks.
> My dear Mother,
> Have just been back to Cambridge for a week's holiday. I tried to arrange a holiday with Champ, but he was booked to go with an economist friend. So I went to Camb. & did some work. Actually Champ turned up there for last week-end. […] Came back to find great excitement as bombs had dropped 100^x away the day after I went. Nobody hurt but old Mr and Mrs Roberts, whom you may perhaps remember, have left their home for time being as ceilings down, and are staying here.[…] I think I shall have to go up to Rossall some time this term to talk to Headmaster about Bob's future. […]
> Yours
> Alan[8]

Alan was also working on a book. In fact, Alan Turing wrote not a single published book in the whole of his career. But in the first year of the war he wrote a 150-page introduction to Enigma, and techniques for breaking it, as a training manual for new recruits. This covered not only Enigma, but also naval bigrams, manual techniques invented by

I. A description of the machine.

We begin by describing the 'unsteckered enigma'. The machine consists of a box with 26 keys labelled with the letters of the alphabet and 26 bulbs which shine through stencils on which letters are marked. It also contains wheels whose function will be described later on. When a key is depressed the wheels are made to move in a certain way and a current flows through the wheels to one of the bulbs. ~~Txxnxdexxxixxdxxkx~~ The letter which appears over the bulb is ~~xxxlxxd~~ the result of enciphering the letter on the depressed key with the wheels in the position they have when the bulb lights.

To understand the working of the machine it is best to separate in our minds

The electric circuit of the machine without the wheels.

The circuit through the wheels.

The mechanism for turning the wheels and for describing the positions of the wheels.

The circuit of the machine without the wheels.

Fig 1

Eintritts walz

The machine contains a cylinder called the Eintrittswalz (E.W) on which are 26 contacts $C_1, \ldots, C_{26}$. The effect of the wheels is to connect these contacts up in pairs, the actual pairings of course depending on the positions of the wheels. On the other side the contacts $C_1, C_2, \ldots, C_{26}$ are connected each to one of the keys. For the moment we will suppose that the order is ~~qxxrtzxixxxdfghjk~~ QWERTZUIOASDFGHJKPYXCVBNML , and we will say that Q is the letter associated with C_1, W that associated with C_2 etc. This series of letters associated with $C_1, C_2, \ldots, C_{26}$

Dilly and much more. It became known as 'Prof's book'. Alan Turing was not a professor – of the 21 men of the professor type named in Denniston's September 1939 letters to the Foreign Office, only nine were actually professors, and indeed Alan would never become a professor – but he had acquired a nickname, and he would be 'Prof' to his Bletchley colleagues and friends from that time.

Prof's book also explained the thinking behind his Bombe. In actual fact, *Victory* was working perfectly, but the problem was that it was producing 'stops' far too often, giving too many suggested wheel configurations/cross-pluggings to be checked: with this performance, it couldn't find the settings so as to produce decrypts within a reasonable time frame. To reduce the number of 'stops' required a really good guessed-at plain-text crib, which would enable several – ideally at least three – loops of replica Enigmas to be wired together. And this was very hard to do at the beginning of the war, when there was only limited Enigma traffic to work with and few breaks from which to build a library of cribs. But Alan Turing was not the only brilliant mind at Bletchley Park, and another mathematician from Cambridge called Gordon Welchman had an insight of great power as well as simplicity, which would allow loops to be created from the feeblest cribs. His idea was to add a cross-wiring arrangement called the 'diagonal board' (which, as built, was neither diagonal nor a board, but we shouldn't be pedantic). When added to Turing's basic Bombe design, the diagonal board led to fewer, better stops. Now they had a machine which really worked, and after May 1940 they had much more material to work with. A second Bombe, called *Agnus Dei*, arrived on 8 August 1940, and from thenceforth the sins of the world could be taken away by means of decrypting Army and Air Force Enigma. It was just as well, for in August 1940 the British were fighting alone.

Professor type meets man of God

Fearing invasion, Alan Turing embarked on one of his famously eccentric escapades. As recounted by Alan's brother John, by now a junior infantry officer who had just escaped from German tanks in northern France:[9]

He invested in some silver ingots just in case there should be a German occupation. He took these to a remote country place pushing them along in an ancient perambulator. Having buried them there he drew a map so that he could find them after the war. The war having ended he enlisted the help of his friend Donald Michie[10] to find this hidden treasure, using for the purpose a home-made metal detector. For once Alan's science had let him down for the heavy ingots were well on their way to Australia.

It wasn't just the silver ingots. For many years, banned from discussing the technicalities of work at Bletchley Park, all people could recount was the oddities of their co-workers. Odd they were – the civilians, at any rate – and Alan Turing seems to have topped the bill. Many anecdotes seem to have involved his bicycle:

- 'He used to cycle to and from work and in the summer he would wear his civilian gas mask to ward off hayfever. This apparition caused consternation to others on the road. Some would search the skies for enemy aircraft and others would don their gas masks just to be on the safe side.'
- 'In the shelter during air-raids he knitted himself a pair of gloves, with no pattern to guide him, just out of his head; he was, however, defeated when it came to completion of the fingers, so he used to bicycle in from Shenley with little tails of wool dangling from his fingertips until one of the girls in his office took pity on him and closed up the ends.'[11]
- 'Every now and then the chain fell off the bicycle. A normal person would then take the machine to the garage and get it mended but for him this would be the absolute last resort; a man ought to be able to confront the universe with his own bare hands and what God put inside his skull so he began to think about it. The first thing he knew was to count how many times the pedals went round and the results of counting suggested a periodicity which he thought could be due to this being a rare event which occurred whenever a particular defective cog on the larger cog wheel was in register with a defective cog on the smaller cog wheel and he investigated and he was proved right, but this was the way he went about everything.'

'Instead of having it mended he would count the number of times the pedals went round and would get off the bicycle in time to adjust the chain by hand.'[12]

Among the young recruits at Bletchley Park in 1940, the Prof was, at 28, an old boy – old enough for his oddities not to matter much. If Dilly Knox, Frank Birch, Alastair Denniston and the other veterans from the first war were the old guard, the new war had grown its own generation of leaders. By virtue of his early arrival date and his reputation, not to mention his great age, Alan Turing was becoming one of them. By 1941 he had become head of Hut 8, responsible for naval decryption.

The occupation of northern and western France by the Germans had opened the whole of the North Atlantic to the U-boats. Now based at Lorient, they were playing havoc with the convoys. Sinkings during the period up to May 1940 averaged 113,000 tons a month; after the fall of France the monthly toll doubled. By the end of 1941 over 5 million tons – 1,124 ships – had gone to the bottom. Fighting the Battle of the Atlantic was Bletchley Park's most urgent, but also its most difficult, challenge. But even the Bombes weren't quite enough to enable Bletchley Park to get on top of naval Enigma. The German Navy used eight coding wheels for their Enigma machine, as contrasted with five in the other armed forces. This, in theory, meant that 336 wheel combinations had to be tested to find the machine settings, rather than 60, requiring 80 hours of Bombe time to break a setting, as compared to 14 hours for Air Force keys. It was time to call upon a man of God.

In the 1740s, the Reverend Thomas Bayes had put forward a theorem about the probability of causes. The man of God was not now fashionable, and it was not because he had been dead for 180 years. It was because any mathematician who followed him was at risk of being branded a heretic. By the 1940s, Bayes's theorem was considered outrageous: the only orthodox way to measure probabilities was to take samples and observe their distribution, in the manner leading to the good old Gaussian Error Function. The inquisition into Bayes's heresy was led by none other than Professor R.A. Fisher, the

Cambridge authority on statistics, he who had said that the subject Alan Turing had chosen for his fellowship dissertation was 'positively repellent'. As befits an inquisitor, Fisher was powerful, irascible and opinionated, and he believed evangelically in Gauss. The reputation of any academic who might stray from the Gaussian Path was at risk.

So the name of the man of God could not be uttered at Bletchley Park. Mr Bayes's theorem was way off the Gaussian Path: applying Bayes's theory, sampling was not necessary to evaluate probabilities. At Bletchley in 1941 the idea that you might take samples and see what happened was laughable: sampling was never going to work with 159 million million million possible Enigma set-ups. Instead, if the testing of wheel combinations on the Bombe could focus on the combinations most likely to be right, it would save hours of time. If only the codebreakers were allowed to guess – ideally making an informed guess – and measure the reliability of the guess. The theorem of the heretical Mr Bayes allowed you to guess.

The starting point for guesswork was the codebreaker's oldest weapon. Frequency analysis has been used by codebreakers for centuries to unravel substitution ciphers, by relying on the unequal reliance of language on particular letters: the same reason that Q in English-language Scrabble is worth ten points but S is only worth one. Frequency analysis ought not to work for Enigma messages, because the scrambling changes with every press of a key on the keyboard – but what if several messages had been enciphered on machines set up the same way? Although the scrambling would change with every new letter of the message, the *changes* would be the same. If two pieces of plain German were each enciphered on Enigma machines set up in the same way, the intercepts would be more similar to each other than a wholly random allocation of letters. If the same letter appears in the same place in the plain-language texts, the same (enciphered) letter will appear in both cipher-texts if the machines are set up identically. So two pieces of cipher-text lined up one underneath the other will have more coincidences than you would otherwise predict. It's the difference between a 1:26 chance that any letter would match and about 1:17; not much, but a start.

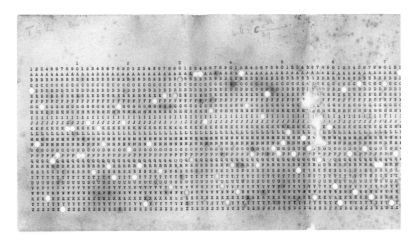

Banburismus. An original 'Banbury sheet' used for early attacks on naval Enigma, found during the restoration of Bletchley Park huts. (© Bletchley Park Trust)

Alan Turing's statistical attack on naval Enigma exploited this difference. Messages were punched as holes into long sheets of paper pre-printed with the alphabet, and pairs of these punched sheets were superimposed and moved sideways from left to right to see where the largest number of overlapping holes appeared. The more overlapping holes, the higher the likelihood that there was a situation of 1:17 correspondence rather than totally random 1:26. This enabled – with a degree of uncertainty – some of the eight possible wheels to be excluded from testing on the Bombe. The process was called 'Banburismus', named for the town in Oxfordshire with the cross and the lady on a white horse, where the mundane process of printing long sheets with rows and rows of alphabets was done. In another nod to Banbury, measures of probability were called 'bans' or 'decibans', using a logarithmic scale to tot up the chances. The process of adjusting guesses based on small observations was distressingly Bayesian. The Cambridge mathematician I.J. Good joined Bletchley Park in April 1940 and was assigned to Hut 8. He is reported to have asked Prof, 'Aren't you essentially using Bayes's theorem?' and Alan confessed that it was so. Fortunately for Alan, the work at Bletchley Park was secret, so Fisher would not find out about the wartime witchcraft of

Banburismus. After the war, Good became a professional defender of
Bayesian methodology, writing several papers on the subject; he had to
do so from the safety of the United States.

Good also described working with Alan Turing at this time:[13]

> When he attacked a problem he liked to start from first principles,
> and he was hardly influenced by received opinion. This attitude gave
> depth and originality to his thinking, and also it helped him to choose
> important problems. In discussions he was excitable, and his voice
> would rise to a high pitch, although he was not in the least quarrelsome.
> Between sentences he had a habit of saying 'Ah-ah-ah-ah-ah …,' which
> made it difficult to interrupt his line of thought, or even to have a line
> of thought of one's own!

Ruthless behaviour

But still the sinkings continued; even Bayes wasn't enough to defeat
naval Enigma. The *Cryptographic History of Work on the German Naval
Enigma* picks up the story:[14]

> Turing was now faced with the following dilemma. There were only
> two ways of getting into a key (1) Cribbing (2) Banburismus. Cribbing
> required some detailed knowledge of the traffic since otherwise
> one could not predict what a message would say; it therefore seemed
> necessary to break a few days on Banburismus first. Banburismus needed
> no knowledge of the content of the traffic but needed at least one
> known bigram table; it therefore seemed necessary to break a few days
> on Cribbing first. A further difficulty was that the bombes – essential
> to complete the break on modern keys – did not start to arrive until
> the Summer of 1940 and the German Air and Army section working on
> Enigma (Hut 6) also needed these machines. Thus the testing of even one
> crib, supposing this to be available, presented a considerable problem. The
> only really satisfactory solution to the problem was (1) a pinch either of
> the key sheets for a month or (rather less valuable) of the set of bigram

tables, combined with (2) maximum bombe production to enable such a pinch to be exploited. Failing a pinch or a really large number of bombes there was little hope of any progress on up to date material.

The attempt by the Allies to forestall the German invasion of Norway in April 1940 had not been a military success. Nevertheless, a German patrol boat *VP2623* had been captured at Narvik on 26 April with its codebooks and some transmitted messages (valuable as cribs). The captured documents confirmed Alan's theory about the bigram processes and allowed some messages to be broken. More captures were needed if the breaks were to continue. Fortunately, British Naval Intelligence included an officer of some ingenuity, namely Commander Ian Fleming, who wanted truth to be stranger than his later fiction. He proposed an operation called RUTHLESS.[15]

> I suggest we obtain the loot by the following means:
> 1. Obtain from Air Ministry an air-worthy German bomber.
> 2. Pick a tough crew of five, including a pilot, W/T operator and word-perfect German speaker. Dress them in German Air Force uniform, add blood and bandages to suit.
> 3. Crash plane in the Channel after making S.O.S. to rescue service in P/L.*
> 4. Once aboard rescue boat, shoot German crew, dump overboard, bring rescue boat back to English port.
> F. 12.9.40

Truth turned out more sober than fiction after all. Although all was prepared, there were no suitable German vessels, and RUTHLESS was called off. Frank Birch, the head of the German Naval Section, reported to the Admiralty:[16]

> Turing and Twinn[17] came to me like undertakers cheated of a nice corpse two days ago, all in a stew about the cancellation of Operation

---

★   Plain language.

Ruthless. The burden of their song was the importance of a pinch. Did the authorities realise that, since the Germans did the dirt on their machine on June 1st, there was very little hope, if any, of their deciphering current, or even approximately current, Enigma for months and months and months – if ever? Contrariwise, if they got a pinch – even enough to give a clue to one day's material, they could be pretty sure, after an initial delay, of keeping going from day to day from then on.

There were other ways to get the material, which were less cinematic but more secure, and the Navy were keen to oblige. A raid on German-occupied Norway in March 1941 secured some useful material from a trawler called *Krebs*; in May 1941 a weather ship called *München* was targeted and her code books and key sheets secured. The *Lauenberg*, another weather ship, was grabbed in June, just after Germany tore up the Molotov–Ribbentrop pact and invaded Russia. The most extraordinary capture of all happened on 9 May 1941, when *U-110*, commanded by *Kapitänleutnant* Lemp, was attacking convoy OB318. Lemp was no novice: he was decorated with the Knight's Cross and he had sunk 96,314 tons of shipping – including one of the first kills of the war, the passenger liner *Athenia* sunk on 3 September 1939. But today was not his day. *U-110*'s periscope was seen by HMS *Aubretia* which fired a pattern of depth-charges. Then HMS *Bulldog* and *Broadway* joined in the hunt. *Bulldog* set a course to ram, and Lemp, knowing that his boat was a goner, gave the order to abandon ship. But the uncooperative U-boat was a large Type IX-B which refused to sink promptly, and Lemp, realising that the British might capture his books, frantically struck out into the icy water to regain his boat and carry out his duty. He never made it, and was never seen again. A boarding party from *Bulldog* went over in a whaler and grabbed everything they could, while the men detailed to rescue survivors from *U-110* bundled them below to conceal what was going on. The haul included an Enigma machine with its rotors as well as the secret books. The men from *Bulldog* swore an oath of secrecy, saw to it that *U-110* sank properly, and whisked their finds across to Naval Intelligence as soon as they reached land.

Square root of minus one

Meanwhile, Hut 8 had done the unthinkable: it had appointed a woman mathematician to join its officer-class codebreakers. The woman was Joan Clarke. Gordon Welchman had supervised Joan when she was studying mathematics at Cambridge, and he recruited her in the spring of 1940. She was allocated to Alan Turing's team in Hut 8, and her job was to test the results of the Bombe which had been analysing the haul of material from *VP2623*. She rapidly 'rose from the ranks of the girls in the big room; but this was obviously because of my degree, and before I had had any chance of proving myself'.[18] Joan was being modest. Her intellect caught Alan Turing's attention; Commander Travis – Denniston's first lieutenant – took steps to have her pulled out of the clerical grades to which women were appointed. Nevertheless, the ingrained resistance to women's achievements remained: pseudo-Germanic terms were usually given to new codebreaking techniques (Turingismus, Yoxallismus and the like, not to mention Banburismus), but when Joan discovered a way to speed up the recovery of Enigma settings she was told it was 'pure Dillyismus'. For the first time in his life, Alan Turing found in Joan a woman he could talk to, on the same level, despite her sex. They tended to do the late shift together; and after some months of chess-playing and general socialising, Alan Turing turned the unthinkable into the unimaginable.

I suppose the fact that I was a woman made me different. We did do some things together, perhaps went to the cinema and so on, but certainly it was a surprise to me when he said – I think his words probably were 'Would you consider marrying me?' But although it was a surprise, I really didn't hesitate in saying yes. And then he knelt by my chair and kissed me. We didn't have very much physical contact. Now the next day, I suppose we went for a bit of a walk together; after lunch, he told me that he had this homosexual tendency, and naturally that worried me a bit, because I did know that that was something that was almost certainly permanent. But we carried on.[19]

Joan Clarke, who was briefly engaged to Alan Turing, relaxing with other colleagues at Bletchley Park. (Reproduced with the kind permission of John Clarke)

Carrying on involved a round of parental visits. Joan's father was a clergyman worried about his daughter's financial security, and Alan's parents were just sniffy. So was John:[20]

> My parents were pretty well accustomed to my landing them with the young, attractive and lively young women with whom I fell in love at intervals of about six months at a time; they used to come for weekends and cheered up my father immensely. But Alan's fiancée was tough going. We parents and elder brother worked like beavers all the weekend on this unpromising female and were exhausted by the exercise (as, no doubt, was she). I have an improbable memory of Alan and his affianced dutifully holding hands in a sandpit, both of them obviously wishing that they could get on with some untried theorem – and that not of the type which would have appealed to me.

It was more complicated, and more sobering, than John knew. Going through the ritual of parental introductions and scrutiny must have been agonising for Alan. At this stage no one in the Turing household had any ideas about Alan's sexuality. John himself had been married since 1934 and had two small daughters, living just around the corner from the senior Turings in Guildford, so at this time the succession of girlfriends to cheer up father was a memory, not the present reality. And life in the senior Turing household was not as calm as it might be. Ethel decided at around this time that she would be known by her second name. Julius moved out to live in the Cromwell Hotel in South Kensington, leaving Sara (as she now was) in Guildford, supervising the grandchildren. It wouldn't have been a fun family visit even in the best of circumstances. After a while reality sank in. Alan and Joan knew it wouldn't work out and the engagement was off. It had been an imaginary number.

Golden eggs

With the aid of the Navy's 'pinches' and a good number of Bombes now in use, decryption of naval Enigma was happening without delay by the summer of 1941. 'A flood of decrypted and translated signals concerning the operational U-boats began to pour into the Operational Intelligence Centre' at the Admiralty.[21] During that summer, Alan Turing and Gordon Welchman were summoned to see Sir Stewart Menzies, now head of the Secret Intelligence Service, who presented each of them with a cheque for £200 for their achievements with Enigma. Better still, Winston Churchill, who loved his secret intelligence, came to Bletchley in person on 6 September to meet the front-line staff, say thank you, and boost morale. Churchill allegedly told the codebreakers that they were the geese that laid the golden eggs. The great man was eager to know how it was done, and Gordon Welchman was told to prepare a short speech:

> When the party turned up, a bit behind schedule, Travis whispered, somewhat loudly, 'Five minutes, Welchman.' I started with my prepared opening gambit, which was 'I would like to make three

points,' and proceeded to make the first two. Travis then said, 'That's enough, Welchman,' whereupon Winston, who was enjoying himself, gave me a grand schoolboy wink and said, 'I think there was a third point, Welchman.'[22]

It seems credible that Commander Travis wanted to shut him up, for Gordon Welchman was getting frustrated with the bureaucracy. One problem with working for a secret organisation is that nobody can explain why resources are needed, because the persons in charge of resource allocation do not 'need to know'. Inspired by Churchill's pep-talk, he decided to act. Or rather, to write a letter to Churchill, get his colleagues to sign it, and ask Stuart Milner-Barry – Welchman's deputy in Hut 6 and chess-player extraordinary – to deliver it. Alan Turing was game, the letter was written, and Milner-Barry took the train to London and an expensive taxi to Downing Street. In his hurry and anxiety Milner-Barry left his identity card behind, but the real effrontery was not him brazenly walking into Number Ten (indeed he subsequently became a very senior official in the Civil Service, so evidently had the right skills); it was the breach of etiquette by the signatories in going over the heads of Alastair Denniston and his deputy, Commander E. W. Travis.

> Hut 6 and Hut 8, (Bletchley Park)
> 21st October 1941

Secret and Confidential
Prime Minister only
Dear Prime Minister,

   Some weeks ago you paid us the honour of a visit, and we believe that you regard our work as important. You will have seen that, thanks largely to the energy and foresight of Commander Travis, we have been well supplied with the 'bombes' for the breaking of the German Enigma codes. We think, however, that you ought to know that this work is being held up, and in some cases is not being done at all, principally because we cannot get sufficient staff to deal with it. Our reason for writing to you direct is that for months we have done everything that we possibly can through the normal channels, and that we despair of any early improvement without your intervention. [...]

We have written this letter entirely on our own initiative. We do not know who or what is responsible for our difficulties, and most emphatically we do not want to be taken as criticizing Commander Travis who has all along done his utmost to help us in every possible way. But if we are to do our job as well as it could and should be done it is absolutely vital that our wants, small as they are, should be promptly attended to. We have felt that we should be failing in our duty if we did not draw your attention to the facts and to the effects which they are having and must continue to have on our work, unless immediate action is taken.

We are, Sir, your obedient servants

A.M. Turing
W.G. Welchman
C.H.O'D. Alexander
P.S. Milner-Barry[23]

Somehow Milner-Barry got past the policeman on the door despite having no ID, and handed the letter to a brigadier who did not sling him out on his ear. The letter was delivered to the great man. Churchill scribbled on a piece of notepaper and included one of his notorious stickers printed with the words Action This Day. His note read: 'Secret. In a locked Box. Gen. Ismay. Make sure they have all they want on extreme priority and report to me that this has been done. WSC 22.x.' None of the four conspirators – to become known as the Wicked Uncles – were fired, and the resources started to flow. There were also reorganisations of the Bletchley Park management; by February 1942 Denniston had been moved 'sideways' back to London to run diplomatic decryption, and Travis was left in sole charge at Bletchley.

In the blackout

Army and Air Force Enigma was producing copious amounts of intelligence. Bletchley Park was constantly trying to recruit more people, not just Wrens to operate the Bombes but professor types as well. Enigma keys changed at midnight, so a good deal of the decryption took place in unsocial hours. For most of the staff at Bletchley Park, shift work was particularly ghastly. Joan Clarke recalled later:[24]

> Most people did not take their weekly leave when working the midnight-to-nine shift, but I can remember Alan Turing coming in as usual for a day's leave, doing his own mathematical research at night, in the warmth and light of the office, without interrupting the routine of daytime sleep.

The coming of the war hadn't prevented Alan from continuing his work on formal mathematical logic. Throughout 1940 and 1941 he was corresponding with M.H.A. Newman on ordinal logics and the lambda-calculus. Writing from his digs at the Crown Inn, Shenley Brook End, Alan wrote periodically to Church with queries. 'Dear Professor Church,' he begins; Church responds, 'Dear Dr Turing'. Alan's relationship with Newman was warmer. 'Dear Newman, Church's notes certainly are rather a mouthful. I have never worked steadily through them myself, but have taken them in much the same spirit as you are doing. Fortunately I was able to go to the fountainhead for information.'[25] Together with Newman, still sitting out the war at Cambridge, he wrote a paper, which Newman sent off to Church for comments in January 1941; it was published in Church's *Journal of Symbolic Logic* in March 1942. Another paper, this time by Alan alone, followed in the same journal at the end of the year. However, that was the last major contribution Alan was to make in symbolic logic. Alan's intellectual interests were destined to take a different direction, because of a decision taken at the highest level in the German Naval Staff.

Towards the end of 1941, hints had been dropped in the decrypted messages of a major change in German procedures. The old Enigma process was going to be thrown out. Now the U-boats were going to use a four-wheel Enigma machine, and the codebreakers' existing methods weren't suitable for this horrific development. The switchover happened on 1 February 1942, and once again Bletchley was blacked out. The sinkings in the Atlantic started to rise once more.

Improvements to the Bombe technology were needed. At the leisurely pace of 17,576 settings every 12 minutes, Bombes couldn't find plausible settings quickly enough with Enigmas using an extra set of coding wheels: the increase to 456,976 possible wheel positions turned 12 minutes into over five hours, even if you could find a way to rig a three-wheel machine to solve a four-wheel problem. Six Bombes took 17 days to break naval Enigma in February 1942. Bletchley needed to add a superfast fourth wheel to its three-wheel Bombes. They turned to C.E. Wynn-Williams, who was working at the Telecommunications Research Establishment, for ideas; he was the expert in electronic counters, using gas-filled tubes which stood in for mechanical components and therefore worked much faster. These could monitor the positions of the fast wheel whizzing past each position in less than a thousandth of a second. Wynn-Williams designed a thing named the Cobra, so called because of its snake-like cable of 2,000 wires connecting it to the regular Bombe. The Cobra had all sorts of problems: one was the habit of its metal brushes bouncing and so missing fast-moving contacts; another was due to electromagnetic fields in the vicinity of the gas tubes, which made the switching unreliable. It was all quite difficult. Wynn-Williams's high-speed Bombe was tried out but in October it was said that 'the first Wynn Williams assembly has not been as successful as was hoped'. Doc Keen was working on a high-speed four-wheel machine too ('it looks as if Keen's machine will exceed expectations'), but under any circumstances production of fast Bombes was still several months away. Meanwhile the U-boats unerringly found their targets, and the British remained in the dark.

A drawback of Alan's regular three-wheel Bombe was that it only produced one plausible set-up for the three coding wheels, and one possible cross-plugging. There were nine more cross-pluggings to find, and then the ring-settings. All this could be done using the same crib and menu that had been used to wire up the Bombe, but the process involved a thing called a checking machine, which was operated manually. In theory the checking could be automated, and for this problem the Post Office Research Station at Dollis Hill were brought in to help. At Dollis Hill Alan Turing was introduced to another engineer, one who would bring Bletchley Park into the computer age before computers had even been invented. The man was called Tommy Flowers.

Alan explained the Bombe-and-checking problem to Flowers. Explaining things was not always Alan's forte, as Donald Michie described in a later interview with Professor Brian Randell:[26]

> You had to get over a hurdle first before you were in the right ballpark at all, and it was very very easy for people to fail to clear that hurdle and consequently to regard Turing as totally incomprehensible, which was a very widespread attitude towards him, and this arose in two ways, one being simply overawed or panicked by a person of very great intellectual penetration. Secondly, his personal peculiarities were so obtrusive, as for instance his style of speaking and his whole appearance, and the way he twitched his head as he spoke and squeaked in a very high pitched grating voice and appeared to stammer, simply fazed some people.

Although most people found Alan incomprehensible, this was not the case with Flowers, who 'never had any trouble with him'. 'I thought he was a charming chap once you got to know him, but he certainly was odd. Turing was always very much – complete in himself. You never felt that he was joining in, that he was dependent on anybody else, but he was a very charming chap.'[27] Despite their effective working relationship, the machine which Alan wanted was not a success: the speed specification was far too low for the task in hand, and the project was abandoned. There was a turf war, or a skirmish, between the British Tabulating Machine Company, who were building Bombes, and the Post Office Research Establishment, who were not.

Notwithstanding, Flowers's talents were not going to be thrown away – he had the impression that Bletchley Park felt guilty that his time had been wasted, and he had now been cleared for working on the most secret operations of the war. His would be a new codebreaking project, which in 1942 was just beginning at Bletchley Park, and it would involve Tommy Flowers and Alan Turing in the genesis of the first all-purpose computing machinery in the world.

Meanwhile, there was a war to fight. On the intelligence front the fighting wasn't going to plan, and turf skirmishes were breaking out in other theatres. Since December 1940 the British had been trying to arrange an intelligence partnership with the United States. The first unveiling of the Enigma secret took place in March 1941, but after then relations had deteriorated. Secrets are not shared willingly, and there was suspicion of non-disclosures and counter-suspicion of indiscreet sharing of secret material. Even when America entered the war it didn't get much easier. Bletchley Park sent its head cryptographer, Colonel John Tiltman, to America in March 1942 to try to convince the Americans to focus on Japanese codes while the British handled Enigma. Given that Bletchley was in a blackout, the Americans weren't in the mood to be convinced. They thought they should sort out naval Enigma for themselves, not surprisingly given that U-boats had been creating carnage with American shipping along the eastern seaboard of the United States. Eventually the British let them have answers to a detailed questionnaire, and a copy of Prof's book. Blueprints for the Bombe were also promised, but those the British didn't deliver; then in mid-1942 there was the Blue Bird incident, involving Colonel B.F. Fellers, who was the US military attaché to the British Army in North Africa.

> On 24 April GC and CS had decyphered an appreciation from Kesselring referring to information he had received from a reliable source to the effect that a British attempt to advance to Benghazi was not possible before the beginning of June.[28]

'Reliable source' is just how the British would describe the provenance of intelligence derived from cracking enciphered messages.

Early on 24 June Sigint* revealed that the Germans were aware, from decrypts of his signals, that in the opinion of the US Military Attaché in Cairo the British had been decisively beaten and that this was a suitable moment for Rommel to take the Delta.

It was bad enough that the US attaché Colonel Fellers had little confidence in the British, but unforgivable that his signals were sent in a cipher broken by the Germans and revealed to Kesselring the Allies' plans for the Battle of Egypt. Insult was added to injury because the revelation came to the British through their own codebreaking activities. Some serious bridge-building was needed to overcome these setbacks. Two American naval officers, Lt Cdr R.B. Ely and Lt (junior grade) Joe Eachus, were posted to Bletchley Park, arriving in July, and both worked closely with Alan Turing. The Blue Bird incident was bad enough to implicate the Americans' cipher security, but it was worse than that. The indications late in 1942 were that British cipher security was also shaky. Although the British were blacked out of naval Enigma, they were reading Italian and Japanese ciphers – and these other decrypts gave the British the fright of their lives. The Axis powers seemed to be able to read the British Naval Cypher No. 3. Not only did the convoys have no idea where the U-boats were, the U-boats knew exactly where the convoys were. It was a disaster of the first order. The Allies needed to sort themselves out, and get back on top of naval Enigma.

Commander Travis worked hard on the problem, and together with Commander Joseph Wenger of the US Navy, a deal was thrashed out. Among other things, the British were to provide 'technical assistance in the development of analytical machinery' and agreed 'in principle to full collaboration upon the German submarine and naval cryptanalysis problems'; the British were 'to obtain certain items of special analytical equipment developed by the U.S.'[29] The quid pro quo was that Britain would leave Japanese naval cryptanalysis to the Americans. To help with the 'technical assistance', Travis agreed that he should send Prof across to liaise with the US Navy Department:

★　Signals Intelligence.

FOR 'OP-20-G' FROM 'G.C. & C.S.' X T163
FOR WENGER FROM TRAVIS
YOUR WB170 X SHOULD BE GLAD IF TURING (WHO IS
NOT A PROFESSOR) COULD COME EXAMINE MACHINERY
X MAKE ANY USE YOU LIKE OF HIM IN CONNECTION
WITH BOMBES X HAVE SUGGESTED HE STAY A WEEK IN
WASHINGTON BUT IF YOU WOULD LIKE HIM LONGER I
SHOULD BE QUITE WILLING[30]

Although the successes of the U-boats in the Atlantic were at their height in November 1942, Alan took a passage on the RMS *Queen Elizabeth*, whose average speed was, at 26 knots, about 8 knots faster than a surfaced U-boat. He arrived in New York for a third time on 13 November 1942. This time he wasn't going for the attractions of Princeton in the fall. He had another mission, which had very little to do with breaking codes. Alan Turing's new responsibility was to prevent the British making mistakes like those of the unwitting Colonel Fellers.

LOOKING GLASS WAR

Alan Turing's trip to America was so secret that, nine years later, in writing to his friend Norman Routledge Alan said that the job he had had during the war 'certainly did not involve any travelling'. In fact, his work between late 1942 and the end of the war remained under official wraps right into the twenty-first century. Even at the time of his departure for the United States in November 1942 it was so secret that he was told to take no documents at all other than the contents of a diplomatic bag; taking this admonition rather too literally Alan had a difficult time with the immigration authorities on arrival in New York:

> I reached New York on Friday November 12th. I was all but kept on Ellis Island by the Immigration Authorities who were very snooty about my carrying no orders and no evidence to connect me with the F.O. They considered my official's passport insufficient in itself. They asked me very minute details about where I was to report etc. I think it might have been better from a security point of view if I had been provided with some kind of document of the kind they wanted.[1]

Alan stayed a few days in New York, where he met with a Canadian engineer called Lieutenant Colonel Pat Bayly. Bayly's Number One project was to improve the security of communications across the Atlantic: between the British on both sides of the ocean, and between the British and the Canadians, all without being overheard by the Americans.

Bayly's focus was messages sent in the teleprinter code. Instead of using Morse, teleprinter messages go out in the five-bit binary Baudot-Murray code. As with all ciphers, if you add the key to the plain-text, you get gibberish; the clever part is that since the Baudot-Murray code is binary, adding the *same* key to the gibberish gives you back the plain-text. Bayly had invented a machine, called the Rockex, which generated a random string of binary digits, which were punched out onto two tapes: one which could be added by the cipher-clerk at the sending end, and another, containing the same key-string, which could be added by the cipher-clerk at the receiving end. Then the tapes would be destroyed, so that the key would never be used again. This method, which is the 'one time pad' system of encipherment, is the only truly secure one – assuming it is properly used. Bayly's machine for producing the 'tapes' which carried the key-string was pronounced by Alan to be secure.

By the end of 1942 – the turning point in the war described by Churchill as 'the hinge of fate' – Alan Turing's job had itself turned about. His meeting with Pat Bayly was a foretaste of something which would occupy the next two years of his secret career. It was becoming the mirror image of its previous shape: Alan was changing from safe-breaker into safe-keeper. From this point on his cryptographic role would mainly be to guard secrets, rather than to uncover them.

Dr A.M. Turing, Ph.D

After Alan's vetting of Bayly's work, it was time to check up on, or, to put it diplomatically, to liaise with the Americans. It wasn't apparent that the Americans wanted to be liaised with, or checked up on, which is probably why Alan had struggled to get off Ellis Island. The liaison mission was to begin with the American cryptanalysts of OP-20-G, the US Navy's equivalent of Bletchley Park. After a few days with Bayly Alan moved on to Washington, and had a few awkward days there. First up was a meeting with the Americans' answer to Dilly Knox.

> As I saw nobody working with pencil and paper, I asked if there was anyone in E[*] who did so. Was introduced to Mrs. Driscoll at this point. I was rather alarmed.[2]

Alan might well be alarmed. Agnes Driscoll was a formidable intellect, who, like Dilly, believed in the power of the pencil. Her attack on naval Enigma had proceeded from first principles, and she believed it possible to find a 'way in' using an eight-letter crib. Unfortunately Alan had shown conclusively that it was in practice impossible to break three-wheel naval Enigma this way: Mrs Driscoll's method would give about 3,000 solutions for each wheel order, with 336 wheel orders to try. He wrote a memo, which in true British fashion did not rubbish her approach, but it concluded with a set of unanswerable questions, suggesting only that the British must have misunderstood her method.[3] At their actual meeting Mrs Driscoll tried the same technique herself, asking Alan 'a great number of questions, to most of which fortunately I did not know the answers', and the moment of danger passed.

As requested by Travis, Alan was also in America to examine machinery. There were obstacles when foreigners wanted to look at secret machines, and Alan found that 'my Princeton Ph.D. was quite useful in enlisting help, so I have decided to go by the name of Dr. Turing officially whilst I am over here'. His first report back to London, on his discussions with Bayly and the alarming Mrs Driscoll, was suitably doctored, beginning 'REPORT BY DR A.M. TURING, Ph. D.' Whether the recipients – Travis and Captain Hastings, a Royal Navy captain, 25 years Alan's senior, veteran of the previous war, and now the liaison officer between Bletchley and the American codebreakers – were likely to share in Dr Turing's brand of humour is not recorded.

[*] Contemporary papers refer to Enigma as 'E'.

Alan's report considers a number of cryptological machines which were in development by the US Navy. He liked the machinery but was much more critical of the thought processes, or rather the lack of them, underlying some of its use. Still, fertile imaginations were being brought in to battle against the ongoing problems of German and Japanese codes and ciphers. Alan inspected machines that used teleprinter tape instead of punched cards for data input and celluloid film coupled with photoelectric cells for comparison of messages. There were frequency counters and decoding machines. Punched-card processes were faster and slicker than in Britain. It was most impressive; his report runs to 28 pages, with many recommendations for improvement addressed to his colleagues back at Bletchley.

Alan was next due to visit Bell Laboratories, the research division of the telephone company AT&T. In many ways this was the counterpart to the Post Office Research Establishment where Tommy Flowers was based, and it was where they were building Bombes for the US Army. Getting into Bell Labs was difficult. For one thing the US Army was not the US Navy; Alan's security clearance was a naval one, and so self-evidently invalid. So, for the time being, Alan went to see the Americans' own four-wheel naval Bombe, which was not at Bell Labs. Although the US Navy reckoned they should be able to move ahead faster than the British with a four-wheel Bombe, it was not proving to be so easy. And the Americans were using an awful lot of equipment.

VISIT to NATIONAL CASH REGISTER CORPORATION of DAYTON, OHIO

On December 21st I visited the works at Dayton, Ohio, where the Bombes are being made, with Commander Wenger, Lieutenant-Commander Engstrom, Lieutenant-Commander Meader, Lieutenant (jg) Eachus and Major Stevens. The weather held up our train and we arrived six hours late at 2 p.m. so that we did not have quite so long there as we might have had, but probably sufficient.

The plans for the Bombes are on the whole essentially the same as ours, but there are a number of minor differences which should be noted.

(A)   As mentioned in my previous report the machine is intended to stop and reverse whenever there is a 'stop', and go back to the position of the stop, and there do further twisting. Engstrom and I are still both rather unhappy about this idea. […]

(B)   Wheel Changing. You may remember that the American Bombe programme was to produce 336 Bombes 'one for each wheel order'. I used to smile inwardly at the conception of Bombe hut routine implied by this programme, but thought that no particular purpose would be served by pointing out that we would not really use them in that way. However it now seems that this programme has actually affected the design of the Bombes, for, assuming that the wheels would not be changed, they have designed the Bombes with different sizes of wheels for the different positions.[4]

The eavesdroppers

The technical visit to Dayton was no doubt all very interesting, but everyone knew the Americans were highly accomplished at engineering. While some input from Prof with his years of experience might be helpful, this type of 'liaison' was not exactly vital, although having him available to answer questions showed commitment to the secrecy alliance. From the British perspective, the primary purpose of Prof's visit was something altogether different. It was not about Enigma or even teleprinter codes. It was about something much more direct and simple as a means of communication, but equally dependent on radio and therefore open to eavesdroppers. It was the problem of the telephone.

As with the British naval codes in the Battle of the Atlantic, so with phone calls. The scrambled telephone calls of Winston Churchill had been intercepted and unscrambled by the German Post Office – the old technology in use at the start of the war was insecure and unfit for purpose. As early as August 1940 Churchill had been worried about switchboard operators listening in, and he was still concerned in

Very substantial equipment. The US Army Bombe: an entire roomful of relay-based switching machinery that emulated all the moving parts and logical structures of the British Bombe.

Bell Labs New York building. Alan had to wait for six weeks while a fight between the top British and American generals broke out as to whether he would be allowed in. During the war, a railway line carrying freight trains ran right through the building.

October 1942, writing to Anthony Eden, 'I do not feel safe with the present free use of the radio telephone either to USA or to Russia.'[5] Bell Laboratories, the home of the US Army Bombe, was working on a new device to make phone calls secure, and it might be the solution. There was, however, a problem. Alan Turing still wasn't allowed into Bell Labs.

AMERICAN RESEARCH AND DEVELOPMENT OF TELEPHONIC SCRAMBLING DEVICE AND RESEARCH OF UNSCRAMBLING TELEPHONIC DEVICES

Although there has been no exchange of information between the British and U.S. on this subject, it was known that the U.S. were carrying out certain experiments and Air-Commodore Lywood, Director of Signals, Air Ministry, raised the question with General Olmstead suggesting that a technical expert might be sent out from England as a consultant with a view to assisting British authorities and making available to U.S. authorities a technical expert of proved ability. On September 24th. Mr. Albert F. Murray, of the Communications Section of the National Defence Research Committee, wrote to the R.A.F. Delegation stating that permission for Dr. A.M. Turing to visit Bell Laboratories in New York had been approved by the Director of Naval Communications and the Office of the Chief Signal Officer. On receipt of this letter, G.C. & C.S. sent Dr. Turing to the U.S.A. but on application being made to Mr. Murray, it was discovered that the matter was complicated and that permission to visit Bell Laboratories could not be obtained for the present. […] I am informed that the construction of the scrambling device is well advanced and is considered of so secret a nature that Dr. Turing cannot be given access to the investigations in Bell Laboratories – this decision having been taken by General Marshall himself.[6]

This was in a memo from Captain E.G. Hastings, RN, to Field Marshal Sir John Dill, the former Chief of the Imperial General Staff, now Chief of the British Joint Staff Mission in Washington. General George C. Marshall was the US Army Chief of Staff. The Bell Labs question couldn't get much higher-level attention than this. Dill wrote to

Marshall in early December 1942 and over the course of the following five weeks, while Alan pottered around Washington and Dayton, they exchanged a further seven letters. Alan Turing's bridge-building liaison mission was turning into an international incident. It boiled down to mutual mistrust on the secret-sharing deal between Travis and Wenger. Every time Marshall thought he had obtained clearance for Alan's visit he was rebuffed. Finally Dill put his foot down. If it was to be a two-way street, Britain would show the Americans everything in Britain, but the Americans would not, on security grounds, be allowed to exploit in America everything they had seen; conversely, America should show the British everything going on in the US, on condition there was no exploitation of it in Britain. It was a sensible compromise, if the Americans agreed to it. If. There was an ultimatum in there – not set out explicitly, but it was there clearly enough between the lines ('perhaps rather crudely worded but I did it in a hurry to catch you before you looked into the matter tomorrow,' wrote Sir John disingenuously). If the Americans persisted in denying Turing access to Bell Labs, the deal for them to get British Enigma intelligence and everything else would be annulled. The Americans blinked. Two days later, in Marshall's absence, his deputy wrote to Dill's deputy: 'I have instructed our Assistant Chief of Staff, G-2, to permit Dr. Turing to visit the Bell Laboratory for the purpose of inspecting the scrambling device experiments which are being conducted there.' On 12 January Alan Turing's name was added to the Clearance List for something called the 'X-61753 Project', with the caveat that he was not cleared for 'Cryptographic U.S. Army'. Alan got into Bell Labs on 19 January 1943 and, apart from a couple of weeks away in Washington, he was there until 15 March.

He might be in the building but the question of security clearance was still rumbling on. Scrambling of phone calls used, at root, the same principles as encipherment of text: putting it into codified form and adding a secret 'key'. The cryptographic key which was added by the X-61753 equipment to the speech was provided by phonographic records, which didn't have nice American music on them but random screeches and noise. This method was, for a time, thought 'operationally

impractical', and instead the US Army Signal Security Branch wanted
to replace the records with an electromechanical converter called
M-228. Alan had not been cleared to see M-228 but 'it does not appear
practicable to exclude certain British representatives, principally
Dr. Turing, from gaining knowledge of the principles and construction
of Converter M-228'.[7] Twenty thousand other personnel were going
to know about M-228's construction and operation, so 'withholding
these features from the British would appear to be somewhat
unimportant'. On 6 February it was decided that M-228 converters
would be sent over to Bell Labs for them to study. 'Bell Laboratories
will acquaint Dr. Turing with the cryptographic principles involved in
the M-228 but will not permit him to examine or conduct any tests
on this equipment in their laboratories. Any and all specific questions
which Dr. Turing may have on this converter will be answered by
representatives of the Signal Security Branch.'

On 5 February 1943 Alan was, at last, allowed to see the US Army
Bombe at Bell Labs. Alan's report went over to Travis on 11 February
under cover of a note apologising for Alan's typing (perhaps unfairly,
since at least compared with Prof's book, it is of reasonable, if not
secretarial, quality) – 'unfortunately time does not permit re-typing
before catching the bag'. Like the bag, the Bombe was fast, 'giving a
3-wheel running time of 7 minutes. These advantages do not seem
to me to outweigh the disadvantage of the enormous amount of
equipment involved.'[8]

He was being sniffy, but in a different sense his imagination was
captured by this machine. All the moving parts that characterised the
British Bombe were reimagined in circuitry – switching, using relays –
provided a digital, logical alternative to moving drums and hard-wired
analogues to Enigma parts. If the Germans introduced new Enigma
rotors, it would not be necessary to manufacture new parts for the US
Army Bombe, since the wiring patterns were a matter of switching
– or programming, just like Alan had foreseen in the *Computable
Numbers* paper six years earlier. Certainly he was not recommending
a changeover of British Enigma-breaking practice, but equally the
US Army machine had a new versatility. Later in the war, it was used

to keep on top of all manner of problems that were beyond British Bombes as well as German innovations aimed at making Enigma more secure; these included solving the wiring of the 'Uncle Dick' settable reflector rotor, the challenge of false stops, and 'dud-busting', which meant finding the missing parts of settings when the message setting on an Enigma intercept was incomplete. Problems like this required additional equipment in Britain; the American way, which started with enormous amounts of equipment, allowed a logic-based approach. Alan had been introduced, by the US Army Bombe, to algorithms brought out of the page and into operational reality.

The Green Hornet

Vast equipment was something Alan was getting used to. For the problem of secure voice encryption, Bell Labs had built something huge. Their device filled an entire room, used 40 racks of equipment, and weighed 50 tons. It needed 13 people to operate it, and it took 15 minutes to set up a phone call. Called Project X-61753 when Alan viewed it, it was later renamed Sigsaly, and then nicknamed the Green Hornet because its enciphered product had a nasal sound a bit like Rimsky-Korsakov's *Flight of the Bumblebee*. It worked by taking samples of the spoken messages and measuring their strength. The amplitude of each sample could be expressed as a number, and then enciphered like text by the addition of a key. At the receiving end, you just reversed the process. Simple enough, except that human speech is not a monotone, speech is not writing, and (as Alan had been learning for several years) encipherment was not wholly resistant to attack.

At Bell Labs, Alan met the mathematician and engineer who explained how all this was solved by the new equipment. The man was called Claude Shannon. Shannon had done his master's thesis on Boolean algebra, establishing that electrical circuits could be used to execute logic problems – the basis for modern computer logic. He had then done a stint with John von Neumann at Princeton. Claude Shannon and Alan Turing are reported to have met frequently in the Bell Labs cafeteria. There was much to talk about. Shannon's areas of interest overlapped significantly with Alan's, if Shannon's output of technical papers during this period is anything to go by:

- Four papers on pulse counting, pulse modulation and pulse shape, all connected with the capture, digitisation and transmission of speech.
- 'A Mathematical Theory of Cryptography', of 114 pages in length, finished in 1945.
- Two papers on calculating machinery, one theoretical and the other practical.

Later, in 1949, Claude Shannon wrote a paper on how to program a computer to play chess. Designing a chess-playing algorithm was at the back of Alan Turing's mind: could a mechanical process be used to carry out the combination of logical and intuitive steps which are needed to play the game? Talking to Shannon about the logical design would have been tremendously good fun, and, from a security perspective, totally safe. But to imagine that this is what they discussed is speculation, and there were no computers at Bell Labs in 1943, nor indeed anywhere else. Work was going on elsewhere in the building to build a Relay Calculator to help with the computations needed to aim anti-aircraft guns successfully, but Alan Turing was not at Bell Labs to look at calculators. He was there to see if the Americans' solution to secure telephony would actually work.

Claude Shannon had cracked the monotone problem of speech encryption, by seeing that it was a problem of sampling. X-61753 listened to the amplitudes of the spoken signal in ten wavebands across the frequency spectrum, and sampled each of these 50 times a second. Each of these samples would then constitute part of the digitised signal to be encrypted. Then the key would be added. And here the second problem came in. Telephone conversations are not like telegrams, which you can decipher at your leisure. To have a real-time conversation, the key needs to be stripped off the enciphered speech at the receiver's end at precisely the same moment as it is put on at the speaker's end. The encoding and decoding machines have to be operating exactly in synchrony. No wonder Bell Labs needed those 40 racks and 50 tons. Thirdly, there was the problem of adding a secure key which wasn't going to be cracked open like Enigma, and whether this was going to be done using phonograph records or the converter M-228.

On 15 February 1943, while Alan was still somewhere among the 40 racks, General Sir Hastings Ismay – the Chief of the Imperial General Staff who had already had to deal with the Wicked Uncles' troublesome request for more resources at Bletchley – sent a note to the Prime Minister:[9]

> A United States Officer has just arrived in London with instructions to install an apparatus of an entirely new kind for ensuring speech secrecy over the radio-telephone. The apparatus is an American invention. We know little or nothing about it, except that it requires three rooms to house it and six men to operate it. [...] The Chiefs of Staff have been considering the position. They think it essential to establish beyond doubt the effectiveness of the equipment. If it is not one hundred per cent secure, it would be extremely dangerous. The only Englishman who has so far been allowed to see it is Dr. Turing of the Government Code and Cypher School. The Chiefs of Staff are not sure that he is sufficiently qualified on all aspects to be able to give a final opinion. [...] The fact that the Americans desire to retain complete control of this apparatus, and to prevent our experts from becoming familiar with it, is perhaps strange. Nevertheless, the Chiefs of Staff do not recommend that any objection should be raised by us at this stage. They feel it will be time enough to ask to be let into the secret when the apparatus has been installed, and has proved its value.

The Prime Minister, whose notes were shorter than his phone calls, replied, 'Good. WSC 16.ii.43.' The Joint Staff Mission sent a Most Secret Cypher Telegram to London a few days later, explaining that there were no British officers in Washington technically qualified to examine the thing, so Alan's verdict, as follows, would have to do:

Bell System depends on electronic translation of speech into numerical code and any standard reciphering process can be applied. It was originally intended to apply a process equivalent to onetime table which would have provided absolute security. In order to simplify construction U.S. propose to adopt modifications and the proposed process is a machine method which should provide adequate security though definitely inferior to onetime table. If the equipment is to be operated solely by U.S. personnel it will be impossible to prevent them listening in if they so desire.

The full report, addressed to Travis, was sent by air mail later. Travis was put on the spot. Was X–61753 all right, or not?

I am in some difficulty in expressing an opinion on the security of the U.S. project X–61753. Dr. Turing's report is incomplete as the authorities at the Bell Laboratories would not, for security reasons, permit him to include certain details and drawings. Dr. Turing left New York on 18th March and I should prefer to await his arrival so that I can consult him before giving a definite opinion.

Subject to the caveats on eavesdropping and machine encipherment, and the secrets of M–228, it was a favourable verdict, and 50 tons of equipment were duly delivered to London so that Churchill could badger Roosevelt with flights of eloquence in private. There was not enough space for X–61753 in Whitehall, so the basement of Selfridges department store was taken over for the purpose. They stuck to phonograph records for the encryption method; M–228 was renamed Sigcum and kept for encryption of teleprinter traffic.

The return of Prof

By the time of Alan's return to Britain in the spring of 1943, Bletchley Park had evolved into a radically different place from four years before. Dilly Knox was dead, and with his passing the sense that codebreaking could be done if you were given enough brainpower, pencils, and squared paper had passed too. Machinery was giving the Enigma settings which enabled Bletchley to produce both decrypts and intelligence. The organisation was now being run by Commander Travis, and it was an intelligence factory, with the various groups (still nostalgically called Hut 6, Hut 8 and so on) now housed in functional, bomb-proof brick buildings and communicating with intercept stations, London and beyond over high-speed teleprinter links.

Towards the middle of 1942, Alan's role at Bletchley had already begun to change. With the mechanisation of decryption, it was no longer right to have the intellectuals running the process. Alan's friend Donald Michie, who joined Bletchley Park in the autumn of 1942, later described the Bletchley legend that grew up around this. It's a legend, and so it's probably a myth, but tales about classical heroes are usually worth retelling:

Although [Alan's] intellectual leadership was absolutely unchallenged, he had no powers of administrative leadership, and in the organisation that worked on the Enigma he was the official head; although Hugh Alexander was a member of the same section, and was superlatively gifted in organisational skills. And this situation just became more and more absurd – and here I am now speaking from hearsay because I was not a member of that section myself, but I had good friends who had been in that and they told me about it – what began to happen was the inevitable, that everybody went to Alexander to know what to do and eventually any order forms would get signed by Alexander although Turing was the titular head. And this was quite characteristic of him, that he wouldn't know how to deal with such a situation. It wasn't that he necessarily objected to being displaced from a position in which he wasn't appropriately placed, but he wouldn't know how, himself, to bring about the transition which other people might take in their stride – they might go to Alexander and say, 'Look Hugh, you're really running this show and I don't like running things so shall we swop around' – but it wouldn't come naturally to Turing. That resolved in the most extraordinary way; he turned up at the entrance to the Park late one

morning and anybody who did had to sign their name in a book, and
one of the columns in the book was for the name of the head of your
section, and he wrote down that day his own name and the time and
then in the head of section column he wrote 'C.H.O'D. Alexander' and
nothing more was said, but finally throughout the whole organisation
all the administrative records were changed. And without a word being
spoken Alexander from that day on was the titular head of the section.[10]

More significant for Alan, though, than any of this, was that the Battle
of the Atlantic had largely been won by the spring of 1943. Alan
arrived back safely; he was lucky in his timing. The first three weeks of
March 1943 were among the worst ever for sinkings, with 97 merchant
ships totalling more than 500,000 gross registered tons going to the
bottom. What the Germans described as 'the greatest convoy battle of
all time' had just concluded. Over a ten-day period, Convoys HX229,
HX229A and SC122 had battled with three wolfpacks – 36 U-boats
in all – which had sunk 22 ships from these convoys. Nevertheless, this
battle was the swansong of the U-boat war. Aided by another capture
of secret material from the foundering *U-559*, the Allies would, from
the end of March 1943, always be in the ascendant in the naval code
war. Not only had the Enigma blackout ended but, with the closure
of the 'air gap', convoys were escorted in much greater safety from
this point on. Admiral Dönitz abandoned U-boat operations in the
Atlantic after May 1943. It was time for Alan Turing to move on.

The Gamekeeper

Hanging beside the stairs at home is a family portrait. It dates from
about 1910 or so. It is not by a distinguished painter, it is rather dark
and a bit scratched, and it is very large, which is why it is by the stairs.
Its subject is Sir James Turing, the ninth baronet. He is holding a
shotgun and on the table beside him is a dead pheasant. This is the sort
of thing you might expect in a portrait of the only man who could
put Alan's formidable Aunt Jean in her place; and if Aunt Jean was

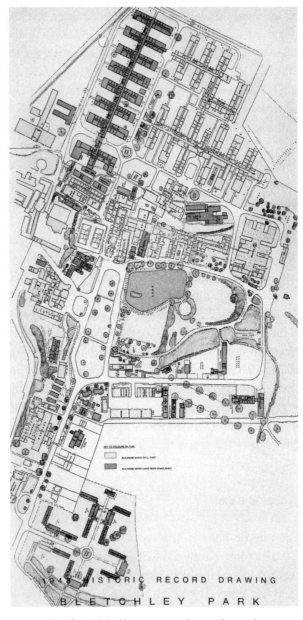

By 1943 Bletchley Park had become an intelligence factory, the workplace for thousands of people. Alan Turing needed a new role. (© Crown Copyright and by kind permission of the Director, GCHQ)

the only woman who could scare Alan's mother you are beginning
to get the picture. We call the picture in question 'The Gamekeeper'.
I am fortunate in being born much too late to experience what
Sir James would have thought of such mockery. In their childhood,
John and Alan Turing were cleaned up and dressed up and made
visits to Sir James in Chichester (and were allowed on outings in
Sir James's red car, complete with its twirly horn and acetylene lamps).
John remembered talking to Sir James about some of the family
portraits, and Alan would have recognised The Gamekeeper. Family
holidays in Scotland and Ireland with Julius and Ethel Turing were
fishing holidays; there are fuzzy photos of John and Alan with freshly
slaughtered trout. The importance of gamekeeping to keep the stocks
secure was well understood by all concerned.

In 1943 it was time for Alan Turing to become the gamekeeper.
Gamekeeping began with the Typex machine. The Germans had not
been alone in developing machines to encrypt and decrypt messages.
With varying degrees of security, machines similar to Enigma, with
rotating coding wheels in an electro-mechanical typewriter-like
box, had been developed at around the same time in a number of
countries. Britain was one, and Britain had poached. In 1934 the
RAF had decided to produce an encryption machine which could
print its output. They selected 'an improved "Enigma" type through
the agency of so-called "Type-X" attachments',[11] and their Typex
machines were in operation by 1936. Typex was very similar indeed in
its concept to Enigma. To be honest, it was almost certainly a rip-off of
German intellectual property. But such niceties as royalty payments to
a potential enemy, in relation to a product that was highly secret, were
not going to trouble the British.

By 1943 the demand for Typex machines had soared: all the
forces in all theatres wanted them, and so did government agencies.
Operational communications with the Americans and Canadians in
the Atlantic were going to be made more secure by using a modified
form of Typex. However, a 'most secret' report written in the autumn
of 1943 mentioned that out of 6,000 staff then working at Bletchley
Park, the resources devoted to the security of Allied communications

were 'the part-time services of only one man plus two or three girls'.[12] Of the armed services, only the Admiralty had scrutinised its own security, and nobody had yet investigated whether, with the improved understanding of cryptanalysis that had been developed in the last ten years, Typex itself was safe. If the British could break open Enigma, Typex itself might equally be vulnerable to attack. Sure, there were technical developments afoot to improve its security: a plugboard (like the one on Enigma), and a pluggable reflector wheel (here anticipating the Germans, who introduced these for Enigma nearer the end of the war). With more services using the machines, the need for confidence in their security was rising too. Back at Bletchley Park, in his new role, Alan was asked to investigate. The Air Ministry wanted to run longer messages through the machine before changing the coding wheels. What was the maximum message length compatible with security? Alan worked out the maximum-length formula, tested it against his experience of codebreaking techniques, and concluded it was all right to double the message length – provided that the pluggable reflector wheel was used.[13]

The problem of encryption which Pat Bayly was working on in America was thus, in all senses, the key. Pat Bayly had also been over to Britain. He was shown round Bletchley Park by Gordon Welchman and then returned the favour when Welchman visited New York. This was the lead-up to a new project for Welchman, Turing and a group of other senior men from Bletchley: 'the design of new Cypher Machines intended to embody all the lessons learnt during this war'.

D.D. (S) Serial Order No. 117
Machine Co-ordination and Development Section
     I am setting up a new Section under Mr. Welchman to deal with all matters arising from the development of new machinery as an aid to Cryptography. [...] He will call together a Committee, which should meet at least once a month, and of which I wish the following to be members :–
     Mr. Welchman (Chairman)
     Professor Vincent

Messrs. Newman, Turing, Freeborn, Wynne Williams [*sic*] and Major Morgan.

Mr. Welchman will at the same time take over all questions regarding the supply etc. of cyphering and deciphering machines. He will delegate the work of Type X machine supply to Major Carr, who is now responsible for this, only himself co-ordinating this matter with the whole subject of cypher machine supply and selection. [...]

E. W. Travis

10th September, 1943[14]

Deceiver of men

In his new job as guardian of secrets, and designer of machines, Alan gravitated towards another secret government establishment, located less than five miles from Bletchley, and hiding under another innocuous cover name. This was the 'Radio Security Service' at Hanslope Park. Here Alan was going to try to design a secure encrypted telephone which weighed less than 50 tons.

Alan started work on his speech system in May 1943. Speech encipherment was not simply for the likes of Churchill and Roosevelt, for whose conferences 50-ton monsters might be acceptable. Alan's new machine was to be used on the go, for 'tank-to-tank and plane-to-plane work'. As well as portability it would have three units: an audio sampler, a key unit to produce the cipher (which, by flipping a switch, could also serve to decipher), and a combiner to add the key to the signal. Alan, being Alan, rolled up his sleeves and got stuck straight in with a soldering iron.

Donald Bayley, newly commissioned into the Royal Electrical and Mechanical Engineers, was ordered to Hanslope Park. He was rather surprised at his first encounter with Prof:[15]

He was a bit slapdash; I was very well-organised. I came into the hut, they said just see what's what to start with. This chap had his shirt hanging out. There were resistors and capacitors, as fast as he'd soldered one on another would fall off. It was a spider's nest of stuff – a complete mess. We made up a 'breadboard' sheet of plywood, you soldered between strips of metal, to make up the board. He hadn't worked on it like that at all, soldered anyhow, and hoped they'd hold together. He was annoyed I mentioned his shirt hanging out. He took it for granted. He said I shouldn't have mentioned it.

The importance of being able to make it yourself had been imbued from Hazelhurst days. Alan's brother John kept a carpentry shop in a garage or a garden shed until the end of his life, constantly making cupboards and bookshelves for leisure; from time to time he even indulged in bricklaying, and built a playhouse for his daughters in Guildford. As for Alan:

He was intrigued by devices of every kind whether they were abstract devices or concrete, and his friends felt it would be better if he kept to the abstract devices but that didn't deter him. He wasn't at all gifted at the concrete embodiment of theoretical ideas but he loved to do it.[16]

Hanslope Park at around the time of World War Two. (Courtesy of Hanslope & District Historical Society)

168

Robin Gandy (centre), in his King's College matriculation photograph from 1938. (By kind permission of the Provost and Scholars of King's College, Cambridge)

Hanslope Park, unlike Bletchley, was run as a military establishment, so his shabby clothes must have stood out markedly. To develop his project Alan really needed help. On 16 June 1943 Alan reported on his resourcing needs for the development of 'Delilah'. He needed more space and a second oscilloscope; he asked that 'provision will be made to enable Lt. Bayley to be assigned to me officially'.[17] Alan's other assistant, also commissioned, was a young mathematician whose degree at King's College, Cambridge, had been interrupted by the war. This was Robin Gandy, who was to become Alan's closest friend.

> When I arrived he had already started building this speech encoder and he liked doing things himself – very much – he regarded it as very important that one ought to be able to do things oneself. He was *fairly* clumsy, and he had to me a very curious habit. It's called a breadboard – actually his was called the bird's nest, it was a great mass of wires, condensers and resistors and so on – and he was always swapping them round to try and improve something or other. And so he would take the soldering iron. He always soldered with a high-tension left arm, I can't think why. My first memory of coming into the shop is there was this rather scruffy looking civilian in an old tweed jacket bent over the bird's nest and every now and again he'd go 'OW! OW!'[18]

Sometimes Prof could take people by surprise in other ways:

> It was at Bletchley [wrote Alan's brother, John] that for some reason Alan was attached to an army unit, where he was treated with that brand of tolerant amusement which the armed forces reserve for boffins. This did not suit Alan at all so when he heard that there was to be a cross-country race he asked modestly if he could join in. The request was granted; all in the mess looked forward eagerly to the Prof trailing in well behind the rest. Of course Alan came in three minutes before anyone else.[19]

Delilah. Combining, power, and key units. The key unit is also shown with its top open to reveal the scrambler wheels at the rear and valves (one removed) at the front. (© The National Archives)

It is said that Robin Gandy named the speech device Delilah, because Delilah was a deceiver of men. With his Hazelhurst grounding in Scripture (which meant the Old Testament, so as to avoid troublesome theology), Alan probably knew the story of Samson and Delilah better than Robin, but he didn't complain that Delilah was a spy working for the other side. In any case, like Delilah, the machine 'pressed him daily with her words, and urged him, so that his soul was vexed unto death',[20] and that probably summed it up for all of them. So Delilah she became.

Delilah's biggest problem was her ability to deceive, or to put it technically, her key unit.

> The system requires a random voltage ($k(t)$) to be produced simultaneously at each end of the transmission path. This problem presents formidable difficulties. Of the possible solutions, the two that received most serious consideration are (a) recording random noise on discs or tape and using those recordings simultaneously at the ends of the transmission path [this is what the Americans had done with X-61753] and (b) generating identical voltages at each end. The first has the advantage that the keys are truly random and identical but has the disadvantage that the mechanical difficulties of starting and maintaining the keys in synchronism are large and, furthermore, the number of discs or reels of tape required becomes prohibitive. The second scheme is the one that has been tried in practice.[21]

The key unit randomised the signal by taking six lumps of noise through networks which generated 26 voltage outputs. Twenty-six is a rather handy number if you want to add further disguise by using coding wheels from a cipher machine – and any cipher machine will do. So the key unit could plug into ciphering wheels, then there were further recombinations, a plugboard, and a modulator to normalise the output signal to sound more like white noise. It was very complicated, but it was very compact and it would be possible to use Delilah with components from any text-encipherment machine.

On her own, however, Delilah was not going to be a sufficiently fruitful source of puzzles to keep Alan Turing occupied for long. Of World War Two's least-known establishments, Hanslope Park has managed to keep its secrets safe far better than its cousin at Bletchley. The Radio Security Service had numerous roles: tracking of illicit radio transmissions, issuing 'black propaganda' targeted at Germany, creating James Bond-style devices for operatives working behind enemy lines and, occasionally, thinking about radio security. The last of these was a broad brief, and Alan's new role as gamekeeper seems to have allowed him to dabble in direction finding, circuit design, randomisation of cipher keys and the production of Rockex machines to encipher teleprinter messages in accordance with Pat Bayly's design, approved by Alan during his American trip.

Gordon Welchman was assigned to work together with Alan specifically on the development of cipher machinery to handle teletype traffic; so, after the autumn of 1943, Welchman too was spending time at Hanslope Park. Balancing the demands of Bletchley and Hanslope might have implied that Alan should remain in his lodgings at the Crown Inn, Shenley Brook End, but the congeniality of working at Hanslope won out. On D-Day, Alan Turing submitted a progress report on Delilah, in which he concluded that the key settings should be changed after every eight minutes of chat; shortly afterwards, Alan moved into Hanslope Park itself, first living in the old house and then later in a cottage which he shared with Robin Gandy. Discretion was needed, possibly even concealment; both Robin and Alan knew personally why it was necessary to be a deceiver of men.

As an epilogue to the story of Delilah, there was some idea that the Post Office had itself invented a speech scrambler. In January 1945 Prof was asked to investigate, although the Post Office were told they could not ask him about the Americans' speech secrecy machine. So Prof went to Dollis Hill again. His report was not encouraging: 'with the ciphering problem they have made practically no progress.' The problem was, none of the British experts who could help, could actually help, as they were all off-side, what with the promises made to the Americans that knowledge of the X–61753's secrets would not be exploited in Britain. Alan took the opportunity of letting the right hand of British bureaucracy (the Cypher Policy Board) know what the left hand was already doing: building a secure speech device at Hanslope Park. Despite this, the Cypher Policy Board was still arguing about developing speech devices several years later.[22] Delilah was destined to remain buried between the pages of the Old Testament.

Even with Delilah out of the picture, or, rather, in the hands of competent engineers like Donald Bayley, there was still work for the gamekeeper. At Bletchley Park Alan was still an important figure. Periodically his expertise on the security of ciphers was called upon – notably when the scare about the British cipher machine Typex arose. Questions about machines, and questions about teleprinter ciphers, were occupying many minds at Bletchley. Since the middle of 1942, the codebreakers had themselves been working on German teleprinter traffic, and now they were using machines to process Fish.

The processing of Fish

Early in 1940 some British policemen listening for German spies had intercepted a rather strange type of transmission emanating from across the Channel. Like Enigma messages, they were enciphered, and so they found their way to Bletchley. Like Enigma, a machine was converting plain-text into cipher-text. That is about where the similarities with Enigma stopped. The messages were sent not in Morse but in the Baudot-Murray teleprinter code – the very code which Pat Bayly's machine was to keep secure. Bletchley Park called this type of traffic 'Fish'. From small beginnings, Fish was going to have a profound impact on the shape of codebreaking at Bletchley Park, the strategic intelligence available to Allied Supreme Command, and the post-war career of Alan Turing.

The British had never seen the machine which was involved in creating Fish and had no idea how it worked. Everything to uncover the secrets of Fish would have to be done from first principles, and by hand. Fortunately for Britain, the Germans made mistakes, and the classic one of retransmitting a garbled message in the same key in mid-1941 gave Bletchley Park their first break. By mind-boggling feats of analysis, John Tiltman and another Bletchley code-master called Bill Tutte reverse-engineered the structure of the German teleprinter cipher machine. The Germans called it the *Schlüsselzusatz*, or cipher attachment, made by the Lorenz company in Berlin. The Lorenz machine worked – like Pat Bayly's machine by overlaying a 'key' of random letters which had to be reversed out to reveal the original. Unlike Bayly's machine, the Lorenz key was supplied by ten wheels, each of which had a different number of pins which could be set to 'on' or 'off' to make electrical pulses whenever contact was made with a pin in the 'on' position. There were two groups of wheels, which were named 'chi' and 'psi' because the Bletchley mathematicians couldn't help using Greek. Chi wheels always rotated between letters, but psi wheels were more erratic, pausing for one or more letters before moving on.

As with Enigma, knowing the machine is not the same as knowing the key. Alan was transferred from his role in Hut 8 in mid-1942 to help out with research on this new and all-but-impenetrable system. His contribution was a technique for revealing pin-patterns, which, as tradition demanded, was named 'Turingismus'. Alan Turing's method began with the idea that you could track the changes introduced by the chi wheels by adding the five-bit code for each letter in the message to the five-bit code for its neighbour. Using the mathematics of binary arithmetic, this would eliminate the effect of the psi wheels (assuming they hadn't moved), because the contribution of the psi wheels to the cipher key was being added a second time – just as it is in decrypting a message. With this insight, you could start looking for the effect of the chi wheels.

Even knowing which pins were on or off did not break the cipher for, as with wheels in Enigma machines, knowing the starting positions of each wheel, and the stepping pattern of the psi wheels, was also essential to uncovering the key. The problem was far, far worse than Enigma: to Enigma's 1.6×10^{20} set-up permutations, the

Lorenz had 1.0×10^{170} – the age of the Universe is supposedly only 4.4×10^{18} seconds. But the chi wheels repeated their influence on the cipher regularly, and this feature, together with another of Alan's ideas – the probabilistic analysis of coincidences, exploited previously in Banburismus – would enable Bill Tutte to design a method for finding the key. Alan's report of December 1942 from Dayton, Ohio, ends up with a paragraph headed 'Tunny'. (In the 1940s 'tunny' was the name British people gave to tuna, when it could still be caught using a rod and line in the North Sea. Tunny was also the codename for one species of Fish.) One message had been 'sent over here' and 'could have been broken by Tutte's original method'. The subtext of Alan's report is that no progress on this cipher had been made by OP-20-G in the US. The British had exclusivity on Fish, but breaking Fish by Tutte's, or indeed any other, method was tough. It was time to put a new man onto the problem.

Newman at Bletchley

M.H.A. Newman had had a difficult time since his sabbatical in Princeton during 1937–38. At Princeton he believed he had found a proof of a mathematical problem known as the Poincaré Conjecture, and presented his proof to the intellectual elite of Princeton shortly before his return. Alas for him, there was a flaw in the proof, and he suffered sleepless nights for his error. The new war with Germany didn't bring peace of mind. Newman's father, Herman Neumann, was a Jewish émigré to Britain from Bydgoszcz, which at the time of Neumann senior's birth was part of the German Empire. Neumann senior had been interned in 1914; on his release, he had gone back to Germany, leaving the young Max and his mother in England to fend for themselves (and change their name to Newman). World War Two was an attempt by history to repeat itself, but it was tying itself in knots in the process. In 1940 the invasion of England by Germany was imminent, and the threat of internment, and much worse, was apparent to anyone of Jewish ancestry. Max Newman sent his wife and two small children to America for its greater safety; his efforts were then directed towards finding work for himself there so he could join and continue to support them. Given the background, it's no surprise that Newman had ended up with 'no' against his name on the emergency professors' list of 1938. In 1942 he came under renewed pressure to change his mind. The Room 40 old boys were brought back into action:[23]

Dear Newman,

There is some work going on at a government institution which would I think interest you and which is certainly important for the War. If you are disposed towards it, would you let me know and a meeting will be arranged to talk it over with someone without either party being committed to anything in advance …

Yours sincerely

F.E. Adcock

Room 47, Foreign Office, London, S.W. 1.

1st June, 1942.

Dear Sir,

Professor Adcock has handed me your letter of May 26th. We are hoping that one of our Principals will be in Cambridge one day during the week of June 8th. He is away for a few days, but when he returns I will ask him to make some definite appointment with you.

The post would certainly be a very important one from the point of view of the War.

I am not certain at the moment what attitude would be taken by the authorities concerned, about your father's nationality, but that can however be investigated if your conversation with our Principal is mutually satisfactory.

Yours faithfully,

Nigel de Grey

By mid-August it was settled. The billeting officer wrote to Newman to say he 'had in mind a very nice billet in a modern house with constant hot water, only a few minutes walk from here'. Within a few weeks, shortly before Alan Turing left for America, Newman was installed as part of the team working on Fish.

To begin with, Newman was a fish out of water, whether hot or cold, constant or otherwise. According to his son William:[24]

> Max was initially assigned to the Research Section, joining Tutte and others working on Tunny. Part of his work involved decrypting messages by the existing slow hand methods, which were somewhat akin to solving crossword puzzles. Max found the company congenial, but the work frustrated him at times and left him feeling ineffectual. He even thought of returning to Cambridge. It was around this time, however, that Max made his first breakthrough – the idea of mechanising Tutte's method using high-speed electronic counters. He took his proposal to the Bletchley Park management. The whole scheme must have seemed hopelessly overambitious at the time, but Max won his superiors round, and in December 1942 was put in charge of developing an experimental machine.

The message would be punched as holes in teleprinter tapes, and the machine would use photoelectric cells to count pulses as the holes whizzed by. The experimental machine to tackle Tunny was called the 'Heath Robinson' – named for the cartoonist whose absurd jerry-built fantasy machines illustrate the Professor Branestawm books – but it ripped up the paper tape and had all sorts of other operating problems. However, Alan's role, alongside M.H.A. Newman, on Welchman's Machine Committee brought him close to this project, and thus enabled Alan to bring into being one of the most important partnerships of the Tunny war, that between Newman and Tommy Flowers. And so it was at Bletchley Park that electronic computing machinery was first developed in Britain.

Schoolboys and their crazes

When Tommy Flowers saw the Heath Robinson he knew immediately that the engineering solution was wrong. What was being done unreliably with simultaneous reading of two punched tapes could be done much more safely with a single tape; the content of the other tape could be stored electronically, using vacuum tubes, then called valves. His machine design was called the Colossus. The data feed from the second 'tape' was programmed into the machine using a panel of switches. The prototype Colossus was working in December 1943 and subsequent Colossi broke messages in time to give confidence to the Allies about their deception plans relating to the Normandy landings the following year. However, this was routine – Colossus could do a whole lot more, according to Flowers:[25]

> It just changed the whole picture. We were able to start off on a new line altogether; we could do so many things and of course much of what we were doing was just intuition, and it can be seen now to have anticipated what was done later on – it was just intuition – such as when they wanted to change the logic and we provided – they wanted programmable logic – and we provided them with a big panel with a lot of keys on it and by throwing the keys they could – the mathematicians – could program the machine – the keys did the 'and' and 'or' functions – and we didn't do any multiplying; we didn't need a multiply but we added 'and' and 'or' functions and put them in series and parallel and so forth, and they were quite happy. In fact they were like a lot of schoolboys with a new toy when we first gave it to them; they thought it so wonderful they were playing with it for ages just to see what you could do with it.

The codebreakers were trying to get Colossus to do long multiplication, just for the hell of it. Flowers went on to say of this work, 'it led us to the computer field for Turing'. The Normandy landings symbolised a reversal of fortune, and it became legitimate to imagine a world after the war. One of Flowers's tasks was to consider the applications of electronics in peacetime; computing machinery was one of these, and Flowers and Turing began to think about the design of a multi-purpose computing machine at about this time.

Rather closer to Hanslope than Bletchley was the pub at Wolverton, where, on a Friday evening in the latter part of the war, you might have found Alan Turing playing chess with Donald Michie.[26]

> He was keen on playing chess, which he wasn't very good at and, because of the way that Bletchley Park had been recruited, other people there either didn't play chess at all or they tended to be chess masters so that he couldn't find anybody to give him an even game and I was, as it happens, the only person around in the immediate environment who was bad enough.

Playing chess was only part of it. They were also talking about algorithms for machines to play chess.

> People of his own age tended to regard this as all a bit unfortunate that such an outstanding intellect and mathematical logician should allow himself to be led astray by childish and science fiction-type speculations about mechanised thought, but for young people like myself, and I.J. Good, Peter Hilton and many others, we were very turned on indeed and quite inspired by these ideas. I recall that he was quite narrowly concentrated on computer game playing as being a suitable arena in which to test these ideas. It was quite often that some of us went for long walks on Sundays or on leave days, days off, and talked about game playing and I think that nearly all the ideas that one finds in Shannon's 1950 paper in one form or another came up, mainly between Turing and Good I would say.

As the war came to a close, Alan went with Donald Michie to try to locate his buried ingots – as we know, without success. However, his war service was recognised with the award (in 1946) of the OBE (Officer of the Order of the British Empire). Gordon Welchman also received the OBE, and it was offered to M.H.A. Newman as well, but he turned it down. According to his son William, Newman had been incensed by the faint praise implied by such a lowly honour in the case of Alan Turing. 'I was offered something as a matter of fact but I said I didn't wish to have it. Turing got the OBE, which I thought really a "wonderful" thing to offer a man for what he did. I mean, Good Heavens, he changed the course of the war and I thought all these decorations were so ludicrous that I felt justified in declining the one they offered me. I think to offer a man like Turing the OBE, which he accepted rather as a joke I must say, was fantastic.'[27] Gordon Welchman had been promised some sort of recognition by both Denniston and Travis, and had even heard a rumour that he had been recommended for a knighthood. Bureaucracy soon put paid to that. Officials' awards depend on their grade, and an OBE was as good as it was going to get. There was, additionally, the problem of recognising achievements in clandestine service. The vow of secrecy was permanent, and unwanted attention would follow if a higher award had been made. Sara Turing was extremely proud of Alan's gong (though he, characteristically, kept it in his toolbox); with Mother making an embarrassing fuss, Alan probably saw the advantages of discretion more readily than Gordon Welchman.

Frankenstein's castle

Victory in Europe was declared on 8 May 1945. Tommy Flowers had been waiting to go to America to see for himself the progress being made on computing machinery there, but there were procrastinations and excuses. Eventually his telegram arrived: he was expected there on 15 July. But then an intervention, from America, upset his plans again. General George C. Marshall never issued orders directly to Tommy Flowers, or even Alan Turing, but once again he was going to direct the secret war in Alan's direction. On 7 August 1944 he had written to the Supreme Commander:[28]

Dear Eisenhower:

Following up my radio to you of August 7th concerning the organization of an American team to participate with the British Government Code and Cipher School in an investigation of German Signal Intelligence activities, I am enclosing a list of subjects for inquiry. The attached tab sets forth in itemized form the matters which we believe should receive primary attention. [...]

Faithfully yours,

G. Marshall

SCHEDULE OF SUBJECTS FOR INVESTIGATION

1. Complete cryptographic and cryptanalytic data on file at German centers, as well as equipment and operating instructions pertaining to the same. [...]

6. Speech secrecy equipment, cryptographic facsimile encipherment, and all non-Morse cryptographic equipment as used both on wire lines and on radio circuits.

The investigation of German signals intelligence had begun as soon as the Western Allies crossed the Rhine. Marshall's program was called TICOM, standing for the Target Intelligence Committee. Shortly after the German surrender, Tommy Flowers and Alan Turing were sent overseas as part of the TICOM effort, thereby putting paid to Flowers's computing-machinery trip. The departure was to take place on 15 July, and instead of America they were going to the devastated heartland of Germany – to find out what secrets the Germans had.

CONTROL COMMISSION (GERMANY), BRITISH ELEMENT
FIELD INFORMATION AGENCY, TECHNICAL, (FIAT)
REAR HEADQUARTERS
c/o U.K. BASE, A.P.O. 413

14 July 1945.

SUBJECT: TRAVEL AUTHORITY NO. FIAT 30.

TO: All concerned.

1. The following personnel are authorised to travel by military aircraft on or about 16 July 1945 to PARIS, France, to carry out the instructions of:–

    CG, U.S. Group, Control Council, and

    Head, Control Commission, Germany, (BE)

and upon completion thereof to return to present station:– […]

    Mr. T.H. FLOWERS BRAE/122/1 Br Post Office […]

    Mr. A.M. TURING DWQD/2304 Br Foreign Office […]

        s/t/ D. J. NIELSON, Major, G.S.

This is a certified true copy:

EDWARD I. FRANKENSTEIN,

Captain, Signal Corps.[29]

Tommy Flowers described the journey:[30]

It was an Anglo-American party and because we were going to Patton's area it was American led; we came under the American Army. They provided the transport and everything else. We were supposed to meet up in Paris which we did after some delays, and then go to Frankfurt by road, which we did, and then get some sort of clearance or other from Frankfurt, which we did after a great deal of trouble. I just enjoyed the trip. Then we blasted our way. We started out from Frankfurt about five o'clock in the afternoon to do a hundred and eighty miles before dark, which our driver did his best by putting his foot down and going hell for leather, and there were still bomb holes in the road which had only just been filled in, so it was a nightmare journey, but we just made it.

Their destination was the *Laboratorium Feuerstein*, which became the subject of several reports by US Army officers. Here, at Ebermannstadt near Nuremberg, was a special engineering facility – 'a huge outfit unbelievably well equipped' – under the direction of Dr Oskar Vierling. On the one hand, Dr Vierling had joined the Nazi Party 'for

reasons of expediency, but seems to have been conspicuous by his fail-
ure to attend meetings and take any part in party activities'. However,
'Professor Vierling will be arrested by the military government section as soon as they can bring it about. He is charged with being a
member of the SS and with having had Gestapo railroad a few workers.' Moreover, 'an investigation of the personnel of the Laboratorium
Feuerstein disclosed that eight of the supposed mechanics working in
the laboratory were SS troops in civilian disguise'.[31] Protected by the
US Army, Alan Turing and Tommy Flowers were unlikely to find themselves railroaded, whatever unpleasantness that might involve. They
had come to see the secret lab, and it was evident that the Germans
had been catching up fast on the Allies. Alan Turing produced a brief
report for his American superiors, with a typical seasoning of super-
iority and mischief:[32]

Impressions of Feuerstein

The Feuerstein Laboratory is in a magnificently romantic setting,
on the top of a small Bavarian mountain far from any other buildings,
and in the appropriate style of architecture for filming 'Frankenstein'.
Any visitor to the laboratory who was properly conditioned by tales of
scientific marvels produced there might well expect to see an electronic
man peering at him out of the windows as he drove up.

After this romantic beginning the projects actually being carried out
in the lab. appear very disappointing. There is nothing being done there
which is really original although some projects might be described as
new to us. The techniques involved were (as a whole) not merely not
new but slightly outmoded.

On the speech secrecy side, in which I was chiefly interested, there
was nothing giving high security. The Baustein scrambler gives the
same sort of security as the P.O. Inverter, i.e. it is only secure against the
casual listener. The 'triple wobbling' system is somewhat analogous to
the public transatlantic telephone, both as regards the security achieved
and the nature of scramble produced. [...]

Vierling himself was working, or proposed to work, on yet another
speech project. This he described as a 'speech writer', and it was

Burg Feuerstein: the fantasy castle where Dr Vierling was developing secure communications technology.

intended to write down the words spoken into it in an appropriate phonetic notation. Such a development would be valuable as a basis for a secure speech scrambler. We had the impression at first that this was to be based on some new knowledge about the nature of speech discovered by Vierling. We questioned him on this, but were unable to discover any original work on speech that he had done, unless one believed his claim to have really written a paper published under the name of his professor in Hanover (Wagner). […]

Prof's report was, however, not destined for inclusion in the official TICOM records. William F. Friedman, the Americans' chief cryptanalyst (who had vetted Alan for his Bell Labs visit in 1943), decided against, and it languished in the file relating to Vierling's lab. Friedman hadn't suppressed it. He had visited the Vierling lab ('an important TICOM target'), arriving at the same time as Alan Turing. All the details were in the official military reports, and Alan's paper did not add anything new. After his trip to Germany, Friedman went to Bletchley Park for a debriefing. It was the end of an era.

My second visit to GC & CS can hardly be said to have been as interesting as my first: V-E Day and the imminence of V-J Day had diminished activities and operations to but a mere shadow of their former stature. An air of the graveyard and tomb hung over each of the 'huts' and buildings. Gone was the bustle, hurry, sense of urgency, and hum of wheels turning; every day fewer faces were seen. However, I found the visit interesting nevertheless and was glad of an opportunity to renew acquaintance with many old friends, all of whom endeavored to impress me with their earnest desire to continue our collaboration during the peace and to cement further the cordial relations that existed at the end of the war.[33]

It is tempting to speculate as to what Alan Turing and Tommy Flowers discussed as they jostled over the bomb craters on their way to Ebermannstadt. Another project at Feuerstein, according to the American report on the investigation, was the development of a 'Calculating Machine which would instantaneously solve equations to the power of N^6. [...] The machine was to be used for solving equations for the design of wings of high speed planes and in the design of projectiles, which formerly took 14 days to solve.' Shortly before they left for Germany, Alan had been shown a significant paper written by his old Princeton professor, John von Neumann. This report contained the outline for a design of a stored-program computing machine. The plan, when they got back to Britain, was for Turing and Flowers to turn von Neumann's paper into a reality. Together, they were going to build the first full-function British electronic computer, and it was going to be far more versatile than something which could solve equations to the power of N^6 in less than 14 days.

8

LOUSY COMPUTER

In June 1945 Alan Turing had had a most interesting conversation with a man called J.R. Womersley, who had with him a rare copy of a new paper bearing the name of John von Neumann. This document had the uninspiring and obscure name *First Draft of a Report on the EDVAC*, but its contents were electrifying.

At the Moore School, Philadelphia, not more than an hour's drive from Alan's alma mater at Princeton, they had started work in 1943 on a machine called ENIAC – the Electronic Numerical Integrator and Computer – to number-crunch the most secret equations of the war. The equations had been written by John von Neumann to model shock waves to help the men designing the atomic bomb. Like a Bombe, the ENIAC had to be programmed by being plugged up with cables and switches, but unlike the Bombe it was a multi-purpose machine. It was electronic rather than electro-mechanical, and it was capable of tackling any problem. ENIAC was not completed until 1945, and when ready it filled the best part of a house. It was described in 1946 by Brigadier General Ford of the US Army as a 'crude prototype' which would not fulfil the requirements of the future.[1] Yet ENIAC had been a vitally important project, perhaps as important as Colossus, in pointing the way for electronic computation. Like Colossus, what ENIAC did was count, and counting is at the

John von Neumann, whose path crossed with Alan Turing's at many stages, standing in front of the IAS computer in 1952. Von Neumann's seminal paper on the logical structure of computers was essential to Alan's own design of the ACE. (© Alan Richards photographer, from the Shelby White and Leon Levy Archives Center, Institute for Advanced Study, Princeton)

root of all arithmetical computation. Because it was electronic, and superfast, ENIAC used counting – lots and lots of it – to do what pre-war task-specific analogue machines had done, and better, and with more versatility. The *First Draft of a Report on the EDVAC* was von Neumann's appraisal, based on discussions with the ENIAC team, of how a proper universal computing machine should be designed. And designing and building a proper computing machine was exactly what Alan Turing was planning to do with Tommy Flowers.

The EDVAC was the Electronic Discrete Variable Automatic Computer. It didn't exist, yet, but it was going to make ENIAC obsolete when it did. The EDVAC wasn't just another horrible acronym; unlike other calculating machines, it was going to use the concepts set out by Alan Turing in his paper, our old friend *Computable Numbers*.

The machine which Alan sketched out in *Computable Numbers* was more than a programmable machine capable of many different mathematical tasks – it also used the concept, anticipated by Kurt Gödel, that the instructions given to the machine were themselves a species of data. So the program didn't need to be wired or plugged or switched at the back of the machine, while the data were fed in somewhere else: everything was data, so everything could be fed in. *Computable Numbers* allowed for universal computing machines with stored programs. The very idea was revolutionary. For a generation of people brought up with very expensive, temperamental, inaccurate single-purpose analogue machines, the notion that you could build a single machine of fixed structure which would do any task, and do it reliably, was the realm of science fiction, and self-evidently it couldn't be done. John von Neumann's report set out to prove the naysayers wrong. He described the architecture for a machine which, unlike ENIAC or Colossus or the Bombe or any pre-war calculating machine, had a stored program.

ACE

The official origins of early British computing are in the minutes of the Executive Committee of the National Physical Laboratory (NPL).[2] On 21 March 1944, the Committee met at the rooms of the Royal Society, and reported that 'there was a general consensus of opinion that a Mathematical Department should be set up and that it would, in effect consist of two parts (a) to deal with mathematics of a computational type, and (b) statistical work'. J.R. Womersley knew about computing machinery – he had written a paper on mechanical methods for solving partial differential equations with Professor Douglas Hartree before the war. In those days, computing machinery was specifically engineered to the problem in hand, and 'differential analysers' were built by various people, including Hartree, who used Meccano to make one in Manchester. Womersley, who had read Alan Turing's paper on *Computable Numbers*, was chosen in September 1944 to head the Mathematics Division of the NPL and to develop its computing laboratory. In February 1945 Womersley went to the USA. He saw IBM's relay-based computing machinery at Harvard and he saw the ENIAC. Womersley wrote home that he had seen 'Turing in hardware'. On his return, by his account:

> 1945 June   J.R.W. meets Professor M.H.A. Newman. Tells Newman he wishes to meet Turing. Meets Turing same day and invites him home. J.R.W. shows Turing the first report on the EDVAC and persuades him to join N.P.L. staff, arranges interview and convinces Director and Secretary.

Alan Turing was appointed in September 1945 and immediately began work on his own report, for a design of Britain's answer to the EDVAC. Given that neither country had yet built an all-purpose stored-program computer at this stage, the only thing the British could improve on immediately was the choice of acronym. The British machine was going to be called ACE, or the Automatic Computing Engine, so named by Womersley in a conscious allusion to Charles Babbage's Difference Engine (a reconstruction of which can be seen at the Science Museum) and conceptual all-purpose Analytical Engine.

Alan Turing joined the NPL on 1 October 1945 and spent the next two months designing a programmable electronic computer. The report was delivered to Womersley, who convinced the Director of the laboratory that the project was feasible. (It may be significant that his memo, under cover of which Alan's report was sent, also enclosed a supplementary paper, which was 'an attempt to state a practical case for the equipment. In view of the unique nature of the equipment this is difficult, but I believe that in this direction the promised support of Commander Sir Edward Travis, of the Foreign Office, will be invaluable.' Womersley knew nothing of the goings-on at Bletchley Park, and it's unlikely that he knew anything about Travis first hand. Alan was pulling a string to ensure his machine would not be ruled out as having no practical uses.) In March 1946 it was Alan's turn to explain it; the proposal was now before the Executive Committee of the laboratory.

The full-sized ACE, under construction at last; but it didn't become operational until 1958. (Science & Society Picture Library)

Dr. Turing explained that if a high overall computing speed was to be obtained it was necessary to do all operations automatically. It was not sufficient to do the arithmetical operations at electronic speeds: provision must also be made for the transfer of data (numbers, etc.) from place to place. This led to two further requirements – 'storage' or 'memory' for the numbers not immediately in use, and means for instructing the machine to do the right operations in the right order.

Delays in the machine

Memory, and programming. Neither of these problems had been satisfactorily attempted before. Flowers's Colossus did use valves for memory, but, as the Executive Committee heard:

> Dr. Turing said that a storage system must be both economical and accessible. Teleprinter tape provided an example of a highly economical but inaccessible system. It was possible to store about ten million binary digits at a cost of £1, but one might spend minutes in unrolling tape to find a single figure. Trigger circuits incorporating radio values on the other hand provided an example of a highly accessible but highly uneconomical form of storage; the value of any desired figure could be obtained within a microsecond or less, but only one or two digits could be stored for £1. A compromise was required; one suitable system was the 'acoustic delay line' which provided storage for 1000 binary digits at a cost of a few pounds, and any required information could be made available within a millisecond.

So the delay line was chosen. To store data, acoustic pings would be sounded at one end of a long tube of mercury; the sound wave would travel slowly (actually very fast, but at geological pace relative to the electronics of the operating parts of the computer) to the other end, where a sensor would pick it up, amplify it, and send it by wire back to the beginning of the tube. The delay line was both a blessing and a curse. Sure, it solved the cost–benefit equation neatly. But it hugely complicated the task of programming, Alan Turing's other main requirement. He didn't attempt to explain programming to the Executive Committee of the NPL. They were still wondering what the uses of this machine would be, but they approved the project.

Now it was the turn of Sir Charles Darwin (the grandson of the more famous Charles Darwin, but a serious scientist in his own right) as Director of the NPL, and he had to explain it to his parent government department:[3]

> An example of the sort of problem that could be solved is the calculation of ballistic trajectories. It is estimated that a full trajectory from muzzle to strike, worked out by small arcs, should be solved in half a minute. Or again a large number of simultaneous equations, as in a geodetic survey, could be solved in a few minutes: or the distribution of electric field round a charged conductor of specified shape. [...]
>
> In view of its rapidity of action, and of the ease with which it can be switched over from one type of problem to another it is very possible that the one machine would suffice to solve all the problems that are demanded of it from the whole country.

Alan Turing's paper had already described some problems which the ACE could solve. Prudently, he started with range tables, as noted by Sir Charles, but ACE would also be able to solve simultaneous equations, multiply matrices ('this has important applications in the design of optical instruments'), 'count the number of butchers due to be demobilised in June 1946', solve simple jigsaw puzzles, and most

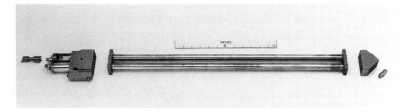

Delay line. Memory in the earliest computers – including Alan Turing's ACE design – relied on the slow speed at which a sound wave travels along a tube of mercury. (© Science & Society Picture Library)

ambitiously 'given a position in chess the machine could be made to list all the "winning combinations" to a depth of about three moves on either side'. ACE would be something more than a fast calculator for arithmetic. Alan's report was not in any sense a copy-out of von Neumann's EDVAC report.

- Alan's paper on the Electronic Calculator was not supposed to be a theoretical analysis. Von Neumann outlined general logical principles for the design of any multi-purpose computing machine; Alan's paper takes it to the next stage, describing the actual components and their engineering requirements and has a practical focus all the way through. There are sections on memory, arithmetical functions, circuitry, logical control, interfaces and programming. If you want more background, he says, 'it is recommended that it be read in conjunction with J. von Neumann's "Report on the EDVAC"'.
- Von Neumann's *First Draft* did not contain much on the subject of programming. Alan's paper has a long section on this topic which includes sample programs.
- The logical design advocated by Alan was tailored to fit the constraints imposed by the technology. This meant for complexity in programming. 'The logical complexity of the ACE is not surprising since Turing had a preference for this type of activity to engineering,' explained Herman H. Goldstine, von Neumann's right-hand man on his own computer project.

John von Neumann's *First Draft* was based around the need for a better, faster calculating machine, for doing numerical computation. He was hardly alone in this: both the Mathematics Division at NPL and the Mathematical Laboratory being started up at Cambridge expected computing machinery to replace the differential analysers and other analogue machines which had been devised exclusively for solving numerical problems. Turing's vision was more ambitious. He saw the ACE as a machine for doing anything at all – anything capable of being rendered into logical notation, digitised and subjected to numerical processing. You could do that for speech, so you could probably do it for anything at all.

Alas, all this was just so much fantasy. Now the war was over it was impossible to get anything built. Tommy Flowers had agreed to build the ACE at Dollis Hill, where he had created Colossus, and this was confirmed by his boss. Two Colossus engineers worked on ACE for a few months but the rules of procurement had changed. The British telephone system needed to be upgraded, and this was Flowers's day job. The resources of the Dollis Hill telephone laboratory were going to be cut off. This being the 1940s, the NPL turned to other public-sector research establishments, but without avail. 1946 was a wasted year.

Equipment versus thought

The lack of actual computing machinery didn't stop people trumpeting about their computers in the press or having conferences to discuss the new generation of machinery which hadn't yet been built. On 7 November 1946 the *Daily Telegraph* ran a story, placed by the NPL's parent department, that 'Britain is to make a radio "brain" which will be called "Ace"', and how much better the ACE was going to be than 'the American invention called Eniac'. The next month Alan gave a series of lectures on the ACE in London, and at the start of January 1947 Alan attended another computing conference, this time at Harvard in the United States. He was the only British delegate among over 300 at Harvard, but some of his old acquaintances were there: Joe Eachus, Claude Shannon, and a handful of mathematicians, as well as the expected ENIAC team. Despite – or possibly because of – his position as outsider, Alan intervened in the questioning after several presentations. All his comments were concerned, one way or another, with the problem of memory in early computers, and after a talk on transfer of data between external and internal memory he raised a familiar theme:[4]

Dr. Turing: I should like to suggest a slightly different approach to this problem which we are applying in England. We are trying to make greater use of the facilities available in the machine to do all kinds of different things simply by programming rather than by the addition of extra apparatus. Without going into the details of the machine, I am afraid I cannot really state quite what happens, but I can give a very rough outline. We have in the machine a number of flip-flop circuits which are used to store one digit at a time. The flip-flop and recording head are allowed to operate for the required period of time, 200 microseconds. During that 200 microseconds arrangements are made by the ordinary computing techniques to pick out the next pulse that one desires to record. And so it continues. This is an application of the general principle that any particular operation of physical apparatus can be reproduced within the EDVAC-type machine. Thus, we eliminate additional apparatus simply by putting in more programming.

While in America, Alan spent some time at the IAS in Princeton, talking to John von Neumann and others about the EDVAC. Alan was there 'for several weeks, during which time he argued that the mercury delay lines used as a memory could not work. His argument was based on various signal-to-noise ratio considerations and seemed most convincing. In fact, he persuaded us, but fortunately experiment and experience proved him wrong.' This is curious, given that ACE was being designed with delay-line memory, and it was also the solution chosen for other pioneering computer equipment.

In the meantime, Alan's London lectures over the winter had left some observers cold:

On a series of Thursday afternoons in Dec 1946 & January 1947, Turing delivered a course of 7 lectures on the design of the ACE at the Ministry of Supply in London. I attended the first one or two, but then decided that I could employ my time more suitably than in hearing about the details of the ACE, which I regarded as a very odd machine.[5]

The reason it was odd was the just-in-time programming designed around the delays inherent in delay-line memory. The oddity was noted by Dr M.V. Wilkes, who was setting up the Mathematical Laboratory in Cambridge, which was aiming to build a computing machine of its own. Wilkes had been invited to the Turing lecture series by Womersley, who had told Wilkes that 'we are very anxious indeed to have all the help and co-operation we can from you. Could you come next Wednesday, lunch here, and talk the matter over with Turing and myself?' This was in the spirit of the times, when the vision of the NPL Mathematics Division was to use computing machinery as a service bureau to assist the mathematicians, and the wider scientific community, with their computational problems. It was a good idea for there to be several bureaux around the country developing their own machines: several bureaux would ease capacity bottlenecks, and there would be sharing of different ideas developed in different laboratories. Wilkes sent over a four-page outline of his plan, which Alan Turing was asked by Womersley to criticise. There was just one problem. Alan Turing and Maurice Wilkes could not abide one another.

Mr Womersley

I have read Wilkes' proposals for a pilot machine, and agree with him as regards the desirability of the construction of some such machine somewhere. I also agree with him as regards the suitability of the number of delay lines he suggests. The 'code' which he suggests is however very contrary to the line of development here, and much more in the American tradition of solving one's difficulties by means of much equipment rather than by thought. I should imagine that to put his code (which is advertised as 'reduced to the simplest possible form') into effect would require a very much more complex control circuit than is proposed in our full-size machine. Furthermore certain operations which we regard as more fundamental than addition and multiplication have been omitted.

On the surface, and in public, strict British politeness was at all times maintained. However, it became notorious that they antagonised each other. Maurice Wilkes was an exact contemporary of Alan's. His name appears four below Alan's in the list of mathematics tripos finalists for 1934, as one of the mathematical superheroes now familiar to us as B-star wranglers. Wilkes's background was very different, though: Wilkes's father had been a 'clerk' (in fact chief administrator) for the Earl of Dudley, and a world away from a Raj upbringing which put the Turing parents in a position of command. Like Alan, Wilkes liked machines and tinkering with them; unlike Alan, he was good at it – he was more of a physicist than a pure mathematician, and did his thesis on radio in the ionosphere, a subject which was valuable during the war years when Wilkes worked on radar. Before the war, Wilkes had mastered the delicate machinery of differential analysers (his machine was also made of Meccano parts); in 1937 he became University Demonstrator in the Mathematical Laboratory at Cambridge. One might be snobbish about the status of Demonstrator, which is the most inferior of academic appointments, but Prof didn't have any university post at all before 1948. After the war Wilkes was back in his Cambridge lab and preparing to create a computation service for the university. To Wilkes, service was an honourable calling. For Alan, such utilitarian ambitions may have seemed very drab; but they were, in fact, just like the plans of the NPL.

I.J. Good, who visited the NPL with Alan's lifelong supporter M.H.A. Newman in 1946 to swap ideas about logical design, also despaired of the approach he was taking:[6]

His really great handicap was that he could not forbear to work everything out for himself. He really had to invent the whole of mathematics for himself, and this is very fine and impressive you see, and all this, but I mean, there simply isn't time for it, and every now and then one would come across this in this computing machine of his. It was a sort of nightmare. It worked in a sense but he didn't think of all the things that had happened, and the human frailties of the operators, and he would always cling to his thing. He invented an extraordinary series of names for the 32 operations of the alphabet and he would never vary these things and he always put these extraordinary things into all his books and papers and everything, and everybody was supposed to learn these symbols.

Lousy computer

Just-in-time programming was very abstruse, and very fiddly, and not at all suitable for someone whose written work had a habit of being sloppy and inaccurate. Alan Turing needed an assistant. Jim Wilkinson had graduated from Trinity College, Cambridge, as senior wrangler in 1939. He was therefore as good a mathematician as you could get, and he was easily recruited for the project to build an electronic computer, as he later explained to Dr Christopher Evans:[7]

> EVANS: How did you first come into contact with Turing? Was it at NPL?
> WILKINSON: Yes. I'd heard of him at Cambridge but I knew him more as an eccentric than anything else. I didn't really know very much about his work. But when Goodwin asked me if I would come to NPL I came over here, I chatted with Turing, and I soon became very enthusiastic about the project. Of course I didn't know very much about the ideas that were in the air at the time then of building digital computers, so this was my first contact. And it seemed to me just the sort of thing that I was looking for to make the numerical solution to partial differential equations a reasonably effective proposition. At that point I decided that I would come to NPL. I came here in May of 1946, and I was assigned half-time to Alan Turing to work with him. We were to work on the logical design of an electronic computer and on the development of what he referred to as 'tables of instructions' for solving basic mathematical problems. The other half of my time was to be spent in the desk computing section with Dr Goodwin and Les Fox at Oxford, acquiring the necessary expertise in the numerical solution of mathematical problems.

The delay in getting the ACE built created unwelcome tensions at the NPL, a fact which was still being discussed thirty years later:

> EVANS: I'd like to ask you about the atmosphere in the other parts of the lab and how other people − senior people − felt about this particular project. Who were the people who were basically 'for' research of this kind, and who were the people who were inclined to be a bit dismissive of it?
> WILKINSON: if we take the Division itself, most of the real work in Mathematics Division in those days was done by the desk computing section. They were interested in the project and very impressed with Turing as a mathematician, he was a very impressive mathematician. He picked up ideas on numerical analysis. (He was a lousy computer incidentally, one of the worst performers on a desk computer it's ever been my misfortune to work with.) But his brilliance was immediately obvious and they believed it to be a practical project.

In a later speech, Wilkinson also described his experience of working with Alan Turing:[8]

> It was impossible to work 'half-time' for a man like Turing and almost from the start the periods spent with the computing section were rather brief. The joint appointment did, however, have its useful aspect. Turing occasionally had days when he was 'unapproachable' and at such times it was advisable to exercise discretion. I soon learned to recognize the symptoms and would exercise my right (or, as I usually put it, 'meet my obligations') of working in the computing section until the mood passed, which it usually did quite quickly.

Wilkinson was speaking in 1970. His comments on Turing's output of academic papers − by which professorial productivity is measured − are interesting as a reflection of what people then knew:

> I feel bound to say that his published work fails to give an adequate impression of his remarkable versatility as a mathematician. He had only twenty published papers to his credit, written over a period of

some twenty years. Remarkable as some of these papers are, this work represents a mere fraction of what he might have done if things had turned out just a little differently. In the first place there were the six years starting from 1939 which he spent at the Foreign Office. He seemed not to have regretted the years he spent there and indeed we formed the impression that this was one of the happiest times of his life. Certainly it was there that he gained his knowledge of electronics and this was probably the decisive factor in his deciding to go to N.P.L. to design an electronic computer rather than returning to Cambridge. Mathematicians are inclined to refer to this period as the 'wasted years' but I think he was too broad a scientist to think of it in such terms.

A second factor limiting his output was a marked disinclination to put pen to paper. At school he is reputed to have had little enthusiasm for the 'English subjects' and he seemed to find the tedium of publishing a paper even more oppressive than most of us do. For myself I find his style of writing rather refreshing and full of little personal touches which are particularly attractive to someone who knew him. When in the throes of composition he would hammer away on an old typewriter (he was an indifferent typist, to put it charitably) and it was on such occasions that visits to the computing section were particularly advisable.

According to Wilkinson, the decision not to set up a hardware section at the NPL from the outset 'appeared to me to be a deplorable decision even at the time'. Nothing had yet come of the attempt to outsource the engineering to other governmental bodies. Finally, Sir Charles Darwin brought the hardware development back in-house, and to the disgust of Alan Turing it was proposed to scale it back and have an engineer called Harry D. Huskey build a small-scale 'test assembly'. Huskey was an American who had worked on the ENIAC, and might therefore be assumed to know his stuff. The test assembly – what these days might be called a 'proof of concept' – would be fit for testing the engineering and the feasibility of Alan's programs, but it wouldn't be up to any serious computing task. From Alan's viewpoint the test assembly was a waste of effort.

On the one hand the Test Assembly was to be a small computer in its own right, involving much more equipment than was strictly necessary to test the fundamentals of Turing's design, and yet on the other it fell far short of being the ACE. Probably Turing saw Huskey's project as diverting effort from his own. According to Wilkinson, Turing 'tended to ignore the Test Assembly', simply 'standing to one side'. Woodger[9] described how he 'was writing a program for [Version H] when Turing came in … looked over my shoulder and said, "What is this? What's Version H?". So I said, "it's Huskey's." "WHAT!" … [T]here was a pretty good scene about that.'[10]

In fact, the test assembly would evolve, after more machinations, into a small working machine called the 'Pilot' ACE. That, however, would take a few more years.

Robots and scrap iron

With the atmosphere at NPL becoming increasingly tense, and with no machine to test out the trial programs he and Jim Wilkinson were writing, Alan needed something else to do.

Sir Edward V. Appleton, G.B.E., K.C.B., D.Sc., F.R.S.,
Department of Scientific and industrial Research,
Park House,
24, Rutland Gate,
London, S.W. 7

23rd July, 1947

Dear Appleton

As you know Dr. A. Turing, S.P.S.O.*, is the mathematician who has designed the theoretical part of our big computing engine. This has now got to the stage of ironmongery, and so for the time the chief work on it is passing into other hands. I have discussed the matter both

* Senior Principal Scientific Officer.

with Womersley and with Turing, and we are agreed that it would be best that Turing should go off it for a spell. Though I have other work he might do here, I judge that it is not quite suited for him, and that a different action would be better.

He wants to extend his work on the machine still further towards the biological side. I can best describe it by saying that hitherto the machine has been planned for work equivalent to that of the lower parts of the brain, and he wants to see how much a machine can do for the higher ones; for example, could a machine be made that could learn by experience? This will be theoretical work, and better done away from here. The proposal then is that he should be allowed to be away for a year, which he would spend at Cambridge, where he is a fellow of King's. […]

Yours sincerely,

C.G. DARWIN[11]

A machine that can learn might seem rather far-fetched. But once you have grasped the idea that a computer program is just so much data, it is really not so hard to believe in intelligent machinery, however peculiar the idea might have seemed to an audience listening to an Alan Turing lecture in 1946.

It has been said that computing machines can only carry out the processes that they are instructed to do. This is certainly true in the sense that if they do something other than what they were instructed then they have just made some mistake. It is also true that the intention in constructing these machines in the first instance is to treat them as slaves, giving them only jobs which have been thought out in detail, jobs such that the user of the machine fully understands what in principle is going on all the time. Up till the present machines have only been used in this way. But is it necessary that they should always be used in such a manner? Let us suppose we have set up a machine with certain initial instruction tables, so constructed that these tables might on occasion, if good reason arose, modify those tables. One can imagine that after the machine had been operating for some time, the instructions would have altered out of all recognition, but nevertheless still be such that one would have to admit that the machine was still doing very worthwhile calculations. Possibly it might still be getting results of the type desired when the machine was first set up, but in a much more efficient manner. In such a case one would have to admit that the progress of the machine had not been foreseen when its original instructions were put in. It would be like a pupil who learnt much from his master, but had added much more by his own work. When this happens I feel that one is obliged to regard the machine as showing intelligence.[12]

Accordingly, in September 1947 Alan went back to Cambridge to think about machines and whether, and how, they could think. The plan was that Alan would spend his sabbatical year writing his 'theoretical work' on *Intelligent Machinery*. In fact, by the time he got to King's the thinking had already been done. Alan's paper was written up in that September. The operations of computing machines are based on components which react in different ways according to the inputs they receive: arithmetical processes such as adding and dividing are achieved by assembling small sub-groups of components linked together. In his paper on *Intelligent Machinery*, Alan Turing had begun to consider other implications of assembling groups of tiny decision-making units. What if they were connected together unsystematically – into what you might call 'unorganised' machines? The paper goes on to show that unorganised machines can be conditioned – essentially to learn. Alan Turing had invented the idea of the neural network.

The whole idea of 'intelligent' machinery was causing sniggers at the numerically focused NPL. 'Turing is going to infest the countryside with a robot which will live on twigs and scrap iron!'[13]

MAN AS A MACHINE
One way of setting about our task of building a 'thinking machine' would be to take a man as a whole and to try to replace all the parts of him by machinery. He would include television cameras, microphones, loudspeakers, wheels and 'handling servo-mechanisms' as well as some

sort of 'electronic brain'. This would be a tremendous undertaking of course. The object, if produced by present techniques, would be of immense size, even if the 'brain' part were stationary and controlled the body from a distance. In order that the machine should have a chance of finding things out for itself it should be allowed to roam the countryside, and the danger to the ordinary citizen would be serious. Moreover even when the facilities mentioned above were provided, the creature would still have no contact with food, sex, sport and many other things of interest to the human being. Thus although this method is probably the 'sure' way of producing a thinking machine it seems to be altogether too slow and impracticable.

Instead we propose to try and see what can be done with a 'brain' which is more or less without a body providing, at most, organs of sight, speech, and hearing. We are then faced with the problem of finding suitable branches of thought for the machine to exercise its powers in. The following fields appear to me to have advantages:

(i)   Various games, e.g., chess, noughts and crosses, bridge, poker
(ii) The learning of languages
(iii) Translation of languages
(iv) Cryptography
(v)   Mathematics.[14]

His boss was not impressed.

Dear Turing

I have received your paper which has been signed and sent out.

I may say that I read it through with some attention and interest, but spent most of the time cursing you for giving me such a perfectly smudgy copy to read. Next time I hope somebody else and not myself with [*sic*] be the sufferer, but I think the best plan would be to get better carbon paper.

I hope you are enjoying life at Cambridge.

Yours sincerely,

C G Darwin[15]

Sir Charles Darwin, Director of the NPL, who thought Alan's paper on *Intelligent Machinery* unfit for publication. (Courtesy of the National Physical Laboratory)

The facsimile of the paper, helpfully made available online by the present-day NPL, is rather neat – much too well presented to be one of Alan's own typing efforts (such as the draft in the King's College Archive). It's tempting, therefore, to comment that Sir Charles should have checked his own letter before complaining about typing. Actually the problem was a bit more serious than giving Sir Charles a carbon rather than the top copy. The paper bore no relation to the role of the NPL's Mathematics Division as the nation's computing bureau; apparently Sir Charles's real view was that it was a 'schoolboy's essay'. *Intelligent Machinery* was not to be published for another twenty years.

Off scratch

In truth, the thing that had been roaming the countryside was none other than Alan Turing himself, and he had been doing it for some time now. He had developed a taste for long-distance running during his days at Bletchley Park. He would on occasion run across from the NPL to Dollis Hill (about 14 miles), and one day in Teddington the hobby became more of an organised machine.

> We heard him rather than saw him. He made a terrible grunting noise when he was running, but before we could say anything to him, he

was past us like a shot out of a gun. A couple of nights later, we kept up with him long enough for me to ask him who he ran for. When he said nobody, we invited him to join Walton. He did and immediately became our best runner.[16]

It was the period leading up to the 1948 Wembley Olympics. Austerity Britain was not expecting to do astoundingly well, but track athletics was one sport in which Britain might not be dishonoured; unlike thinking machines, running was something which everyone could understand. Later, the Walton Athletic Club admitted Christopher Chataway, an old Shirburnian of a new generation, into its membership. Chataway was (like Alan) best as a three-miler and won the world record in 1955; he also acted as Sir Roger Bannister's pacer in the famous four-minute mile of 1954. As a member of the Club, Alan was swept into a busy programme of race meetings. In 1946 Alan won the three-mile Club Track Championship and the ten-mile Road Running Championship, both in record time. Another race took place on Boxing Day 1946, just before he went off to the Harvard conference, and had enough drama to reach the papers:[17]

3 MILES RACE WON BY ONE FOOT
FAST TIMES AT WALTON
By A Special Correspondent

Excellent weather and a track in first-class condition considerably helped athletes to record fast times in the open handicap meeting at Stompond-lane sports ground, Walton, yesterday.
The Three Miles was a thrilling race in which C. G. Scott (Surrey A.C.), who started from the 10-yards mark, beat the scratch man, A. M. Turing (Walton A.C.), by one foot in the last stride in 15min 51sec.

Athletic prowess also gave Alan something to write to Mother about.[18]

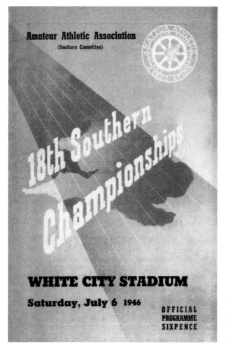

Amateur Athletic Association
programme for July 1946. Alan ran in
the Six Miles but wasn't in the first three.
(Courtesy of Sue and Martin Gregory)

'Good Mornings'
begin with
Gillette

John eats up the miles, gulping pints
of good air; both in sprinting and
shaving he's trained to a hair!

Blue Gillette blades 3d each   including Purchase Tax

A.A.A. Southern Championships Saturday, 6th July, 1946   5

SIX MILES   10.45 a.m.

Standards:
Southern—32 min. 15 sec. A.A.A.—31 min. 30 sec.   **Event
No. 1**
HOLDER: C. T. Carter, Belgrave H.

Amateur Records:
WORLD'S RECORD: 28 min. 38.6 sec.—V. Heino (Finland), 1944.
BRITISH RECORD: 29 min. 38.4 sec.—P. Nurmi (Finland), 1930.
ENGLISH NATIVE RECORD: 29 min. 45 sec.—J. A. Burns, 1936.
SOUTHERN CHAMPIONSHIP: 30 min. 37 sec.—A. F. Purse, 1936.

57. R. F. TOWNROW	...	...	...	...	...	...	Polytechnic H.
62. H. J. ASHTON	...	...	...	...	...	...	Queen's Park H.
69. A. E. FROST	...	...	...	...	...	...	Belgrave H.
87. M. BINGHAM	...	...	...	...	...	...	Finchley H.
35. A. V. MACOY	...	...	...	...	...	Aylesford Paper Mills S.C.
55. A. M. TURING	...	...	...	...	...	...	Walton A.C.
159. S. J. BELTON	...	...	...	...	...	...	Surrey A.C.
169. R. J. RUDDICK	...	...	...	...	...	...	Walton A.C.

1st........... Time:....... min........ sec.   2nd.......   3rd.......

Standards:
Southern................. A.A.A.................

THROWING THE HAMMER   11.30 a.m.

Standards:
Southern—105 feet. A.A.A.—130 feet.   **Event
No. 2**
HOLDER: J. McG. Dolens, L.A.C.

Amateur Records:
WORLD'S RECORD: 195 ft. 6¼in.—E. Blask (Germany), 1938.
BRITISH RECORD: 183 ft. 3 in.—K. Hein (Germany), 1937.
ENGLISH NATIVE RECORD: 172 ft. 0¼in.—M. C. Nokes, 1923.

Judges—J. C. Crump, J. H. Neve, R .W. Thrasher.

70. F. WOOD	...	...	...	...	...	Kent Police S.C.
85. D. H. CULLEN	...	...	...	...	...	London A.C.
93. C. J. REIDY	...	...	...	...	...	South London H.

1st................. Distance :.................ft.................in.
2nd................. Distance :.................ft.................in.
3rd................. Distance :.................ft.................in.

Standards:
Southern................. A.A.A.................

Cunard White Star R.M.S. 'Queen Elizabeth'

My dear Mother,

The sports meeting was a great success, the weather being perfect. I also enjoyed my race (3 miles) thoroughly. I was running off scratch which made me feel rather grand. I managed to take the lead from one Scott in the last lap, and was able to do quite a sprint in the last 220 yards, but Scott put up a better one and beat me by a few feet. A very exciting race indeed.

Yours

Alan

My dear Mother,

Yes, I was running in the Southern Counties Championship at Ascot, but did very badly. Also ran in the Nationals yesterday, and was in much better form, coming in 62nd out of about 300 runners. This probably represents my form fairly well.

It was, however, rather bad form to turn up at Guildford in running kit.

Alan's behaviour as it affected other people was not, in my view, so amusing for those who were at the receiving end. Alan would descend upon any household at any moment of the day or night with or without warning and seldom with more than a few hours notice. When he was stationed at Teddington after the war he discovered that the distance to Guildford corresponded roughly with the marathon distance, so the first we knew of his impending arrival was a badly made parcel containing a change of clothing. About twelve noon he would come running up the steep hill of Jenner Road and straight up the stairs and into a bath.[19]

Nevertheless, provided Alan took his bath at John's house in Guildford, rather than Mother's, all would be well, and Mother was content to read the good things in the paper.

MARATHON AND DECATHLON CHAMPIONSHIPS

The Amateur Athletic Association championships for this year [1947] were concluded at Loughborough College Stadium, on Saturday, with the second and last day of the Decathlon and the decision of the Marathon championship.

MARATHON CHAMPIONSHIP (26 miles 385 yds.) (record: 2 hrs. 30 min. 57.6 sec by H. W. Payne, Windsor to Stamford Bridge, on July 5, 1929; standard time: 3 hrs. 5 min.). – J.T. Holden (Tipton Harriers). 2 hrs. 33 min. 20 1-5 sec., 1; [...] Dr. A. M. Turing (Walton A.C.), 2 hrs. 46 min. 3 sec., 5.[20]

Fifth place ought to have been good enough for the Olympic squad, but it was not to be, owing to a leg injury which troubled Alan for several months in 1948. Alan kept running for the Club at Walton even after he had left the NPL, running in the London–Brighton relays in the same team as Chris Chataway in 1949 and 1950, and continuing as vice-president of the Club until 1954.

Many years later, another member of the Club recalled:[21]

Looking back, he was the typical absent-minded professor. He looked different to the rest of the lads; he was rather untidily dressed, good quality clothes mind, but no creases in them; he used a tie to hold his trousers up; if he wore a necktie, it was never knotted properly; and he had hair that just stuck up at the back. He was very popular with the boys, but he wasn't one of them. He was a strange character, a very reserved sort, but he mixed in with everyone quite well; he was even a member of our committee. We had no idea what he did, and what a great man he was. We didn't realise it until all the Enigma business came out. We didn't even know where he worked until he asked us if Walton would have a match with the NPL. It was the first time I'd been in the grounds. Another time, we went on our first ever foreign trip to Nijmegen in Holland; he couldn't come, but he gave me five pounds, which was a lot of money in those days, and said 'Buy the boys a drink for me'.

Alan Turing boarding a bus with other members of the Walton Athletic Club, 1946. (By kind permission of the Provost and Scholars of King's College, Cambridge)

Pipped at the post. Alan Turing loses the Three Miles by one foot on Boxing Day, 1946. (By kind permission of the Provost and Scholars of King's College, Cambridge)

Alan was also mixing in with the boys back at Cambridge, where there was a new group of young mathematicians. First, there was Neville Johnson, a student from Sunderland, who may have felt out of place in the grandeur of King's; tea in Alan's rooms blossomed into something more, and Neville retained a place in Alan's affections for the rest of his life. More colourful than Neville was Norman Routledge, who was clever, flamboyant and sometimes outrageous. Thus, writing to Alan in 1952:[22]

> My dear Alan,
>
> What a delicious Xmas card you sent me – it was certainly the finest choirboy I've ever had – (although someone else sent me a <u>delicious</u> youth in pyjamas peeping from behind some curtains with a charming inscription about 'Here's wishing you everything you want …').
>
> Am being trained as an ACE operator at N.P.L. – find whole work v. fascinating.

In 1952 Norman was working at the Royal Aircraft Establishment, where they planned to install a computer. Later he would go on to be an inspirational teacher at Eton; meanwhile at King's it was banter and achieving B-star wrangler status and then a PhD. Norman was able to become an ACE operator in 1952, because by then a modified version of Huskey's test assembly had become operational. In early 1948 there was still no computer at the NPL, and still no prospect of one – in fact, the ACE as designed by Alan did not become operational until late 1958. It was all very frustrating. Worse, M.H.A. Newman's laboratory in Manchester had had a small computer actually working since August 1947.

Mr Newman and Dr von Neumann

At one stage, historians of computer development believed that Alan Turing had conferred during his 1942–43 visit to the United States with his old boss John von Neumann: it would make for a nice story if John von Neumann's seminal paper on the EDVAC had been worked up jointly with Alan. Certainly, von Neumann had been influenced by the concepts in Alan's paper on *Computable Numbers*. Stanley P. Frankel, a colleague of von Neumann who had learned how to program ENIAC, said that 'in about 1943 or '44 von Neumann was well aware of the fundamental importance of Turing's paper of 1936 "On Computable Numbers …" which describes in principle the "Universal Computer" of which every modern computer is a realization. Von Neumann introduced me to that paper and at his urging I studied it with care.'[23] However, Alan couldn't have discussed computing machinery with John von Neumann during his 1942–43 visit to America, because while Alan was in the US, John von Neumann was in the UK, and having at least one meeting with a different ex-colleague from Princeton. John von Neumann was in the UK to understand better what makes explosions escalate; it was certainly on his agenda to discuss the state of the art as regards computing machinery. He wrote to his boss Professor Veblen at the IAS in Princeton that he had 'developed an obscene interest in computational techniques',[24] and later he told his UK host that 'I received in that period a decisive impulse which determined my interest in computing machines'.[25] The Princetonian whom von Neumann had met with was none other than M.H.A. Newman, the senior man on the team that was just about to start work on Colossus. Although they didn't meet at Bletchley, and Newman was too discreet to discuss his war work, it is difficult to imagine that von Neumann did not have a discussion about a more neutral topic, one of burning relevance to von Neumann, namely computing machinery.

In 1945, as the war came to an end, Newman was appointed Fielden Professor of Mathematics at Manchester University. Notwithstanding von Neumann's plans for the EDVAC, and not-withstanding the NPL, M.H.A. Newman was planning a computer laboratory of his own, one with a broader vision than just being a number-crunching bureau.

The University, Manchester 13

8 February 1946

Dear von Neumann,

I have been owing you a letter for a long time, since you sent me a copy of your Theory of Games. I can truthfully say that if your book had been less interesting I would have answered sooner. [...] My more particular reason for writing at this moment is computing machines. I have just heard, through Hartree, that you are starting up a machine project in Princeton. I am also hoping to embark on a computing machine section here, having got very interested in electronic devices of this kind during the last two or three years. By about eighteen months ago I had decided to try my hand at starting up a machine unit when I got out. It was indeed one of my reasons for coming to Manchester that the set-up here is favourable in several ways. This was before I knew anything of the American work, or of the scheme for a unit at the National Physical Laboratory. Later I heard of the various American machines, existing and projected, from Hartree and Flowers.

Once the N.P.L. project was started it became questionable whether a further unit was wanted. My view was that, in this, as in other branches of technology, basic research is wanted, which can go on without worrying about getting into production; that with the development of fast machine techniques mathematical analysis itself may take a new slant, apart from the developments that may be stimulated in symbolic logic and other topics not usually in the repertoire of engineers or computing experts; and that mathematical problems of an entirely different kin from those so far tackled by machines might be tried, e.g. testing (say), the 4-colour problem or various theorems on lattices, groups, etc, for the first few values of n. [...] I hope you don't think the field will be getting a bit crowded if still more come in.

Anyhow, I have put in an application to the Royal Society for a grant of enough to make a start. I am of course in close touch with Turing.[26]

In 1946 a new war had broken out, one for talented and experienced people, particularly electronics engineers. In his letter to von Neumann, Newman said that 'good circuit men' were 'both rare and not procurable when found'.

Professor Newman's Proposals for an Electronic
Calculating Machine – 616/2/2.

I have read Professor Hartree's note and feel inclined to agree with him that a group at Manchester parallel with the group working on the pure mathematical aspect of the use of machines of this kind would be a very good thing. [...] So long as we have Dr. Turing I feel that his talent once the machine is constructed, should be employed in the direction of further development of the use of the machine in the most general manner possible [...] So far as I remember Professor Newman's proposals contained a suggestion of a full time electrical engineer at £800 a year. Although I do not know details I imagine Professor Newman has a particular individual in mind, namely, Mr. Flowers at the Post Office Engineering Research Station. Surely Mr. Flowers' first duty is to us [...].[27]

JOHN WOMERSLEY

The NPL had done well to nab Dr Turing.

What Newman had nabbed, instead of Turing or Flowers, was the Colossus itself. The week before VJ Day, on 8 August 1945, Newman asked his superiors at Bletchley Park if he could take with him 'the material of two complete Colossi; and in addition a few thousand miscellaneous resistances and condensers off other machines'.[28] When it was ready for delivery, the equipment sent to Manchester weighed seven tons. These seven tons would give him a 500-yard start in the three-mile race to build an electronic computer.

In early 1946, as projected in his letter to von Neumann, the Royal Society received an application for a grant of £36,000 for Newman to build a computing machine. A committee, including among its members Professor Hartree and Sir Charles Darwin, was appointed to consider the application, and by May the committee had concluded that the application could go forward to the Treasury with their support. Newman had got his funding.

Split atoms and stolen assets

He had done even better than get funding and a lorry-load of components. He had also got Professor F.C. Williams, who had solved the problem of computer memory in a sleeker and more elegant way than the mercury delay line. Williams was using cathode-ray tubes (CRTs) – rather like rudimentary old-style big-box television screens – and exploiting their property that the screen luminesces for a while before the image fades away. Digits could be stored in arrays on CRT screens, read, and refreshed. The data were almost immediately accessible, and on a random basis, so the problem of waiting for a sound wave to trudge up a delay line would not arise. They were trying something similar for the IAS machine at Princeton, but the technology was difficult, which is why Goldstine had been debating delay lines with Alan in early 1947. But Williams was good: by mid-1947 he had made his CRT memory work. So, when Alan had an opportunity to discuss his frustrations with Newman in early 1948, the solution was obvious. 'I stole him away, and made old Darwin very angry because I stole him away from NPL to come to Manchester.'[29] Alan resigned from NPL in May 1948 and went to work for Newman.

Sir Charles Darwin was asked to explain to his Executive Committee why it was that Dr A.M. Turing had resigned from the NPL.

> <u>Director</u> said this was not quite as bad as it appeared as Dr. Turing's work at the laboratory had, in the main, already been done. Dr. Turing had been on leave of absence at Cambridge University, with a general understanding that he would return to the laboratory for two years before taking up a post at a University. During his stay at Cambridge, Dr. Turing had been on half pay from the laboratory to supplement his Fellowship, etc., fees, and he has now produced a report which,

although not suitable for publication, demonstrated that during his stay there he had been engaged in rather fundamental studies.[30]

Alan's move to Manchester was highly significant, and would be life-changing in many ways. Alan would live there for the rest of his life. It didn't mean losing touch with his friends at Cambridge and elsewhere, but for the first time he had a senior university post, he bought a house, and it provided opportunities for both the professional and personal sides of his life. Newman's philosophy about what computers were for was exactly in line with Alan's own vision. So Alan became the Deputy Director of the Royal Society Computing Machine Laboratory at the University of Manchester.

The laboratory was described by Professor F.C. Williams:[31]

> A fine sounding phrase, but what was the reality? It was one room in a Victorian building whose architectural features are best described as 'late lavatorial'. The walls were of brown glazed brick and the door was labelled 'Magnetism Room'.

The brown glazed brick dated from the era of Ernest Rutherford, who had used the building to do his original atom-splitting experiments; the brickwork is still somewhat radioactive. It was not only the surroundings that were rudimentary: so was the computer, often referred to as the 'Manchester baby'. The baby's memory consisted of three Williams tubes (as they were now called), each storing 32×32 bits of data. One tube was taken up with the accumulator and another by the control, leaving precisely 1024 bits for random-access memory. Like an austerity Christmas display, the baby's dreary wires hung from the ceiling in loose gathers, while racks of valves glowed dimly and the CRT displays cast an eerie monochrome flicker among the twigs, scrap iron and other leftovers salvaged from the two old Colossi. Williams again:[32]

> Our first machine had no input mechanism except for a technique for inserting single digits into the store at chosen places. It had no output

mechanism, the answer was read directly from the cathode ray tube monitoring the store. At this point Turing made his, from my point of view, major contribution. He specified simple minimum input facilities that we must provide so that he could organise input to the machine from five-hole paper tape and output from the machine in similar form.

Although it seemed to take up the full 20×20 feet of available space, it did not have as many as 40 racks, or weigh 50 tons, and there were certainly not 13 people to operate it. The Manchester 'baby' computer was not going to be guilty of the American sin of much equipment prevailing over thought. But who cared that it was small and untidy and made of junkyard parts? It was the first electronic full-function computer in the United Kingdom that could actually run a program.

Because of the improvisation, much of Newman's Royal Society grant remained to be spent; £3,000 a year was to be used for salaries, and Alan Turing was paid out of that amount. Sir Charles Darwin might have backed Newman's project with less warmth if he had known this was how things would turn out. Still, Newman had trumped the ACE: Newman's computer was working and, despite its limitations, Newman and Turing could use it to work on a real problem.

300-year-old sum

In September 1588, as the Spanish Armada was limping home from its failed attempt to invade England, the theologian, musicologist and mathematician Marin Mersenne was born in the west of France. One of his many ideas was that numbers of the form 2^n-1 are prime numbers. While it is relatively easy, if very boring, to write out numbers of the form 2^n-1 in ordinary decimal notation (1, 2, 3, 7, and so forth), after a bit the rule breaks down ($2^4-1 = 15$ is not prime). Mersenne's numbers get very big after a while, and it is very tedious indeed to test whether they can be divided by anything and so to find out whether a given Mersenne number is prime. Mersenne had made

'A Marvel of Our Time': the Manchester Electronic Brain, as shown in the *Illustrated London News* in 1949, was cobbled together using leftovers from Colossus. (Mary Evans Picture Library)

a list of numbers of the form 2^n-1 up to $n = 257$ which he asserted were primes. But was he right?

> The first problem that we put onto – the one other thing that I was responsible for, but it's not gone down in history I'm sure, is that the problem was to find something non-trivial to put on to our Manchester machine which had a storage of one thousand and twenty-four digits, not words, and I devised a problem, a method, of testing Mersenne primes, allowing for motor cars parking outside and a few things like that; in spite of that it did calculate. That was, I think, the first real problem that was done. It was very nice because $[2^n-1]$ in the scale of 2 is simply 1 1 1 1 1 1 … and so that's a very nice thing for the computer.[33]

Newman had selected his problem with the same mental dexterity that had characterised his work at Bletchley Park. The Manchester baby flicked through the numbers, trying to divide each one by everything possible, one after another. It took about an hour to reach a verdict for the larger Mersenne numbers. And what was the answer? The Manchester computer showed that Mersenne had got some of his results wrong. $2^{67}-1$ and $2^{257}-1$ aren't prime, but $2^{127}-1$ is. The result was something to be proud of, as *The Times* reported:[34]

THE MECHANICAL BRAIN

ANSWER FOUND TO 300 YEAR OLD SUM

From Our Special Correspondent

Experiments which have been in progress in this country and the United States since the end of the war to produce an efficient mechanical 'brain' have been successfully completed at Manchester University, where a workable 'brain' has been evolved. Not only is it working satisfactorily, but for the first time a machine has been brought to the point at which it can work out problems which it is practically impossible to execute on paper. The Manchester 'mechanical mind' was built by Professor F.C. Williams, of the Department of Electro-Technics, and is now in the hands of two university mathematicians, Professor M. H. A. Newman and Mr A. W. [*sic*] Turing. It has just completed, in a matter of weeks, a problem, the nature of which is not disclosed, which was started in the seventeenth century and is only just being completed by human calculation.

Its appearance is somewhat unprepossessing. It is composed of racks of electrical apparatus consisting of a mass of untidy wires, valves, chassis, and display tubes. When in action, the cathode ray becomes a pattern of dots which shows what information is in the machine. There is a close analogy between its structure and that of the human brain. It differs from other mechanical brains in its method of storing information. The electronic method ensures that information is more readily accessible.

CALCULUS TO SONNET

Mr Turing said yesterday: 'This is only a foretaste of what is to come, and only the shadow of what is going to be. We have to have some experience with the machine before we really know its capabilities. It may take years before we settle down to the new possibilities, but I do not see why it should not enter any one of the fields normally covered by the human intellect, and eventually compete on equal terms. I do not think you can even draw the line about sonnets, though the comparison is perhaps a little bit unfair because a sonnet written by a machine will be better appreciated by another machine.'

It was pretty outrageous to extrapolate from a simple program squeezing the most out of the Manchester machine's tiny processing capability to the composition of sonnets. But Alan had been provoked. In the way that Darwin's evolutionary theory had caused an irruption in the establishment of the nineteenth century, the Mechanical Brain had electrified the conservatives of the twentieth.

Game of sonnets

Every three years an award is made to a meritorious surgeon in memory of Sir Joseph Lister, whose work in the 1880s and 1890s introduced sterility into surgery. The winner in 1948 was a Manchester neurologist, Sir Geoffrey Jefferson. Jefferson's award was made for his 'knowledge of the functions and structure of the nervous system, made as a philosophical biologist, practising neurosurgery'. On 9 June 1949 Sir Geoffrey presented his thank-you speech, known as the Lister Oration. His subject, under the heading 'The Mind of Mechanical Man', was the idiocy of the computer scientists' notion that machines might think.[35]

> A machine might solve problems in logic, since logic and mathematics are much the same thing. But not until a machine can write a sonnet or a concerto because of thoughts and emotions felt, and not by the chance fall of symbols, could we agree that machine equals brain. When we hear it said that wireless valves think, we may despair of language. I venture to predict that the day will never dawn when the gracious premises of the Royal Society have to be turned into garages to house the new Fellows. I end by ranging myself with the humanist Shakespeare rather than the mechanists, recalling Hamlet's lines: 'What a piece of work is a man! How noble in reason! how infinite in faculty; in form, in moving, how express and admirable! in action, how like an angel! in apprehension, how like a god! the beauty of the world! the paragon of animals!'

The man behind the sonnet. Sir Geoffrey Jefferson, who debated with Alan whether machines can think. (Gerald Festus Kelly © Society of British Neurological Surgeons, courtesy of the US National Library of Medicine)

The reporter from *The Times* who was covering the speech was more intrigued by Sir Geoffrey's mention of the Manchester computer than by his gushings about *Hamlet*. He had got in touch with the Computing Department and asked Alan about sonnets. Newman's wife, Lyn, wrote about the episode in a letter to a friend:[36]

Did you see the extraordinary report in the Times two weeks ago on the Manchester Calculating Machine with the fantastic remarks attributed to Alan Turing? And Max's letter the following week trying to clear things up? The Times wired Alan, who isn't on the telephone, to ring their office, and they interviewed him on the phone. He's wildly innocent about the ways of reporters and has a bad stammer when he's nervous or puzzled. It was a great shock to him when he saw the Times – and to Max who had been flying back from Belfast that day. We had a wretched weekend starting at midnight on the Friday night when some sub-editor of a local paper rang up to get a story. By Sunday Max was getting a bit gruff, and when he said, 'What do you want?' to one newspaper, the reporter replied, 'Only to photograph your brain.'

Alan had just contrived to annoy his new boss and there was now a danger of what might, in 1949, have become a media frenzy. M.H.A. Newman duly wrote to *The Times* to try to clear things up, or at any rate restore things to a state of ordinary dullness:[37]

Sir,— it may help to avoid any misunderstanding of the nature of the computing machine now being tried out in Manchester University if you will allow me to add something to the account of it in *The Times* of June 11. It is a 'general purpose' automatic computing machine of the same general type as others which are in various stages of development. All these machines will have the [property] of choosing which instruction to obey next, according to the result of the work so far completed. It is [this] that gives these machines their great flexibility and makes them capable of carrying out from a reasonably small set of instructions the enormous number of simple operations that make up the solution of large problems. It is this feature also which has interested physiologists on the look-out for possible schematic 'models' of the human brain.

He went on to explain about Mersenne primes and make it all seem very mathematical and unpoetic. Good try, but as well as a photograph of the Manchester Mechanical Brain and all its unromantic wiry tangles, *The Times* of that day also carried the following:

Sir,—Your Special Correspondent quotes Mr. A. W. Turing, of Manchester University, as saying that 'the University was really interested in the investigation of the possibilities of machines for their own sake. Their research would be directed to finding the degree of intellectual activity of which a machine was capable, and to what extent it could think for itself.' If one may judge from Professor Jefferson's Lister oration, to which your Correspondent refers us, responsible scientists will be quick to dissociate themselves from this programme. But we must all take warning from it. Even our dialectical materialists would feel necessitated to guard themselves, like Butler's Erewhonians, against the possible hostility of the machines. And those of us who not only confess with our lips but believe in our hearts that men are free persons (which is unintelligible if we have no unextended mind or soul, but only a brain) must ask ourselves how far Mr. Turing's opinions are shared, or may come to be shared, by the rulers of our country.

Yours &c.,

ILLTYD TRETHOWAN

Downside Abbey, Bath, June 11

Game on. Downside is another public school and Sherborne's great rugby-football rival. Shockingly and exceptionally, during Alan's time at Sherborne, Downside had actually won by 38 points to 8, on an occasion when Sherborne was captained by Alan's friend Pat Mermagen. Soon it would be time for a replay.

> It is hard to convey to the modern reader [wrote Maurice Wilkes in 1985] the seriousness with which this debate, which was after all no more than a debate about the use of words, was regarded by all sorts of people. Some people appeared to regard it as an impious act even to attempt to construct a computer. In order to understand the emotion that was released, it is, I think, necessary to remember two things. In the first place, computers exhibited a behavior far more complex than was exhibited by the simple automatic machines with which people were familiar up to that time. The result was that to a non-scientist a computer appeared like magic. It dazzled him, and he was all too ready to believe that it differed from other machines in more than degree. In the second place a discussion about how far a machine can go in imitating human beings can easily turn into a discussion about whether the human brain is to be regarded as nothing more than a machine; this raises religious and ethical issues about which human beings have long argued and felt emotion.[38]

Wilkes may have had cause to be grumpy in June 1949. He was trying to get ready for his own conference on 'automatic calculating machines' to be hosted by the Cambridge University Mathematical Laboratory, at which his own work on the machine called EDSAC – standing for Electronic Delay Storage Automatic Calculator – would be showcased. Various experts (including Newman, Wilkinson, Williams, Wilkes himself, and Turing) would speak. The conference was due to begin only a week after the Newman and Trethowan letters were published in *The Times*.

Alan's presentation at the Cambridge conference was on the 'Checking Process for Large Routines' – in other words, debugging programs, which people were beginning to realise was a non-trivial problem. His paper drew once again on the old *Computable Numbers* ideas: he had proved mathematically *in 1936* that it is impossible to devise a computer program which will tell you for sure whether any other program will go into an endless loop, or, as we say nowadays, whether it will crash. Alas, his point may have been lost on the others, as Wilkes explained:

> At one point in his talk, Turing had occasion to write a few decimal numbers on the blackboard and add them up. At first none of us could follow what he was doing until we realized that he was writing the numbers backwards with their least significant digits on the left. There was quite a fashion for doing this in Manchester and at the NPL with binary numbers, presumably because that was the way the pulses appeared on a cathode ray tube, but to do it with decimal numbers and without comment was a typical Turing aberration. I really believe that it did not occur to him that a trivial matter like that could possibly affect anybody's understanding one way or the other.

Propaganda

Paradoxically, at the same time Alan was working on a new paper, which, almost uniquely for Alan's works, would contain not a single equation. This paper was written in an easy, accessible style, and it was not about mathematics and it was not about the programming of computers. Thwarted by the burial of his *Intelligent Machinery* paper by the NPL, Alan was having another go. This time his paper would be published. Rather than place it among the engineering or mathematical publications, it appeared in the philosophy journal *Mind*.

The new paper would rival *Computable Numbers* for fame: while *Computable Numbers* presented the concept now known as the 'Turing Machine', the *Mind* paper presented the 'Turing Test'.

COMPUTING MACHINERY AND INTELLIGENCE
By A. M. Turing

1. The Imitation Game

I propose to consider the question, 'Can machines think?' This should begin with definitions of the meaning of the terms 'machine' and 'think.' Instead of attempting such a definition I shall replace the question by another, which is closely related to it and is expressed in relatively unambiguous words. The new form of the problem can be described in terms of a game which we call the 'imitation game'. It is played with three people, a man (A), a woman (B), and an interrogator (C) who may be of either sex. The interrogator stays in a room apart from the other two. The object of the game for the interrogator is to determine which of the other two is the man and which is the woman. We now ask the question, 'What will happen when a machine takes the part of A in this game?' Will the interrogator decide wrongly as often when the game is played like this as he does when the game is played between a man and a woman? These questions replace our original, 'Can machines think?'

It will simplify matters for the reader if I explain first my own beliefs in the matter. Consider first the more accurate form of the question. I believe that in about fifty years' time it will be possible to programme computers, with a storage capacity of about 10^9, to make them play the imitation game so well that an average interrogator will not have more than 70 per cent chance of making the right identification after five minutes of questioning. The original question, 'Can machines think?' I believe to be too meaningless to deserve discussion. Nevertheless I believe that at the end of the century the use of words and general educated opinion will have altered so much that one will be able to speak of machines thinking without expecting to be contradicted.[39]

Robin Gandy described the genesis of *Computing Machinery and Intelligence*:[40]

The 1950 paper was intended not so much as a penetrating contribution to philosophy but as propaganda. Turing thought the time had come for philosophers and mathematicians and scientists to take seriously the fact that computers were not merely calculating engines but were capable of behavior which must be accounted as intelligent; he sought to persuade people that this was so. He wrote this paper – unlike his mathematical papers – quickly and with enjoyment. I can remember his reading aloud to me some of the passages – always with a smile, sometimes with a giggle.

In his paper, one after another, Alan demolished the counter-arguments. Very politely, Alan refers to the views of Sir Geoffrey Jefferson, and the business about sonnets:[41]

I am sure that Professor Jefferson does not wish to adopt the extreme and solipsist point of view. Probably he would be quite willing to accept the imitation game as a test. The game (with the player B omitted) is frequently used in practice under the name of viva voce to discover whether some one really understands something or has 'learnt it parrot fashion.' Let us listen in to a part of such a viva voce:

Interrogator: In the first line of your sonnet which reads 'Shall I compare thee to a summer's day,' would not 'a spring day' do as well or better?

Witness: It wouldn't scan.

Interrogator: How about 'a winter's day.' That would scan all right.

Witness: Yes, but nobody wants to be compared to a winter's day.

Interrogator: Would you say Mr. Pickwick reminded you of Christmas?

Witness: In a way.

Interrogator: Yet Christmas is a winter's day, and I do not think Mr. Pickwick would mind the comparison.

Witness: I don't think you're serious. By a winter's day one means a typical winter's day, rather than a special one like Christmas.

And so on. What would Professor Jefferson say if the sonnet-writing machine was able to answer like this in the viva voce?

The debate with Jefferson was not yet finished, however. Alan gave a talk on the BBC's Third Programme (the predecessor of Radio 3) on the subject in May 1951, and in January 1952 the Third Programme hosted a debate between Turing and Jefferson, with Newman participating as well. The whole thing was introduced by Professor Richard Braithwaite of King's College, Cambridge – who had, back in 1933, introduced Alan to the Moral Sciences Club and the subject of philosophy. It is still fresh and lively even after more than 70 years; they discuss whether computers can have appetites, complain about the programs they are given, have a sense of duty, or throw tantrums; and it concludes with Jefferson saying, 'it would be fun some day, Turing, to listen to a discussion, say on the Fourth Programme, between two machines on why human beings think that they think'.[42]

Meanwhile, in Manchester, a new computer had come into operation. This one wasn't a baby, it wasn't at all lousy, and it was too busy to pay attention to thoughtless chatter on the wireless. Too busy writing love letters.

9

TAKING SHAPE

It was all Strachey's fault. Not Lytton, arguably the most overt of the Cambridge Hellenistic homosexuals, or even his brother Oliver, who was more closely connected with Alan Turing as a veteran of Room 40 and a senior codebreaker at Bletchley Park. This Strachey was Christopher, Oliver's son, and another former student of mathematics from King's College, Cambridge. Christopher Strachey had gone up to King's in 1935, while Alan was doing his work on *Computable Numbers*, and since the war he had been teaching maths and physics, most recently at Harrow. But in 1951 he was introduced to Alan's former assistant at NPL, Mike Woodger, and Strachey started producing computer programs. He wasn't interested in solutions of 300-year-old problems relating to prime numbers. Like Alan, Strachey saw the potential for the computer, and his particular interest was games. But to play even children's games the computer needed a grown-up memory.

Since October 1948, when Alan was installed as Deputy Director of the Computing Machine Laboratory, a lot of engineering had been going on. The Manchester baby was being rebuilt as a grown-up computer, to be called the Manchester Mark 1. This was an altogether more professional machine, and the Royal Society grant was put towards a modern building with acceptably low levels of radioactivity in which it could be housed. Technical experts from the Telecommunications Research Establishment – which was not only the home of radar but had an honourable record in producing computing equipment – and a local Manchester firm called Ferranti joined forces to develop a full-capacity machine which Ferranti would then be able to exploit commercially. Unlike the baby, its innards were neatly arrayed and hidden within streamlined metal cabinets. The Mark I looked professional. On the other hand, its programming manual was written by Alan Turing.

Programming the Manchester Mark 1 was not for the faint-hearted. R.K. Livesey, who was assisted by Alan in 1953 with the mathematical aspects of an engineering problem, recalled:[1]

> Programming the Mark 1 was certainly 'machine code programming'. Each machine instruction consisted of 20 binary digits. An instruction was fed into the machine as four rows of holes/blanks on 5-track teleprinter tape, each row corresponding to a character on a teleprinter keyboard. Thus the written form of a program consisted of a sequence of 'words', each of four teleprinter characters. Unfortunately the characters corresponding to the 32 binary numbers 00000 … 11111 were arranged in the entirely arbitrary sequence /E@A:SIU½DRJN FCKTZLWHYPQOBG"MXV£. Anyone who used the machine regularly ended up knowing this sequence by heart – I can still repeat it from memory. And this bizarre programming code was not the only complication facing a user. The Mark 1 had a C.R.T. store, and in a C.R.T. store the trace always goes from left to right. So all numbers were stored and processed with the most [*sic* – he means least] significant digit on the left. (I imagine Turing could have changed this in the original specification of the machine, but he probably had no difficulty in doing arithmetic backwards himself and couldn't imagine it being a problem for anyone else.)

No surprise, then, that the programming manual was later redone in a more user-friendly way (for example, allowing decimal input) with the help of an assistant called Cicely Popplewell. In February 1951,

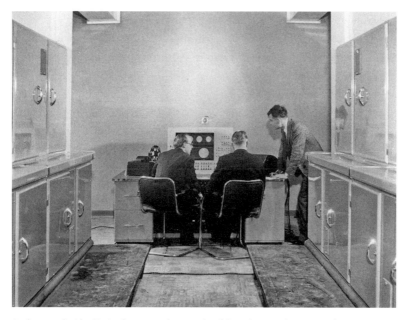

At the console. Alan Turing leans over the console of the rather swanky new Mark 1 computer in Manchester. (© University of Manchester)

the new Manchester Mark 1 was switched on, and Alan Turing made his first entry in the machine's logbook. One innovation of the new computer was a random-number generator: not the kind of thing you needed to churn out trajectories for missile development, but just perfect for computer games. In May, Alan gave his broadcast on the Third Programme. Christopher Strachey was listening in, and fired off a four-page letter about teaching (something about which he had some experience) as applied to machines (about which he was learning); oh, and mentioning his program for the Pilot ACE to play draughts. This was doomed – it had exhausted the small machine's memory – but the Manchester Mark 1 could do what the Pilot ACE could not. Alan provided the programming manual for the new Manchester Mark 1 computer, and Strachey translated his program. He also persuaded the computer to play *Baa, Baa, Black Sheep*. The random-number generator could also be deployed in the serious business of love letters:[2]

Darling Sweetheart

You are my avid fellow feeling. My affection curiously clings to your passionate wish. My liking yearns for your heart. You are my wistful sympathy: my tender liking.

Yours beautifully

M. U. C.*

Honey Dear

My sympathetic affection beautifully attracts your affectionate enthusiasm. You are my loving adoration: my breathless adoration. My fellow feeling breathlessly hopes for your dear eagerness. My lovesick adoration cherishes your avid ardour.

Yours wistfully

M. U. C.

All this was a step on the road to the programmer's Holy Grail: to write a program which could play a decent game of chess. Ever since those discussions in the pub in Wolverton had this been an objective. Donald Michie had been trying to write a chess algorithm:[3]

Alan told me that he and Champernowne had constructed a machine to play chess, in the sense of a complete specification on paper for such a machine. One could call it a 'paper machine' from which one could laboriously calculate move by move what the corresponding electronic machine would do were it constructed. Each move required perhaps half an hour's paper work as compared with the fraction of a second which a real machine would need. During a stay in Cambridge, Shaun Wylie[4] and I constructed a rival paper machine which we christened 'Machiavelli', from our two names, Michie-Wylie. On behalf of Machiavelli we then issued a challenge to the Turochamp (our name for the Turing-Champernowne machine), the game to be played by correspondence.

I.J. Good had found out about the Machiavelli already.[5]

---

* Manchester University Computer.

16 Sep 48

Dear Prof,

Pardon the use of the typewriter: I have come to prefer discrete machines to continuous ones.

I visited Oxford last week-end. Donald showed me a 'chess machine' invented by Shaun and himself. It suffers from the very serious disadvantage that it does not analyse more than one move ahead. I am convinced that such a machine would play a very poor game. […]

Yours, with best wishes,

Jack

Sept 18, 1948

Dear Jack,

The chess machine designed by Champ & myself is rather on your lines. Unfortunately we made no definite record of what it was, but I am going to write one down definitely in the next few days with a view to playing the Shaun-Michie machine. […]

Yours

Prof

History doesn't reveal whether the TuroChamp bested the Machiavelli. It does reveal that Champ could find Alan exasperating at times:[6]

My wife and I had invited Alan to stay with us at Shotover around Christmas. One morning an envelope arrived containing a piece of perforated tape, and the postmark (Manchester) led me to suppose that this was Alan's eventual response to our invitation. Four hours of hard work broke the code and I learnt that he would arrive at 2 a.m. the next morning, and that a parcel of food which he was sending must be unpacked and immediately dealt with according to some specified instructions. My satisfaction in deciphering the message was damped the next day when Alan explained it had only taken him half a minute to type the message on to the tape, as it was in standard teleprinter code, and I gathered he had hardly supposed it would occupy more than a few minutes of my time to reverse the process.

Chess Champ. David Champernowne in about 1959: Alan Turing's lifelong friend, mathematician, economist, and co-designer of the chess-playing algorithm TuroChamp. (By kind permission of the Provost and Scholars of King's College, Cambridge)

With the power of the Manchester Mark 1, moving from a paper algorithm to an electronic program became a possibility. The time was also right and everyone was onto the problem: Claude Shannon had written his paper in 1950, as had one of the computer experts from the NPL (Donald Davies, who had been able to deliver the working Pilot ACE). Alan began work on converting the TuroChamp into code, but the task wasn't completed. Instead, Dietrich Prinz, one of the Ferranti engineers, wrote a working chess program which ran on the Manchester machine in 1951. Alan's own written contribution to the chess-program literature came as part of a chapter on 'Digital Computers Applied to Games' published in 1953.

Jack Good's correspondence with Prof wasn't just about computers playing games. For example:

3 Oct 48

Dear Prof,

I have just read Adrian's 'The physical background of perception' (Oxford, 1947, pp. 96: lectures at Magdalen, Oxford). On page 9 it is stated that there are 10oooooooooo nerve-cells in the integrated nervous system. Presumably the vast majority are in the brain. There is an interesting passage on page 92: '... we can still accept the hypothesis that the physical basis of a memory is in the nature of a resonance pattern which may be established in local circuits throughout the whole of the cortex'. I like the idea of resonance patterns in spite of its vagueness. Have you heard of the TRANSISTOR (or Transitor)? It is a small crystal alleged to perform 'nearly all the functions of a vacuum tube'. It might easily be the biggest thing since the war.

> With best wishes and good luck in your new job,
>
> Jack

While all the fuss was going on about thinking machines, considerable thought was going into questions of neurology. It was no accident that the wireless debates had involved Sir Geoffrey Jefferson: certainly, he had weighed in on the question of sonnets, but as one of the country's foremost brain surgeons who had patched up soldiers with head wounds in two world wars, he had more claim than most to know what he was talking about. The other side of the question was how the brain thinks, and how it controls the body. If you regarded the body as a kind of machine …

Pattern recognition

In 1948 Norbert Wiener published a book. Wiener was a mathematician at the Massachusetts Institute of Technology – with the impeccable academic lineage of having studied with Russell in Cambridge and Hilbert in Göttingen; later on he worked with Claude Shannon, John von Neumann and others connected with the early development of computers. Wiener's book was called *Cybernetics, or control and communication in the animal and the machine*. Wiener opens up the crossover area where machines and animals have similar characteristics. He discusses how animals perceive and recognise things (by sampling, the same way that Shannon's proposal for voice encryption worked, perhaps?); he explores methods of communication and language, and he compares computers and the nervous system. He also uses plenty of equations.

We have already spoken of the computing machine, and consequently the brain, as a logical machine. It is by no means trivial to consider the light cast on logic by such machines, both natural and artificial. Here the chief work is that of Turing. [Wiener cites *Computable Numbers*.] We have said before that the *machina ratiocinatrix* is nothing but the *calculus ratiocinator* of Leibniz with an engine in it; and just as modern mathematical logic begins with this calculus, so it is inevitable that its present engineering development should cast a new light on logic.[7]

Wiener had visited NPL and discussed the idea of a thinking machine, or *machina ratiocinatrix*, with Alan Turing then, even though there was no hardware realisation of it at that stage. Despite the shortage of hardware, and the abundance of Latin, the ideas in Norbert Wiener's book had caught on. On a stifling September evening in 1949, a group of neuroscientists, engineers and physicists were concluding the inaugural meeting of a new society, called the 'Ratio Club', in an echo of Wiener's Latin tag. The purpose of the society was to discuss the new topic of cybernetics. It had few rules: one was that there should be complete freedom of expression, and another was that there should be no professors (because professors induce deference). It was invitation-only, and slightly anti-establishment; perhaps a bit like the Apostles, except without the aesthetes, spies and pretentiousness. As the first meeting broke up, it was suggested that some mathematicians be invited to join their number, to 'keep the biologists in order'.[8] Alan Turing (who was still not a professor) was suggested, the proposal was unanimously supported, and thereafter Alan assiduously attended its meetings. Later in 1950 I.J. Good also joined. In April and December 1950 Alan gave talks. One was on 'Educating a Digital Computer', covering the issues discussed in *Computing Machinery and Intelligence*, and was 'remembered as being particularly good with Turing on top form stimulating a scintillating extended discussion'.

Yet computing and machine intelligence were only part of what was interesting at the Ratio Club meetings. Some of the other presentations given to the Club heralded a shift in the direction of Alan's own interests. The biologists were giving new order to the mathematicians.

The Ratio Club. This high-energy group of non-professors debated the crossover area between maths, computing and biology. *Back row (l–r):* Harold Shipton, John Bates, W.E. Hick, John Pringle, Donald Sholl, John Westcott, Donald Mackay. *Middle row:* Giles Brindley, Tom McLardy, Ross Ashby, Thomas Gold, Albert Uttley. *Front row:* Alan Turing, Gurney Sutton, William Rushton, George Dawson, Horace Barlow. (By kind permission of the Provost and Scholars of King's College, Cambridge)

- 19 January 1950: 'Why is the Visual World Stable?' The presenter was Donald Mackay, a physicist interested in both machine intelligence and neuropsychology.
- 16 March 1950: Introductory talks from Ross Ashby and Horace Barlow. Barlow was a neuroscientist, a nephew of Sir Charles Darwin, but a member of the Club for his expertise in vision and neurology. Ashby had been corresponding with Alan Turing in 1946, about the potential for modelling adaptive processes on the unbuilt ACE, and writing papers, of which Alan Turing had a good collection, on subjects like adaptation and neural networks. One was entitled *Design for a brain*. Another in the collection is Ashby's later paper from 1952, entitled *Can a mechanical chess-player outplay its designer?*
- 18 May 1950: 'Pattern Recognition'. The presenters included Grey Walter, a natural sciences graduate of King's College, Cambridge, who had overlapped with Alan as a student there, and was now working on his invention, a robotic 'tortoise' which could find its

way back to its 'hutch' where it could recharge its electric supply; Albert Uttley, who had worked at the Telecommunications Research Establishment during the war, developing computing equipment; also Donald Mackay, Thomas Gold (then developing a theory on the workings of the inner ear) and Horace Barlow.

- 21 September 1950: 'Noise in the Nervous System'. The presenter was John Pringle, who had been an undergraduate and fellow alongside Alan at King's. He had proposed Alan for membership of the Club, and was now a neurobiologist.
- 5 April 1951: 'Shape and Size of Nerve Fibres'. The presenter was William Rushton. His work was on electrical excitation of nerve cells, but he was working on vision and, in particular, colour-blindness.

By the beginning of 1951 Alan's interest in patterns in biology had surfaced in a correspondence he was conducting with one or two professors, who were therefore barred from the Ratio Club. One of them was the scientist Professor J.Z. Young, best remembered for his experiments with the giant nerve of the squid. Young had given the 1950 Reith lectures on the BBC, on the subject of 'Doubt and Certainty in Science'. Lecture 2 was called 'Brains as Machines'; Lecture 7 was entitled 'The Mechanistic Interpretation of Life'. Among the influential sources cited by Young were someone called 'A.S. Turing' and Norbert Wiener. Part of the correspondence between Young and Turing was about the ability to recognise things:[9]

Dear Turing,

I have been thinking more about your abstractions & hope that I grasp what you want of them. Although I know so little about it I should not despair of the matching process doing the trick. You have certainly missed a point if you suppose that to name a bus it must first be matched with everything from tea-pots to clouds. The brain surely has ways of shortening this process by the process – I take it – you call abstracting.

Yours

John Young

Dear Young,

I think very likely our disagreements are mainly about the uses of words. I was of course fully aware that the brain would not have to do comparisons of an object under examination with everything from teapots to clouds, and that the identification would be broken up into stages, but if this method is carried very far I should not be inclined to describe the resulting process as one of 'matching'. [...]

I am afraid I am very far from the stage where I feel inclined to start asking any anatomical questions. According to my notions of how to set about it that will not occur until quite a late stage when I have a fairly definite theory about how things are done.

At present I am not working on the problem at all, but on my mathematical theory of embryology, which I think I described to you at one time. This is yielding to treatment, and it will so far as I can see, give satisfactory explanations of –

i)   Gastrulation.
ii)   Polygonally symmetrical structures, e.g., starfish, flowers.
iii)   Leaf arrangement, in particular the way the Fibonacci series (0, 1, 1, 2, 3, 5, 8, 13, ...) comes to be involved.
iv)   Colour patterns on animals, e.g., stripes, spots and dappling.
v)   Patterns on nearly spherical structures such as some Radiolaria, but this is more difficult and doubtful.

I am really doing this now because it is yielding more easily to treatment. I think it is not altogether unconnected with the other problem. The brain structure has to be one which can be achieved by the genetical embryological mechanism, and I hope that this theory that I am now working on may make clearer what restrictions this really implies. What you tell me about growth of neurons under stimulation is very interesting in this connection. It suggests means by which the neurons might be made to grow so as to form a particular circuit, rather than to reach a particular place.

Yours sincerely,

A.M. Turing

Alan Turing was trying something nobody had done before: to explain, in mathematical terms, the reasons for patterns seen in organisms. In February 1951 Alan wrote to his former colleague Mike Woodger at the NPL:[10]

> Dear Woodger,
>   Our new machine is to start arriving on Monday. I am hoping as one of the first jobs to do something about 'chemical embryology'. In particular I think one can account for the appearance of Fibonacci numbers in connection with fir-cones.
>   Yours,
>   A.M. Turing

Another professor may have had a hand in the changing direction of Alan's work. M.H.A. Newman had also moved back from the development of computing machinery as an end in itself. He was turning his attention back to topology, which was the subject of a textbook he had written in 1939. Topology is about shapes, spaces and surfaces, knots and folding. The maths involved is hard, but the subject is very visual, and it's about multi-dimensional spatial problems.

Together with Bertrand Russell, Newman was also pushing for Alan's election to a fellowship of the Royal Society. Alan was elected in March 1951 on the basis of his *Computable Numbers* paper. Congratulations came in by every post: from Mr Darlington, his headmaster from Hazelhurst, from Sir Charles Darwin and from Sir Geoffrey Jefferson. Mother sent a Greetings Telegram:[11] '– GREETINGS ALAN TURING FRS HOLLYMEADE ADLINGTON ROAD WILMSLOW = LOVING CONGRATULATIONS WELL DESERVED HONOUR = MOTHER +++' Alan also wrote to Philip Hall, his former tutor at King's in Cambridge, thanking him for his congratulations.[12]

> It is very gratifying to be about to join the Olympians.
>   The 'waves on cows' is just an example in my mathematical theory of embryology which I am busy on now. 'Waves on leopards' are rather

more elementary. A leopard skin, before the spots arrive is supposed an infinite thin sheet containing two chemical substances with concentrations U,V which react and diffuse. [Alan then sets out some equations.] What particular solution you get will depend on random disturbances just before instability started. Roughly speaking you get a random solution. By assuming there is black where $Z > Z_0$, yellow for $Z < Z_0$ you get very reasonable leopard skins. Certain slight variations of assumptions give you giraffes, zebras, cows. Cows are dappled. [...]

I hope I am not described as 'distinguished for work on unsolvable problems'.

A horse is not spherically symmetrical

Living things tend to start life as formless, spherical objects, like fertilised egg-cells or globs of embryonic cells. But as they grow and develop, shape and differentiation appear – the process of morphogenesis. How can that be? How would the embryo know to make itself symmetrical for some things (left and right) and to limit the number of things like arms and fingers, and yet allow blotchy patterns on animal skins? To answer these questions needed a theory. Rudyard Kipling's *Just So Stories*, with their nonsense explanations for how the elephant got its trunk and how the leopard got its spots, had been nursery reading at Baston Lodge. Alan Turing knew about the problem from the very beginning.

An embryo in its spherical blastula stage has spherical symmetry, or if there are any deviations from perfect symmetry, they cannot be regarded as of any particular importance, for the deviations vary greatly from embryo to embryo within a species, though the organisms developed from them are barely distinguishable. One may take it therefore that there is perfect spherical symmetry. But a system which has spherical symmetry, and whose state is changing because of chemical reactions and diffusion, will remain spherically symmetrical for ever. It certainly cannot result in an organism such as a horse, which is not spherically symmetrical.[13]

Now, Alan thought he had the solution. Tiny fluctuations in the concentration of biochemicals could make a difference. The trick is to introduce some instability, which, after a period, restabilises. This could be done by imagining two different biochemicals – morphogens – which were produced, diffused, and destroyed, at different rates. Now Alan could bring on the equations. There was only one problem. Equations would frighten the biologists. It would not be wise to assume that the biologists would all be as receptive as the Ratio Club members or J.Z. Young to being kept in order by mathematicians like A.M. Turing. So, in his paper, Alan would have to present both the key – the maths to demonstrate rigour – and also the decrypt to convince the biologists.

Certain readers may have preferred to omit the detailed mathematical treatment of §§ 6 to 10. For their benefit the assumptions and results will be briefly summarized, with some change of emphasis. The system considered was either a ring of cells each in contact with its neighbours, or a continuous ring of tissue. The system was supposed to be initially in a stable homogeneous condition, but disturbed slightly from this state by some influences unspecified, such as Brownian movement or the effects of neighbouring structures or slight irregularities of form. It was supposed also that slow changes are taking place in the reaction rates (or, possibly, the diffusibilities) of the two or three morphogens under consideration. These might, for instance, be due to changes of concentration of other morphogens acting in the role of catalyst or of fuel supply, or to a concurrent growth of the cells, or a change of temperature. [...] The conclusions reached were as follows. After the lapse of a certain period of time from the beginning of instability, a pattern of morphogen concentrations appears which can best be described in terms of 'waves'. There are six types of possibility which may arise.

(a) [...] This is the least interesting of the cases. It is possible, however, that it might account for 'dappled' colour patterns, and an example of a pattern in two dimensions produced by this type of process is shown in figure 2 for comparison with 'dappling'. [...]

(d) There is a stationary wave pattern on the ring, with no time variation, apart from a slow increase in amplitude, i.e. the pattern is slowly becoming more marked. In the case of a ring of continuous tissue the pattern is sinusoidal, i.e. the concentration of one of the morphogens plotted against position on the ring is a sine curve. The peaks of the waves will be uniformly spaced round the ring. [...] Biological examples of this case are discussed at some length below.

Alan's examples caused him some trouble, because 'isolated rings of tissue are very rare'; but he pointed to the tentacles of the freshwater polyp *Hydra* and the leaves of the woodruff plant as capable of being explained by his theory. What Alan's paper discussed next was 'chemical waves on spheres'. This was the problem of gastrulation – how a ball of embryonic cells folds in on itself – the beginning of turning a sphere into a horse.

The treatment of homogeneity breakdown on the surface of a sphere is not much more difficult than in the case of the ring. The theory of spherical harmonics, on which it is based, is not, however, known to many that are not mathematical specialists. Although the essential properties of spherical harmonics that are used are stated below, many readers will prefer to proceed directly to the last paragraph of this section.

You bet they would.

The operator ∇^2 will be used here to mean the superficial part of the Laplacian, i.e. $\nabla^2 V$ will be an abbreviation of

$$\frac{1}{\rho^2}\frac{\partial^2 V}{\partial \phi^2} + \frac{1}{\rho^2 \sin^2 \theta}\frac{\partial}{\partial \theta}\left(\sin\theta \frac{\partial V}{\partial \theta}\right),$$

where θ and ϕ are spherical polar co-ordinates on the surface of the sphere and ρ is its radius.

The computing of morphogenesis

With his new status as a fellow of the Royal Society, Alan's ground-breaking paper on *The Chemical Basis of Morphogenesis* was published in the Philosophical Transactions of the Royal Society in August 1952. Within days of publication, he received this from C.H. Waddington, Professor of Genetics at the University of Edinburgh:[14]

> I was extremely interested to read your recent paper on the chemical basis of morphogenesis. It is very encouraging that some really competent mathematician has at last taken up this subject. Although parts of your discussion were rather above my head, I found the general arguments extremely interesting and suggestive.
>
> I rather doubt, however, whether the kind of processes with which you were concerned play a very important role in the fundamental morphogenesis which occurs in early stages of development. Even in a case like the regeneration of tentacles in Hydra the final result seems to me more regular than one would expect from your type of mechanism.
>
> The most clear-cut cause of your type of mechanism seems to me to be in the arising of spots, streaks and flecks of various kinds in apparently uniform areas such as the wings of butterflies, the shells of molluscs, the skin of tigers, leopards, etc.

Although, as predicted, the maths was going to defeat the biologists, they had understood the conclusion clearly enough. Reaction-diffusion and maths could explain some of the basic observations about development of living organisms. And, what was more, it might be possible to go beyond the mere theory by using the Manchester computer to try out some numerical examples. That was going to be the next stage in Alan Turing's work.

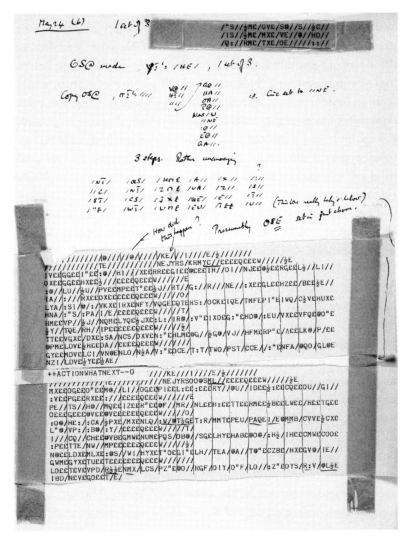

How did this happen? Alan's exasperation at a problematic routine. But the computer was not the only machinery going wrong for Alan Turing after the beginning of 1952.

The computing potential of the Manchester Mark 1 machine deserved its own conference, which took place in July 1951. Maurice Wilkes and Tommy Flowers attended, and a variety of papers were presented; consistent with the ambitions of Newman and Turing, these weren't entirely focused on technicalities of hardware design, logic or programming. Newman himself put forward ideas, which seem to have been rooted in the Bletchley experience, that automatic computers made new approaches to mathematical problems possible. For example, that a random walk 'Monte Carlo' method could be used to solve partial differential equations, and that 'probability methods might throw at any rate a feeble light on problems so large that rigorous methods leave them in complete darkness'.[15]

The final paper was one of great significance, presented by J.M. Bennett and J.C. Kendrew. As with Alan's developing ideas on morphogenesis, Bennett and Kendrew were exploring the zone where biology and computing might cross over. Bennett was Wilkes's first research student, who had been programming the EDSAC since its first days; Kendrew went on to win a Nobel Prize for unravelling the atomic structure of myoglobin using X-ray crystallography. Their paper at the Manchester computing conference described how you could get to the structure from the pattern of spots on an X-ray film, via a program run on the EDSAC. What they were describing was how to use the computer to create a 'contour map'. The contour map was exactly what Alan wanted the Manchester computer to produce to help him with the next stage in his work on the mathematics of organism development. Having set out the basics in his theory of morphogens, he was now going to tackle the remaining parts of the agenda he had set himself in that letter to J.Z. Young. This was a much tougher assignment: to set out the mathematical theory underlying the shapes of plants.

The first few months of 1952 buzzed with activity. In January Alan's conversation with Sir Geoffrey Jefferson, M.H.A. Newman and Professor Braithwaite of King's was broadcast. The first draft of *The Chemical Basis of Morphogenesis* came back from the reviewers with comments, and had (as is usual with scientific papers) to be revised and resubmitted. On 8 February Alan was to go to London to present his (as yet unpublished) work on reaction-diffusion models of morphogenesis to the Ratio Club, explaining how it could be developed through computer modelling. But, despite their apparent importance, none of these things was foremost in Alan Turing's life at that time. Alan Turing was an established logician, mathematician, and computer scientist. He had just created an entirely new science applying mathematics to developmental biology. He had been given an OBE for his secret war work and elected to a fellowship of the Royal Society. Yet, on the day before he was to give the talk at the Ratio Club, Alan Turing's entire world was turned upside down, because Alan Turing had met a young man in the street.

10

MACHINERY
OF JUSTICE

John Turing wrote that 'if the episode of "the burglar" had not proved, ultimately, so fatal to Alan, I suppose this might have been regarded as farcical'.[1] Indeed, it was tragedy, not farce. The facts were set out in the police statement which was read out in the Wilmslow Magistrates' Court on 27 February 1952.[2]

Detective Constable Robert Wills said he went to Turing's home with Detective Sergeant Rimmer on February 7. He said to Turing: 'On February 3 you visited Wilmslow Police Station and gave information about two men, who you alleged, had broken into your house. We have made inquiries, and now have some information. Would you please give us his description?' Turing replied: 'He's about 25 years of age, 5 ft. 10 inches, with black hair'. Constable Wills said: 'We have reason to believe your description is false. Why are you lying?'

The episode of the burglar

Alan's house had indeed been burgled. Alan had lost '2 medals, 3 clocks, 2 shavers, 2 pairs of shoes, 1 compass, 1 watch, 1 suitcase, 1 part bottle of sherry, 1 pair of trousers, 1 shirt, 1 pullover, and 1 case of fish knives and forks together of the value of £50.10.0.'[3] Accordingly, on 20 February 1952, one Harold Arthur Thacker had been committed to stand trial for the burglary at the forthcoming Knutsford Quarter Sessions. The following week, on 27 February, the court was not concerned with the burglary. It was concerned with Alan Turing.

> An Affair. Turing, it was alleged, replied: 'I tried to mislead you about my informant. I have been an accessory to an offence in this house. I have had an affair with him and I have regarded his conduct as a form of blackmail and have consulted my solicitor about him. His name is Arnold Murray. I picked him up in Oxford Street, Manchester.' Constable Wills read out a statement alleged to have been made by Turing in which he said he had committed an offence at his home with Murray. In an alleged statement Murray said he met Turing in Oxford Street and 'knew what he was by the way he talked'.[4]

If Thacker was the burglar, who was Murray, and what on earth was going on? Murray was the young man Alan had met in a pub in the Oxford Road and brought home to Wilmslow. Murray had presumably tipped off Thacker about the riches strewn around in Alan's house. Alan's statement doesn't sound like himself, but that is the way of police statements; the fact is that, in talking to the police about the burglary, Alan had told the constable how he thought he knew the identity of the thief – one of Murray's unpleasant friends – and had tried to protect Murray from liability as an accessory with the false description. But now the police were far more interested in why Alan should be harbouring apparent low-lifers like Murray. They were bound to ask themselves what possible reason there could be for Murray to be in Alan's house in the first place. And the possible reason made Alan an accomplice to whatever Murray had done together with Alan.

Norman Routledge while at King's in the early 1950s. One of Alan's more flamboyant friends, he later went on to become a revered maths teacher at Eton. (By kind permission of the Provost and Scholars of King's College, Cambridge)

In February Alan wrote to Norman Routledge in reply to his jokey letter about Christmas cards and Norman's career:[5]

> My dear Norman,
>
> I don't think I really do know much about jobs [...]. However I am not at present in a state in which I am able to concentrate well, for reasons explained in next paragraph.
>
> I've now got myself into the kind of trouble that I have always considered to be quite a possibility for me, though I have usually rated it at about 10:1 against. I shall shortly be pleading guilty to a charge of sexual offences with a young man. The story of how it all came to be found out is a long and fascinating one, which I shall have to make into a short story one day, but haven't time to tell you now. No doubt I shall emerge from it all a different man, but quite who I've not found out.
>
> Glad you enjoyed broadcast. [Jefferson] certainly was rather disappointing though. I'm rather afraid that the following syllogism may be used by some in the future
>
> > Turing believes machines think
> > Turing lies with men
> > Therefore machines do not think
> > Yours in distress
> > Alan

He also wrote to Robin Gandy, whose doctoral thesis Alan was supervising. Robin was supportive, as expected: 'How wretched; I can only say I hope you have a good lawyer & will get off; also that I think that other people are much less inclined to hold these things against one than is usually supposed.'[6] Unfortunately, some of those other people thought differently. Alan, forever the innocent in worldly matters, had not seen the unfortunate trend in policing in the early 1950s.

> While in 1937/38 the total of 4,448 indictable sexual crimes was made up of 73 per cent. heterosexual and 27 per cent. homosexual offences, by 1954, when the total had increased to 15,636, the respective proportions were 59 and 41 per cent. For every 100 homosexual crimes

recorded by the police in 1937/38, 232 were recorded in 1947, as many as 407 in 1951 and no fewer than 530 in 1954.[7]

During a period of some fifteen years covered by the Second World War and its immediate aftermath, homosexual offences of an indictable character increased between fourfold and fivefold. Offences of gross indecency between males went up from 320 to 1,686. The drive against homosexuals proceeded on a relatively minor scale until 1951, when it suddenly began to be intensified as the result of an incident of international proportions. This was the flight of the two British diplomats Guy Burgess and Donald Maclean in March 1951 and their defection to the Soviet Union.[8]

Burgess and Maclean were Cambridge Apostles, their flight was high profile, and the Americans had asked the British to weed out homosexuals from the security services because they were open to threats of blackmail. Whether there was indeed a link from those facts to the increase in prosecutions in the early 1950s is not proven; certainly there is no evidence that the Manchester police were mindful of these things, or even aware that Alan held secrets of far more significance than those pertaining to his private life. Their action was just part of what has been called 'the Purge': a massive crackdown on homosexuals instigated by the Home Secretary, Sir David Maxwell Fyfe, who regarded gay men as 'exhibitionists and proselytisers and [...] a danger to others'.[9]

So, on 27 February, Turing and Murray were also committed to follow Thacker to the Knutsford Quarter Sessions, to stand trial for gross indecency. Alan was bailed for £50; Murray was remanded in custody. Alan's photograph appeared in the local weekly paper. John picks up the story:[10]

One morning there arrived a letter for me from Alan – a remarkable thing of itself, neither a postcard nor a telegram. I opened it and the first sentence read 'I suppose you know I am a homosexual.' I knew no such thing. I stuffed the letter in my pocket and read it in the office. There followed the story of 'the burglar'. Alan then consulted his University friends, who strongly advised him to defend the case, instruct leading Counsel and heaven knows what else. In the meantime, would I kindly inform our mother of the situation? The short answer to that was that I would not. So I dropped everything and went to Manchester where I consulted Mr G., the senior partner in a leading firm of Manchester solicitors. He in turn saw Alan's solicitor, Mr C., who persuaded Alan to plead guilty.

At the end of the following month the Knutsford Quarter Sessions convened. A brief survey of the court's business in the years spanning Alan Turing's trial reveals its sad and petty nature.[11] The cases of burglary outnumber all other offences by some wide margin. Sexual offences are, though, common enough. Between January 1950 and January 1953, the court had to deal with no fewer than 21 defendants accused of gross indecency with another man. At this distance of time the details of each case are foggy, but we do have the defendants' pleas and the sentencing records. Not a single one of the 21 pleaded 'not guilty' (for comparison, one in three defendants accused of indecently assaulting a woman pleaded not guilty during this period, and a good number of them were acquitted or found guilty only of a lesser offence). As to sentencing, the courts put ten of the 'gross indecency' offenders on probation or conditionally discharged them, sent five to prison and handed out fines to the remaining six. One appalling case involved a man who was convicted, in September 1952, on two counts of gross indecency and a further count of attempting 'to commit suicide, against the Peace of our Sovereign Lady the Queen her Crown and Dignity'. This unfortunate individual was given a three-year prison sentence for the gross indecency offence and an additional sentence of six months (to run concurrently) for his suicide attempt. This is the system in which Alan Turing would find himself – a system in which mental distress could lead to a prison sentence.

Alan Turing and Arnold Murray, described in the court file as a spectacle frame maker, each faced six counts of gross indecency with the other. Not only was each of them accused of committing three acts of gross indecency, on three different dates, but each of them was additionally accused of being 'party to the commission of an act of gross indecency' with the other. This is curious: it is the only case of 'gross indecency' in this period which has this dualism – this risk of double jeopardy – in the indictment. Sentencing, in Alan's case, was different, too. But, before sentencing, there were pleas in mitigation.

Alan's former second-in-command in Hut 8 was called to testify as a character witness. This was C.H.O'D. Alexander, one of the Wicked Uncles of Bletchley Park who had written to Churchill in 1941. Alexander was now head of cryptanalysis at the highly secret GCHQ, as the Government Code & Cypher School had now become, and the mind boggles at the security difficulties involved. Alexander kindly mentioned that Alan was a 'national asset'. Another witness was M.H.A. Newman. With such luminaries on his side it was plain that the defendant was someone out of the ordinary.

The *Alderley, Knutsford and Wilmslow Advertiser* had nearly enough copy to fill a whole column:[12]

UNIVERSITY READER PUT ON PROBATION
To Have Organo-Therapic Treatment

[...]

PARTICULARLY HONEST

Maxwell H. A. Newman, a professor of pure mathematics at Manchester University, called as a witness for Turing, said Turing was particularly honest and truthful. 'He is completely absorbed in his work, and is one of the most profound and original mathematical minds of his generation,' said Newman.

Mr Lind Smith, defending Turing, said: 'He is entirely absorbed in his work, and it would be a loss if a man of his ability – which is no ordinary ability – were not able to carry on with it. The public would lose the benefit of the research work he is doing. There is treatment which could be given to him. I ask you to think that the public interest would not be well served if this man is taken away from the very important work he is doing.'

Defending Murray, Mr Emlyn Hooson said: 'Murray is not a university reader, he is a photo-printer. It was he who was approached by the other man. He has not such tendencies as Turing, and if he had not met Turing he would not have indulged in that practice and stolen the £8.'

The court did not need long to decide the matter. Taking up Lind Smith's suggestion, the judge made the following order.[13]

Turing:– Placed on Probation for a period of Twelve Months. To submit for treatment by a duly qualified medical practitioner at Manchester Royal Infirmary.
Murray:– Bound over to be of good behaviour for Twelve Months. When passing sentence, the Court took into consideration at the request of the prisoner, one outstanding offence, which he admitted.

Hollymeade (on the left), Alan Turing's home in Wilmslow. (© Claire Butterfield)

Murray's additional offence was that 'at Wilmslow, in the County of Chester, in the dwellinghouse "Hollymeade", Adlington Road, feloniously did steal £8 in cash, the property of Alan Mathison TURING. Contrary to Section 13 of the Larceny Act, 1916.'

Treatment of offenders

So Alan, the victim of the theft, was put on probation, and Arnold, who may have been a spectacle frame maker, or even a photo-printer, but was certainly dishonest, was let off – freer even than the other young men, similarly convicted, who had not even asked for a theft to be taken into consideration. Can this have been right? Given the differences in sentence at the Quarter Sessions, one might be tempted to assume that what happened to Alan Turing was exceptional, that he had been singled out for special treatment. What was the law?

> The punishment prescribed by law for homosexual offences is imprisonment. This is in accordance with customary legislative practice; but the general criminal law provides other methods by which the courts can deal with persons brought before them on criminal charges. These methods apply to persons convicted of homosexual offences just as they apply to other offenders. Probation is frequently used by the courts in dealing with homosexual offenders, and 24 per cent. of the persons convicted during 1955 of homosexual offences punishable by imprisonment were put on probation.[14]

Probation was still relatively new in 1952. In some form it had existed since 1887, essentially providing for an offender who was bound over – obliged to pay a fine if a further offence was committed during a given period – to be under the supervision of a named person. With the Criminal Justice Act 1948, the law was reformed and codified. The first two sections show its liberal intentions: they fall under the heading 'Abolition of penal servitude, hard labour, prison divisions and sentence of whipping'. Next come ten sections on 'Probation and Discharge'. Section 3 was about probation, which said that 'the court may, instead of sentencing [a convicted person], make a probation order, that is to say, an order requiring him to be under the supervision of a probation officer for a period to be specified in the order of not less than one year nor more than three years'. Further: 'a probation order may in addition require the offender to comply with such requirements as the court considers necessary for securing the good conduct of the offender or for preventing a repetition by him of the same offence or the commission of other offences'.

But 'treatment' such as was ordered by His Honour Judge J. Fraser Harrison was not 'requirements for securing good conduct or preventing the commission of other offences'. 'Treatment' was something for people with mental disorders:[15]

4. *Probation orders requiring treatment for mental condition*

(1) Where the court is satisfied, on the evidence of a duly qualified medical practitioner appearing to the court to be experienced in the diagnosis of mental disorders, that the

Revelations in the *Alderley, Knutsford and Wilmslow Advertiser*, 29 February 1952. (Manchester Evening News)

University Reader Sent For Trial With Another Man

AT a special court in Wilmslow on Wednesday, Alan Mathison Turing (39), F.R.S., single, University reader, of Adlington Road, Wilmslow, and Arnold Murray (19), unemployed, B o n c a r n Drive, Wilmslow, were committed for trial at Knutsford Quarter Sessions on March 31, on three charges of gross indecency.

Detective Constable Robert Wills said he went to Turing's home with Detective Sergeant Rimmer on February 7. He said to Turing: "On February 3 you visited Wilmslow Police Station and gave information about two men, who you alleged, had broken into your house. We have made inquiries, and now have some information. Would you please give us his description?"

Turing replied: "He's about 25 years of age, 5 ft. 10 inches, with black hair".

Constable Wills said: "We have reason to believe your description is false. Why are you lying?"

AN AFFAIR

Turing, it was alleged replied: "I tried to mislead you about my informant. I h a v e been an accessory to an offence in this house. I have had an affair with him and I have regarded his conduct as a form of blackmail and have consulted my s o l i c i t o r a b o u t him. His name is Arnold Murray. I picked him up in Oxford Street, Manchester.

Constable Wills read out a statement alleged to have been made by Turing in which he said he had committed an offence at his home with Murray.

In an alleged statement Murray said he met Turing in Oxford Street and "knew what he was by the way he talked".

Turing told him he worked on the Electronic Brain at Manchester University. The statement gave details of alleged offences at Turing's home on three dates.

MATERIALLY CORRECT

When a copy of Murray's statement was served on Turing he was alleged to have said: "The statement is materially correct".

Turing reserved his defence and Murray said he had nothing to say.

Turing was allowed £50 bail, but Murray was remanded in custody. Murray was granted legal aid.

mental condition of an offender is such as requires and as may be susceptible to treatment but is not such as to justify his being certified as a person of unsound mind under the Lunacy Act, 1890, or as a defective under the Mental Deficiency Act, 1913, the court may, if it makes a probation order, include therein a requirement that the offender shall submit, for such period not extending beyond twelve months from the date of the order as may be specified therein, to treatment by or under the direction of a duly qualified medical practitioner with a view to the improvement of the offender's mental condition.

It is quite evident from the inconsistency of the sentences being dished out at the Knutsford Quarter Sessions that in 1952 the courts could not make up their minds whether homosexual offences were being committed because the offenders were wicked, or because they were unbalanced. Alan Mathison Turing, MA, PhD, OBE, FRS, was ordered to receive 'treatment by a duly qualified medical practitioner' with a view to the improvement of his mental condition. He was going to be dealt with as a mental case.

It was textbook thinking in the post-war period that homosexuality is a form of mental abnormality, calling for therapeutic measures. In various pieces of published research, doctors earnestly tried to find the link. Doctors D. Curran and D. Parr studied records of 100 of their homosexual patients: 'only' 49 per cent showed significant psychiatric abnormalities. Thirty per cent of these cases were on the doctors' books because of a criminal charge.[16] Dr F.H. Taylor studied 96 men who had been remanded to Brixton Prison on being charged with a homosexual offence. Thirty-four out of the 66 'pseudo-homosexuals' had some form of mental abnormality.[17] In a third analysis 'the proportion of homosexual cases with associated psychiatric abnormality was estimated at 57 out of 113 cases'.[18] The good doctors were chasing their tails by assuming the thing they were trying to prove. The abnormality they had discovered was homosexuality itself.

The received wisdom was bunk. An academic study was carried out at Oxford University on offenders convicted in 1953 who were ordered to have probation with 'treatment' under Section 4. The 414 offenders who received Section 4 orders also included people of both sexes, convicted of theft, indecent exposure, heterosexual offences, violence and attempted suicide. The breakdown of 'medical diagnoses' of these unfortunate people shows no meaningful difference in diagnosis between the 11 per cent who were homosexual offenders and the remainder of the group, giving the lie to the idea that homosexuality is a special clinical condition.[19]

Cycling, chemicals and the couch

Thus in 1952, if you were not going to be punished for gross indecency, you could be ordered to be treated for your mental condition. As to the purpose of the treatment, according to the Wolfenden Committee, appointed in 1954 to conduct an inquiry into the law and practice relating to homosexual offences:

> There are broadly three possible objectives: (i) a change in the direction of sexual preference; (ii) a better adaptation to the sexual problem and to life in general, and (iii) greater self-control. Treatment is not generally specifically aimed at achieving only one of these objectives.

'Treatments' attempted for a homosexual condition have included severe and fatiguing bicycle riding, surgery, visits to prostitutes, aversion therapies of various types (electric shocks, sniffing repulsive chemicals, fluid deprivation, inducement of anxiety etc.), hypnosis, fantasy satiation, religion, drugs and psychoanalysis. In Alan Turing's case, cycling was not suggested; the treatment he got consisted of drugs and psychoanalysis. It could, possibly, have been worse: aversion therapy using electric shocks was reported to be successful in 1967.[20]

Various types of drug have been suggested over the years for the treatment of homosexuality. Earnest researchers had startling disregard for the interests of their subjects. One example is probably more than enough:[21]

> A 1940 report claimed that the administration of metrazol was capable of liberating the fixation of libidinal development responsible for homoerotic dispositions and making psychosexual energy free once more to flow through regular physiological channels. In this study, men and women from the ages of nineteen to thirty-four were treated with metrazol, inducing grand mal convulsions up to fifteen times per person. In one case, though nine treatments seemed to have eliminated all homoerotic desire from a man, he was subsequently convulsed six more times in order to, additionally, eliminate all feminine traits from him as well.

Rather less extreme were experiments with hormone treatment. At first, homosexual men, thought to be too feminine, were given testosterone, but this didn't work: it appeared to heighten sex drive rather than change its direction. So then the researchers tried the opposite, to see whether oestrogen would depress sex drive. By 1949, they concluded that this, by contrast, did work:[22]

> The Criminal Justice Act, 1948, has emphasised the duty of the community to provide treatment for the habitual sexual offender. We decided to offer a course of hormone therapy to abolish libido temporarily in persons complaining of an uncontrollable sexual urge that had led to trouble. Libido was rapidly removed in all our thirteen cases. In view of the non-mutilating nature of this treatment and the ease with which it can be administered to a consenting patient we believe that it should be adopted whenever possible in male cases of abnormal and uncontrollable sexual urge.

One might complain that the Criminal Justice Act in fact said nothing about sexual offenders, let alone their prescribed treatment. One might also take issue with 'non-mutilating', in light of the observations made in earlier literature about the side-effects of hormone treatment. But the authors of this article in *The Lancet* were countering 'a widespread demand that habitual sexual offenders should be castrated'. The side-effects previously noted had included, 'after 75 days' therapy a swelling was felt below each nipple, and subsequently well-marked gynaecomastia developed. At the end of the treatment double testicular biopsy showed degenerative changes.' So, if you were a man given Stilboestrol, the drug of choice, you were likely to grow breasts and suffer genital degeneration.

The judge sitting in the Knutsford Quarter Sessions may or may not have had these thoughts at the back of his mind when passing sentence on 31 March 1952. In any case, it's not at all certain that he applied the law according to the book.

The administration of justice

A person put on probation under Section 4 of the Criminal Justice Act 1948 should have been shown to have a mental condition, which is susceptible to the treatment proposed. A medical report, or the spoken evidence of a medical practitioner, is the first step in the process. In Alan Turing's case, there is no indication that any such medical report or evidence was provided. Surely the no-juicy-bits-omitted *Alderley, Knutsford and Wilmslow Advertiser* would have mentioned something as significant as a mentally disordered university reader? And it was not only the procedure that was deficient. The actual treatment he received was probably illegal too. The Criminal Justice Act itself said that the court could not detail 'the nature of the treatment' in its order (and, it should be noted, the judge's order did not specify it), so how the organo-therapic treatment reported by the *Advertiser* came to be mentioned at all is unclear. Furthermore, under the Act, a probationer could refuse to undergo surgical, electrical or other treatment if it was reasonable to do so. There was even a law as to what was reasonable:

BILL OF RIGHTS – 1 W&M c.2

An Act declareing the Rights and Liberties of the Subject and Setleing the Succession of the Crowne.

The Lords Spirituall and Temporall and Commons pursuant to their respective letters and Elections being now assembled in a full and free Representative of this Nation takeing into their most serious Consideration the best meanes for attaining the Ends aforesaid Doe in the first place (as their Auncestors in like Case have usually done) for the Vindicating and Asserting their auntient Rights and Liberties, Declare That [...] excessive Baile ought not to be required nor excessive Fines imposed nor cruell and unusuall Punishments inflicted.

In 1689 the question of what amounted to 'cruell and unusuall Punishments' was first considered in the English courts. One Titus Oates had been complicit in the Popish Plot and convicted in 1685. His sentence was a fine of 2,000 marks, pillorying four times annually, life imprisonment, defrocking, being whipped from Aldgate to Newgate, and from Newgate to Tyburn two days later. In 1689 he petitioned for release from this sentence, and was pardoned and pensioned off. Unfortunately the case gave little guidance to judges in future centuries. To my mind, allowing a subject liberty only on condition of taking hormone injections and receiving psychotherapy might count as 'excessive Baile' and almost certainly as 'cruell and unusuall Punishment'.

In 1791 the Eighth Amendment to the United States Constitution was adopted. Exactly tracking the wording of the United Kingdom Bill of Rights 1688, this too prohibits cruel and unusual punishments. And, as you might expect in the United States, there is a lot of jurisprudence and commentary on what constitutes a cruel and unusual punishment. Any sentence which is new or 'contrary to usage' may be regarded as 'unusual', and the Amendment has been used to challenge a wide range of sentencing practices and prison conditions, and to improve the lot of offenders. The same principles ought also to apply by virtue of the European Convention on Human Rights. I do not think that it was legal to force Alan Turing to undergo hormone treatment.

The more justifiable part of the 'treatment' was the psychotherapy. A study by Dr Mary Woodward was published in an issue of the gloriously named *British Journal of Delinquency* in 1958, which has a blazon across its front cover bearing the words 'Special Number on Homosexuality'. Maybe that is enough to tell you all you need to know. Dr Woodward's patients were the homosexuals, mostly referred by the courts and probation officers, whom she treated in 1952 and 1953. Dr Woodward says that psychotherapy alone was the treatment given in all but 'five cases, which were also treated with the hormone method'. Her results are noteworthy, because, according to her conclusions, psychiatric treatment actually worked.[23]

> Treatment appears to be most successful (resulting in a loss of the impulse) with bisexuals who are under 30 years in age, who have not started overt homosexuality until their late 'teens and have not a very long habit of activity. This result can, however, be achieved with older patients, provided they are co-operative and can be given treatment over a long period. Although the strength of the homosexual impulse is little diminished, behaviour can be changed in the direction of greater control or discretion among older homosexuals with a long history of persistent activity.

For every psychiatrist like Dr Woodward, eager to find that their therapy was successful, there were plenty who knew that a finding of 'success' said more about the state of mind of the psychiatrist than that of the patient. Lytton Strachey had complained in a letter written in 1923 that 'psychoanalysis is a ludicrous fraud'.[24] The author of the Oxford University study referred to previously wrote: 'psychiatry to-day suffers from the exaggerated expectations of the general public. Mental treatment, like prison, cannot be expected to turn a recidivist thief into a reliable cashier or a confirmed homosexual into a happy husband and father.'

So, Alan's sentencing was procedurally flawed, partly illegal, and ineffective as to the rest. Not that much of this would have registered with any court in 1952 given the prevailing social attitudes. There was not much point in applying for the sentence to be quashed, as this would probably have resulted in Alan being sent to prison, ghastly publicity, and him losing his job. Furthermore, by being put on probation, Alan's conviction did not count as a 'conviction' by virtue of Section 12 of the Criminal Justice Act. Being put on probation, and being 'treated' because he had a 'condition', was illogical and wrong in principle, but it was the easiest way for him to keep his job and forget the whole nasty business. M.H.A. Newman was more than just a character witness for Alan at the end of March 1952. The University of Manchester has not retained personnel files from this era, but it seems that Newman was sufficiently autonomous in his department to square things with the university authorities.

The remaining question now was how Alan Turing would cope. To Philip Hall, who had congratulated him on his Royal Society fellowship a few months before, he wrote:[25]

Dear Philip,

Your letter very welcome. I am afraid I didn't make my communication very clear. I am both bound over for a year & obliged to take this organo-therapy for the same period. It is supposed to reduce sexual urge whilst it goes on, but one is supposed to return to normal when it is over. I hope they're right. The psychiatrists seemed to think it useless to try and do any psycho-therapy.

The day of the trial was by no means disagreeable. Whilst in custody with the other criminals I had a very agreeable sense of irresponsibility, rather like being back at school. The warders rather like prefects. I was also quite glad to see my accomplice again, though I don't trust him an inch.

Yours ever

Alan

So, Alan was going to take it with fortitude and good humour, if with scepticism when it came to the psychotherapy. Donald Bayley, his old colleague from Hanslope Park, said that Alan regarded the whole business as a 'joke', but this jollity may have been old-fashioned grinning and bearing it. At least the newspapers had been kind to Alan: apart from the intrepid *Alderley, Knutsford and Wilmslow Advertiser* there was little coverage, for there was a bigger crime story to fill the pages of the popular press that day. At the Old Bailey a male nurse, an Indian married to a German woman, was on trial for poisoning his wife's food, with the assistance of the housekeeper with whom he was having an affair. That was much more fun to read about than another routine 'gross indecency' sentencing, even of an FRS.

Orthogonal trajectories

The FRS had significant work still to do on his theory of morphogenesis. Having dealt with animal spots in his 1952 paper, it was time to turn to the problems of organism development in plants. Mapping the behaviour of chemicals diffusing across a two-dimensional surface had provided a possible explanation for the appearance of blotches on animal skins. But what about three-dimensional things like fir cones and the position of leaves on plant stems? This was the problem of phyllotaxis. Confusingly enough, important work on phyllotaxis had been done by a man called Church. Not, in this case, Alonzo Church, but Arthur Henry Church, who had written a book called *On the Relation of Phyllotaxis to Mechanical Laws* in 1904.

The first part of Church's book is entitled 'Construction by Orthogonal Trajectories' – in other words, looking at things sideways. Church explained that you could map the nodes from which leaves emerge from a plant stem onto a two-dimensional sheet, by imagining that you had made a vertical cut along the stem and unpeeled the skin. The nodes tend to spiral up the plant in opposite directions, but when laid out on the unpeeled sheet they sit in straight parallel lines, with the leaves at uniform intervals. These are called 'parastichies'. The number of parallel spirals – parastichy numbers – seem to belong to the Fibonacci series, as Alan had noted in his letter to J.Z. Young. Similarly, the arrangement of seeds in a sunflower head is typically one of spirals in opposite directions, and the numbers of spirals are also typically from the Fibonacci series. But what determines where a leaf node sprouts, or where a sunflower seed is positioned?

As Bernard Richards, Alan's last research student, observed, Alan's own thought process was to look at problems 'orthogonally'. Alan's reaction-diffusion theory might be able to explain all this.

> According to the theory I am working on now there is a continuous advance from one pair of parastichy numbers to another, during the growth of a single plant. During the growth of a plant the various parastichy numbers come into prominence at different stages. One can also observe the phenomenon in space (instead of in time) on a sunflower. Church is hopelessly confused about it all, and I don't know any really satisfactory account, though I hope to get one myself in about a year's time.[26]

To get to a satisfactory account, Alan would have to solve the partial differential equations on which his theory was based. By choosing a variety of inputs, the equations could be solved numerically using the Manchester Mark 1 computer. The output data were written onto graph paper by hand, and the graph paper was shaded to show points of concentration. Alan was using the idea of the contour map to model the growth and development of plants.

A short story

Mrs Dixon was the cleaning lady at the Royal Society-funded Computer Laboratory in Manchester. It was all in a day's work dealing

Phyllotaxis and Fibonacci –
The Turing drawings

Alan Turing's beautiful drawings in the King's College Archive in Cambridge were never written up by him, and considerable posthumous effort has been put in by scholars – notably Jonathan Swinton – to interpret them. They connect directly to the work done by Church, but Turing's theory went far beyond Church's work, which was largely descriptive and analytical. Church was trying to fit biology and mechanics together. Church saw the problem of shape as one of packing: how and where would a growing plant fit in the next floret or leaf node. Alan was going further: could his chemical theory of morphogenesis explain the emergence of florets and nodes in the places where they appear, and thus reveal the reasons behind Fibonacci series being found in fir cones and sunflowers?

The diagrams shown here illustrate some part of what Alan was doing with his mathematical models:

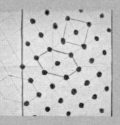

The first image is a split-and-unpeeled stem of a hypothetical plant. Spirals of leaf nodes can be followed upwards going left to right and (rather steeper in gradient) right to left. There are three spirals going left to right and five going right to left: adjacent Fibonacci numbers. The drawing also shows a lattice structure. Lattices emerge from the reaction-diffusion theory the same way that growth-points appear on a ring (as Alan had shown for the tentacles of *Hydra* in his paper on the *Chemical Basis of Morphogenesis*).

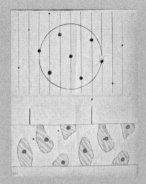

This image shows another unpeeled stem. Jonathan Swinton interprets the spots in the part of the drawing as growth-points whose positions on the stem are constrained like beads moving along a wire. Where they stabilise will depend on a small number of factors, including mutual proximity. The bottom part of the drawing appears to be the computer-generated solution to Alan's equations, redrawn by him as a map of concentration of chemicals; the top part of the drawing is a simplified representation identifying the components of waves which make up the pattern.

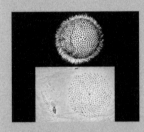

The upper image is a photograph of a sunflower head in the King's College Archive. The lower image is Alan's schematic redrawing, with the seed positions numbered. Spirals are clearly visible in both clockwise and anticlockwise senses. For sunflowers, the number of spirals in either sense typically falls somewhere on the Fibonacci series.

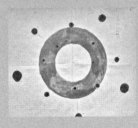

The final image is a theoretical representation of the growing tip of a stem. The doughnut shape is the 'apical meristem' just beneath and around the growing tip of a new stalk or in the centre of a flower like a sunflower or a daisy, which is the area in which growth and decision-making occurs, leading to the sprouting of leaves or florets. This schematic assumes that the florets appear in positions determined by the Fibonacci angle (close to 137.5° - a figure arrived at from the ratio of successive numbers in the Fibonacci series). But why do they do so?

Reaction and diffusion are not sufficient to explain Fibonacci numbers, as Alan's draft paper on applying morphogen theory to phyllotaxis acknowledges. Alan recognised that growth – the change in shape over time – would also change the geometry. The Kjell computer routine introduced an additional term into the equations to bring this into account; Professor Swinton thinks this may have been the key to the Fibonacci problem.

Alan Turing's phyllotaxis drawings were much neater and more attractive than his usual scruffy work done for his own benefit. It seems quite likely that the plan was for these to be used to illustrate a new paper, one that, with the rest of his work on Fibonacci numbers, was never completed.

Jonathan Swinton's appreciation of Alan Turing's drawings can be found in his book, *Alan Turing's Manchester*, published by Deodands Ltd.

with the untidy professors who left their notes about and got excitable if the blackboard was cleaned. She also expected science fiction to become reality in a place where they were operating an electronic brain. But to find an empty pair of trousers in the middle of the floor, like a time-travel scene with a vanished body, was a rather close encounter with the surreal.

Prof, the owner of the trousers, had simply gone for a run. He was supposed to change in his office – the Royal Society grant hadn't extended to changing rooms – and how the trousers had come to be where they were would remain a mystery. One person the runner encountered in the Cheshire countryside was Alan Garner, who later found fame as a writer of fiction for children. He was interviewed in 2012:[27]

> GARNER: It must have been about 1950, and when I was that age, which would have been 16–17, I was a serious athlete. And in those days people didn't go round clogging up the roads with jogging, so when I was out training, for me to see somebody else running was a very strange experience. And so I fell into talking with the strange man, who was quite a different shape from me: I was tall and thin, and he was stocky with a great barrel chest. It was strange to see him running because he didn't run, he was hammering the road: he was running into the ground, not over it. And he had a very extraordinary voice. It was an aristocratic English voice, high pitched, but he had the most remarkable sense of humour. I realised immediately once we got talking that we had quite a lot in common, which was a sense of the absurd. And that's how it grew. So we'd make loose agreements, you know, 'Will you be out running on Tuesday? Okay, I'll see you then.' And this went on for nearly three years until I went to do my military service.
>
> INTERVIEWER: Was it mainly running, when you would get together and talk with him?
>
> GARNER: It was *only* running. And I realised that was why he was doing it. He was thinking. He was using running to think.

Lyn Newman, Max's wife, was also part of Alan's inner circle after his move to Manchester. She too had a literary streak and was accepted on the fringes of the Bloomsbury group. Before the war she had produced a literary journal read by the likes of Virginia Woolf, Graham Greene, John Maynard Keynes and others. When her children were older she went on to write some more substantial books, as well as the foreword to Sara Turing's biography of her famous son. Alan was good with the children, as Newman's son William described:[28]

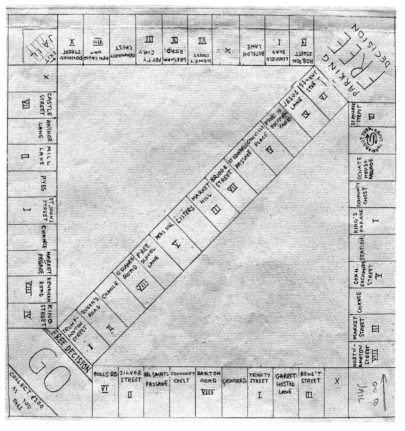

Monopoly, Newman-style. Alan was trounced by M.H.A. Newman's young son William, playing on this board of William's design. (© Bletchley Park Trust)

Alan now became a close family friend of ours. Despite his shyness he seemed to me more approachable than the other mathematicians who visited us. His choice of presents on my birthdays was especially thoughful and generous: a splendid steam engine one year, a little hobbyist's toolkit another. He played games with me and Edward,[29] and lost ignominiously to us at Monopoly. He came with us on a brief spring holiday in Criccieth, North Wales, where we rented a house. I remember Alan running on the beach, disappearing into the far distance and coming racing back. When he later bought a house in Wilmslow he would sometimes run the dozen or so miles from there to our house in Bowdon. Once I heard a noise in the early hours of the morning and went to the front door to find Alan dressed in running gear. He wanted to invite us to dinner and, thinking us all asleep but having nothing on which to write, was posting through our letter box an invitation scratched on a rhododendron leaf with a stick.

There was more to the game of Monopoly than this simple account might suggest.

I remember a later phone call from Alan, asking me if Edward and I had a Monopoly set. I replied that we did, and was delighted when he suggested we three might play a game when he next visited. At the time it didn't occur to me to mention that our 'set' was home-made, with a 'board' drawn by me on a sheet of paper. I could also have told him that its layout was somewhat unorthodox – I'd added an extra row of properties, diagonally connecting the 'GO' square to the square on the opposite corner. I cannot recall why I'd done this, but I may have wanted to provide a choice of routes. In the end Alan lost – neither Edward nor I showed him any mercy.[30]

And there was a bit more to the jog along the beach, too:

One afternoon of overcast skies and threatened rain, Alan changed into blue shorts and disappeared for a short time. When we asked him where he had been he pointed out a promontory of Cardigan Bay seven or eight miles north-west, inaccessible by road. We might have entertained the idea of walking there, but not without carrying a meal and macintoshes with us, scarcely without resting an hour or so on the way. For us it would have been a day's outing, but Alan did it between lunch and tea. From that day – although his normal walking gait was uninspired and almost shambling – we all felt awed, as if Mercury had joined our circle of acquaintances.[31]

Lyn Newman persuaded Mercury to read *War and Peace* and *Anna Karenina* – something to add to Alan's diet of reading which had, apart from the likes of John von Neumann, been limited to Jane Austen. There was another literary figure in his life, too: Alan had taken a holiday with Robin Gandy in 1948, a short let on a house in, predictably enough, Wales. A non-mathematician was in the party – P.N. Furbank, who was a scholar of English from Emmanuel College, Cambridge. Nick Furbank fitted in surprisingly well, maybe because he knew E.M. Forster, who was living at King's; he would go on to become Forster's biographer. Nick became a frequent participant in holiday expeditions and one of Alan's close friends. Maybe as a result of rubbing shoulders with authors, Alan ventured briefly into the uncertain world of fiction himself. There survives a six-page manuscript, which is not dated but seems likely to have been written in mid-1952. Here is the start:[32]

Alec Pryce was getting rather exhausted with his Christmas shopping. His method was slightly unconventional. He would walk round the shops in London or Manchester until he saw something which took his fancy, and think of some one of his friends and whether ^ who would be pleased by it. It was a sort of allegory of his method of work (though he didn't know it) which depended on waiting for inspiration.

When applied to Christmas shopping this method led to ^ variety of emotion just as much as when applied to work. Long periods of semi-despair wandering the stores, and every half hour or so, but quite erratically, something would leap out from the miserable background. […]

Alec had been working rather hard until two or three weeks before. It was about interplanetary travel. Alec had always been rather keen on such crackpot problems, but although he rather liked to let himself go rather wildly to newspaper men or on the Third programme when he got the chance, when he wrote for technically brained readers his work was quite sound, or had been when he was younger. This last paper was real good stuff: better than he'd done since his mid twenties when he had introduced the idea which is now commonly known as 'Pryce's buoy'. Alec always felt a glow of pride when this phrase was used. The rather obvious *double-entendre* rather pleased him too. He always liked to parade his homosexuality, and in suitable company Alec could pretend that the word was spelt without the 'u'. It was quite some time now since he had 'had' anyone, in fact not since he had met that soldier in Paris last summer. Now that his paper was finished he might justifiably consider that he had earned another young man, and he knew where he might find one who might be suitable.

- - -

Ron Miller was distinctly bored. He had been out of any job for two months, and he'd got no cash. He ought to have had 10/- or so for that little job he had helped Ernie over. All he had had to do was to hold the night watchman in conversation for a few minutes whilst the others got on with it. But still it wasn't really safe. Being questioned by the police was very uncomfortable.

Yielding to treatment

There was some self-analysis going on. In November 1952 Alan wrote to Robin Gandy that he had 'decided to have another, and rather more co-operative go at a psychiatrist. If he can put me into a more resigned frame of mind it would be something.' Without telling Mother, but at the prompting of Lyn Newman, Alan began consulting Dr Franz Greenbaum. Dr Greenbaum was a refugee from Nazi Germany who had settled in Manchester in 1939. He was trained in the Jungian tradition, which meant that perpetrating Lytton Strachey's 'ludicrous

Dr Greenbaum. (© Barbara Maher)

Looking Glass Message. Alan sent Robin Gandy letters printed on the Manchester computer, programmed to act as a typewriter. (© The Estate of P.N. Furbank and reproduced by kind permission of the Provost and Scholars of King's College, Cambridge)

AMT/D/4/6
Early 53.

```
//////////TO/R/G/
GANDY/TWENTY/NINE/CHESTRRFIELD/STREET/LEICESTER//////////DERR/RO
BIN///////////////THEY/HAVE/AT/LAST/FOUND/SOMEONE/TO/REFEREE/YOU
R/THESEIS/VIZ/BRAITHWAITE//////I/THINK/IT/WOULD/BE/BEST/IF/WE/HAD/
THEORAL/AT/CAMBRIDGE//AND/AM/WRITING/O/BRAITHWAITE/TO/SUGGETT/THIS
I/HAE/TO/GO/TO/A/CONFERENCE/AT/TEDDINGTON/ON/WEDNESDAY/TWENTY/FIFT
H/MARCHSO/WOULD/LEIK/TO/MAKE/IT/THE/WEEK/EBD/BEFORE/THAT/OR/THE/MO
NDAY/OR/TUESDA//I/SHALL/PROBABLY/STAY/WITH/NICK//////////HAV
E/HAD/ANTOTHER/GO/AT/THE/UNITY/OF/SCIENCE/ESSAY////I/THINK/THE/DUP
LICATE/TYPRS/MIGHT/BE/QUITE/INPORTAMT////DON"T/THEY/ANSWER/THE/QUE
STION/ABOUT/"WHAT/ISTIME/"/////////I/WAS/AMUSED/ABOUT/"IMPENETRAB
ILITY"/AT/FIRST/I/THOUGHT/IT/WAS/A/REFERENCE/TO/"THROUGH/TH/LOOKIN
G/GLASS/WHERE/HUMPTY/DUMPTY/SAYS/"IMPENERTABILITY/////THAT"S/WHAT
/I/SAY"/BUT/ON/LOOKING/UP/THE/REFERENCE/THOUGHT/PROBABLY/NOT/////
```

Love
Alan.

Gr letter on d. after.

fraud' was not part of the plan. Dr Greenbaum would take Alan's sexuality as he found it. Alan himself may not have seen the purpose of the consultations in quite the same light as his doctor. In December he reported to Nick Furbank that he had had a dream 'indicating rather clearly that I am on the way to being hetero, though I don't accept it with much enthusiasm either awake or in the dreams'. However, a resigned frame of mind was Dr Greenbaum's objective, and in any case, the discussions helped.

Alan was corresponding frequently with Robin Gandy, sometimes using the rather unorthodox medium of computer print-out. The Manchester computer was not provided with handy word-processing software, so each character to be printed had to be programmed into the machine. Programming the machine just to print out a note for Robin was, in some sense, a labour of love.[33]

> ////////////TO/R/O/GANDY/TWENTY/NINE/
> CHESTRRFIELD/STREET/LEICESTER///////////
> DEAR/ROBIN////////////////THEY/ HAVE/AT/LAST/
> FOUND/SOMEONE/TO/REFEREE/YOUR/THESEIS/ VIZ/
> BRAITHWAITE////// […]
>
>   Love
>   Alan.

Fortunately for Robin, Richard Braithwaite from King's (who had not only helped see Alan elected to a fellowship years before, but also moderated the Third Programme debate with Sir Geoffrey Jefferson) had stepped up to be his examiner. That, though, was not the principal thing on Alan's mind early in 1953, as he agonisingly set out in another computer-generated message:

Dear Robin
Sorry it really isn't possible to make your oral any earlier. Braithwaite won't have read it before the very end of March. […] Your last letter arrived in the middle of a crisis about 'den norske Gutt' so I have not been able to give my attention yet to the really vital part about the

theory of perception (but will do so at once). I was rather glad you didn't give me any detail of G's account of the interview. I suppose it was the one a few weeks ago, you meant. Will be able to stand it later.
Ever

> Alan

There was indeed a crisis. 'Den norske Gutt' (the young Norwegian) was Kjell Carlson, whom Alan had met on a holiday to Norway late in 1952. The holiday had been taken with a view to meetings which were illegal in England, and it seemed that the holiday had been a success. In 1953 Alan was naming his computer routines after Kjell and other things Norwegian (Ibsen, NorMast, NorPrint, MiddleKjell and so on). Alan explained the crisis in a letter to Norman Routledge:[34]

My dear Norman,

Thanks for your letter. I should have answered it earlier.

I have a delightful story to tell you of my adventurous life when we meet. I've had another round with the gendarmes, and its positively round II to Turing. Half the police of N. England (by one report) were out searching for a supposed boy friend of mine. It was all a mare's nest. Perfect virtue and chastity had governed all our proceedings. But the poor sweeties never knew this. A very light kiss beneath a foreign flag, under the influence of drink, was all that had ever occurred. Everything is now cosy again, except that the innocent boy has had rather a raw deal I think. I'll tell you all when we meet in March in Teddington. Being on probation my shining virtue was terrific, and had to be. If I had so much as parked my bicycle on the wrong side of the road there might have been 12 years for me. Of course the police are going to be a bit more nosy, so virtue must continue to shine.

I might try to get a job in France. But I've also been having psycho analysis for a few months now, and it seems to be working a bit. Its quite fun, and I think I've got a good man. 80% of the time we are working out the significance of my dreams. No time to write about logic now!
Ever

> Alan

Kjell. Theory.

We are concerned with a partial differential equation.

$$\frac{\partial U}{\partial t} = I U + G U^2 - H U V + \Phi(U) + J\left(\cos\frac{\pi z}{h} - 1\right) U$$

$$\frac{\partial V}{\partial t} = \varkappa(U^2 - V) + \mu \frac{\partial^2}{\partial z^2} H(U)$$

where $\Phi(U)$, Φ and I-J are linear operators invariant under congruences of the two-dimensional space. In effect they are functions of ∇^2.

As an approximation we replace the second equation by one of form.

$$V = \Lambda(U^2)$$

Suppose now that it is assumed that U and V are periodic in z with period $\frac{2\pi h}{}$ and in x with period $2\pi\rho$. Then

$$U = \sum A_{m,n}\, e^{i\left(\frac{mx}{\rho} + \frac{nz}{h}\right)}$$

$$V = \sum D_{m,n}\, e^{i\left(\frac{mx}{\rho} + \frac{nz}{h}\right)}$$

$$\text{if } \frac{\partial U}{\partial t} = \sum K_{m,n}\, e^{i\left(\frac{mx}{\rho} + \frac{nz}{h}\right)}$$

and if

$$\Phi(U) = \sum \phi\left(\frac{m^2}{\rho^2} + \frac{n^2}{h^2}\right) A_{m,n}\, e^{i\left(\frac{mx}{\rho} + \frac{nz}{h}\right)}$$

and

$$\Lambda(U) = \sum \lambda\left(\frac{m^2}{\rho^2} + \frac{n^2}{h^2}\right) A_{m,n}$$

The Kjell routine. Alan Turing named his phyllotaxis programs for the Manchester computer for Kjell Carlson. This page from his manuscript notes sets out the theory. (© The Estate of P.N. Furbank and reproduced by kind permission of the Provost and Scholars of King's College, Cambridge)

Alan was acting. If Alan could put on a stiff upper lip for Donald Bayley, he could also camp it up for the flamboyant Norman Routledge. Nothing remains to explain the remark about 'G's account of the interview' in Alan's computer print-out message to Robin Gandy. Moreover, police being nosy before the expiry of the year on probation was not what Alan needed; it would ensure he remained on their watch-list after the 12 months was up. To Robin, in a letter dated 11 March 1953, he was less forced:

> The Kjell crisis has now evaporated. It was very active for about a week. It started by my getting a P.C. from him saying he was on his way to visit me. At one stage police over the N of England were out searching for him, especially in Wilmslow, Manchester, Newcastle etc. I will tell you all one day. He is now back in Bergen without my even seeing him! For sheer incident it almost rivals the Arnold story.
>
> I've got a shocking tendency at present to fritter my time away on anything but what I ought to be doing. I thought I'd found the reason for all this, but that hasn't made things much better. One thing I've done is to rig the room next bathroom up as electrical lab. Am not doing very well over your vision model.
>
> Went down to Sherborne to lecture some boys on computers. Really quite a treat, in many ways. They were so luscious, and so well mannered, with a little dash of pertness, and Sherborne itself quite unspoilt.
>
> Love
>
> Alan

Sherborne recorded its own thoughts on the occasion:[35]

THE ALCHEMISTS

The Society met for the first time this term on Monday, March 9th [1953], at the Green when a paper on the Electronic Brain was read by Mr Turing. Several members of the audience had foreseen the possibility that they might not understand a word of what was said, but they could not have been more mistaken. Mr Turing made a very clear analogy between a stupid clerk, with his mechanical calculating device paper to write his workings on and his instructions, and the Electronic Brain which combined all these in one. All that was necessary was to put the instructions into a tape machine and the mass of wires, valves, resistors, condensers and chokes did the rest, the answer appearing on another tape. The Brain was, however liable to make mistakes and subtle checking devices were included to detect them. As yet it cannot do anything of its own accord, nor is it able to rectify its own mistakes. Slides were shown of the general layout of the machine and also of some previous ones made in the last century. The questions at the end of the meeting showed how much the Society had grasped the principles underlying the workings of the Electronic Brain.

It seems that the final sentence can be read in more than one way. Not all the well-mannered boys may have been mistaken about their inability to understand the Electronic Brain.

Perplication

There was also an attempt to grasp the principles underlying the workings of the human brain. With the Kjell crisis over, Alan had settled into the sessions with Dr Greenbaum. By May 1953, Alan wrote to Lyn Newman saying, 'Greenbaum has been making great strides in the last few weeks. We seem to be getting somewhere near the root of the trouble now.' He also told Lyn that 'it was worth anything to have his life remade'.[36] As was his way, Alan was making friends with the Greenbaum children too. In May 1953 Alan provided Maria Greenbaum, Dr Greenbaum's six-year-old daughter, with some hints for the holidays on how to solve a solitaire puzzle. Fortunately for Maria, the instructions were not in back-to-front 32-character code; quite the contrary, they were written in a very clear way and with a specially invented notation so she could work out what to do.

A set of Alan's own notes on mathematical notation came up for auction in 2015, costing the buyer over a million US dollars. This is one paper of at least two which Alan wrote about reforming mathematical notation. Alan claimed it was difficult to understand the thinking behind traditional dy/dx usage for differential calculus, which might seem a bit rich from the Prof who used to write in Gothic German. Alan's notebook was written up during the war, when he was working alongside Robin Gandy. It is interesting in part because Gandy himself wrote in it, when he inherited it after Alan's death: 'it seems a suitable disguise to write in between these notes of Alan's on notation; but possibly a little sinister; a dead father figure, some of his thoughts which I most completely inherited.' In 1955, like Alan before him, Robin had decided to write down his dreams; in Alan's case, Dr Greenbaum had requested Alan to do so to assist with his analysis. Robin had also been trying to improve the conventions of notation himself:[37]

> Dear Robin,
>   Shall look forward to seeing you May 30. Have only been asked for reference by Cambridge so far. Can't say I'm exactly surprised by the unsatisfactory response of your audience, re notation. I got just such a reception when I talked about deduction theorem at Bristol, about 3 or 4 years ago. It's certainly rather discouraging.
>   Treasure hunt date suits me fine.
>   Yours
>   Alan

The treasure hunt referred to was not another attempt to dig up silver ingots imprudently buried during the war. These were practical games, with a hint of Lewis Carroll, as described by Sara Turing in her biography of Alan:[38]

> Some of the clues were of Alan's invention. Thus he prepared, for each competitor, a bottle containing red liquid, either malodorous (labelled 'The Libation') or drinkable ('The Potion'): when the bottle was emptied the next clue was revealed – written in red ink on the back of the label. As another clue he made up the word '*perplication*'. Over his copy of *Les Faux Amis ou les Trahisons du Vocabulaire Anglais*

he put a convincing dust cover inscribed with the title, 'Dictionary of Uncommon French Words'. He then inserted the word *'perplication'* with an explanation in French involving references to Maimonides and treasure hunters. This done, he prevailed on a bookseller to place it on one of his shelves.

The clue in French may have been prompted by Alan's recent reading matter, Stendhal's *Le Rouge et le Noir*, recommended by Nick Furbank, who was a participant in the treasure hunts. In a letter to Nick, written in confident French, in which he comments on the book, Alan tells him he is planning to make his will. Alan asks Nick to be his executor: 'je voudrais bien qu'un ami sympathique se concerne de mes lettres et mes petites affaires, en cas d'aucun malheur.'[39]

In July 1953 Alan went to hospital to have his oestrogen implants removed. In another letter to Nick written at this time he says he wants a permanent relationship, mentioning the 'problem of etiquette'

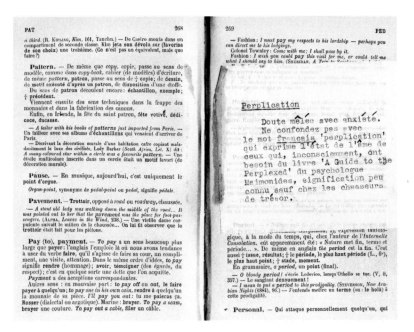

Treasure hunt. Alan's clue in an obscure French dictionary. (Author)

of 'how to behave in a variety of different types of company, to which one doesn't really belong oneself'. 'Perplication' was, according to Alan's dictionary entry, French for doubt mixed with anxiety.

As well as such 'petites affaires', there was greater business to attend to: a new hunt for the sources of shapes of secret living things. In the summer of 1953 Alan took on a new research student, Bernard Richards. Bernard was a 21-year-old mathematics graduate whose task was to solve Alan's morphogenetic equations using the techniques of classical analysis. The problem to which the equations would be applied was a deep one, from the darkest, remotest places on earth.

11

UNSEEN WORLDS

On 7 December 1872 a ship sailed from Sheerness. She had three masts and an auxiliary steam engine and displaced 2,300 tons. For a warship she was rather weakly armed, carrying only two guns. However, she carried six scientists, and her mission was not an aggressive one, unless you happened to live at the bottom of the sea. For her purpose was to explore the mysteries of the deep ocean and test some of the wilder notions of science, in particular a theory by one Darwin concerning the evolution of living things. She was HMS *Challenger*, and she was away from home for over three years, which was time enough to do an awful lot of dredging.

Wonderful ooze

The official report of the voyage of HMS *Challenger* runs to 50 volumes. Some volumes, such as XVIII, are in several parts, too big to bind in a single book. It sounds dry. It isn't. The Preface to Volume XVIII begins:[1]

> The significance of the Radiolaria in regard to the relations of life in the ocean has been increased in a most unexpected manner by the

discoveries of the Challenger. Large swarms of these delicate Rhizopoda were found not only at the surface of the open ocean but also in its different bathymetrical zones. Thousands of new species make up the wonderful Radiolarian ooze, which covers large areas of the deep-sea bed, and was brought up from abysses of from 2000 to 4000 fathoms by the sounding machine of the Challenger. They open a new world to morphological investigation.

Part 3 of Volume XVIII consists entirely of illustrations of the weird and fascinating creatures dredged up from the wonderful ooze. Some look so alien that they could only be from the fevered imagination of a science-fiction writer; in fact it took the biologist Professor Ernst Haeckel ten years of peering down a microscope to catalogue, measure and draw them. They captured Alan Turing's imagination, and opened a new world to morphological investigation. Bernard Richards picks up the story.[2]

To some it might seem an anomaly that two topics, namely high-speed electronic computers and tiny sea creatures, at opposite ends of the scientific spectrum, can be connected by computer science. The late Dr. Alan Turing proposed that the many shapes observed in minute sea creatures, the species 'Radiolaria', could be explained by postulating the diffusion of saline into a growing spherical body resulting in tentacles ('spines') growing out at equilibrium. The present author took this postulate of Turing's and set out to prove, or otherwise, the validity of this theory by solving the differential diffusion equations and examining the resultant observable shapes.

One can introduce U, a substance which represents a 'growth dimension' e.g. the radius of the sphere, and V an alien invader-chemical which is anti-growth, a sort of poisoning factor. One then sets up the diffusion equations for the state of affairs in the single cell as regards these two substances. It is assumed that V will diffuse uniformly into the cell.

The starting point is therefore the two equations:

$$\frac{dU}{dt} = \Phi(\nabla^2)U + GU^2 - HUV$$

$V = (\tilde{U}^2)$, the mean value over the sphere.

The mathematics hereafter becomes very complicated and very long. It can be found in great detail in some 30 pages in the thesis 'Morphogenesis of Radiolaria', written by the author. Given a solution for U, it is necessary to discover what three-dimensional shape this produces. This is not an easy thing to do when one not only needs to know where the spines are on the sphere but also the diameter of the sphere and the length of the spines which protrude therefrom. Here the computer played a role.

The computer involved, the Ferranti MARK 1, had no visual display output facilities, but only a very primitive line-printer restricted to numerical and alphabetic characters. So it was decided to use that printer to print contour maps of the surface.

The contour maps predicted the position of spines on 6- and 12-spined Radiolaria species. There was still more to discover in the field of botany as well. Alan Turing was also working on a new project: an outline of the development of the daisy. The daisy is like a sunflower: the yellow bit in the middle is in fact made up of hundreds of little florets, arranged in spirals. The florets have to be packed in, and the morphogen equations might explain how the arrangements come about.

God's holy pantomime

On 11 February 1954 Alan Turing made his will. There were to be pecuniary legacies for the family and for Mrs Clayton, his housekeeper; Robin Gandy was to get his papers, and the estate was otherwise to be split five ways, between Mother, Robin, Nick Furbank, David Champernowne and Neville Johnson.

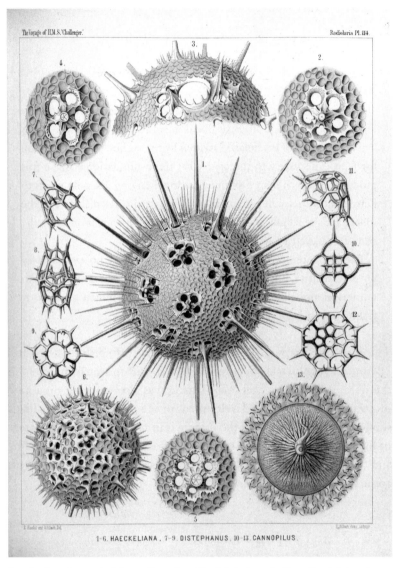

Samples from the wonderful ooze. Examples of Radiolaria drawn by Ernst Haeckel show how weird the creatures can be. (Science & Society Picture Library)

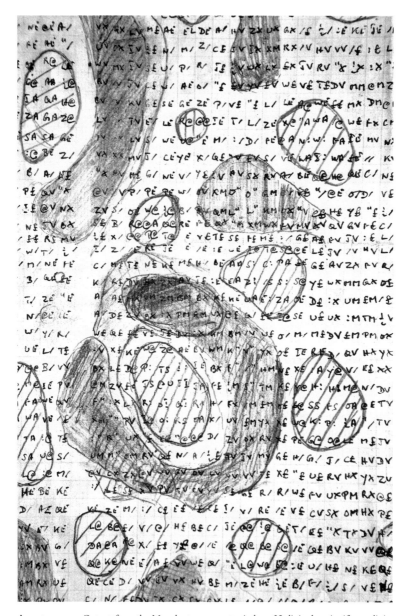

A contour map. Output from the Manchester computer in base 32 digits, less significant digit first, indicates levels of chemical intensity and can be converted into a map. (© The Estate of P.N. Furbank and reproduced by kind permission of the Provost and Scholars of King's College, Cambridge)

To his friends and neighbours he seemed to be in good spirits, and he was beginning to work on something new and highly ambitious.

Dear Robin,

It's a long time since I've heard from you. Have you got yourself a boy or something? Or are you writing out your consistency proof?

I've been trying to invent a new Quantum Mechanics but it won't really work. How about coming here next week end and making it work for me?

Yours

Alan

I'm getting slightly hetero, but it's fearfully dull.[3]

In March 1954 Alan sent Robin Gandy a set of postcards, each containing epigrammatic and whimsical 'Messages from the Unseen World'. They were a bit like treasure-hunt clues. Numbers I and II have not survived, but here are the rest:

III   The Universe is the interior of the Light Cone of the Creation

IV   Science is a Differential Equation. Religion is a Boundary Condition

V   Hyperboloids of wondrous Light
Rolling for aye through Space and Time
Harbour those Waves which somehow might
Play out God's holy pantomime

VI   Particles are founts

VII   Charge $= \frac{e}{\pi}$ arg of character of a 2π notation

VIII   The Exclusion Principle is laid down purely for the benefit of the electrons themselves, who might be corrupted (and become dragons or demons) if allowed to associate too freely.

On Monday 7 June 1954, on a wet Whitsun weekend, and without warning, Alan Turing died.

During the Whitsun holiday [wrote John, Alan's brother], I had taken
one of my daughters to the cinema and arrived home about 10.30 p.m.
In my absence the Manchester police had telephoned to say that Alan
had been found dead in his house. Late as it was I telephoned to the
ever kindly and shrewd Mr. G., who promised to meet me at the station
in Manchester the next morning. He took me to the police and thence
we went to the mortuary where I identified Alan's body. He had taken
cyanide. By great good fortune my mother was on holiday in Italy and
did not return home until after the inquest.[4]

The date for the inquest had been set with remarkable haste. The
note of the phone call which came through while John was at the
cinema late on Tuesday shows that the inquest was due to take place
on Thursday, only two days later. But the unseemly haste might have
been a blessing:

Mr. G. advised me strongly not to instruct Counsel to appear at the
inquest and told me of the unhappy course which some other cases
had taken before this coroner, a retired doctor who could not abide
lawyers. The possibility of establishing death by accident was minimal;
the best we could hope for was the considerate verdict of 'balance of
mind disturbed'. He was right and I accepted his advice. At the inquest
itself this soon became apparent: there were present some eight or
nine reporters, some from the national press, with pencils poised and
waiting for the homosexual revelations. They were disappointed. I gave
evidence briefly. The coroner asked me a few perfunctory questions.
The verdict was as anticipated.

In 1954 self-murder was still a crime, and the newspapers of the time
even report cases of afflicted persons who were on trial for having
attempted to commit suicide. Criminal suicide could have lasting
legal consequences, such as invalidating a life insurance policy. But if
the deceased person had killed himself while the balance of his mind
was disturbed, then it was not a criminal act. The 'unhappy course'

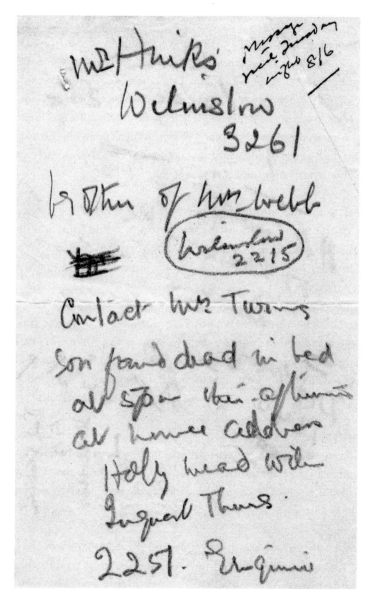

Sara Turing was in Italy, and John Turing was at the cinema, when news of Alan's death reached Guildford, only 36 hours before the inquest was due to take place. (By kind permission of the Provost and Scholars of King's College, Cambridge)

referred to by Mr. G. was this: instead of the hoped-for verdict of accident, the case would go the other way, and Alan would be found to have committed a 'felo de se'. This, together with the risk of revelations feared by John, would have escalated the family's grief to nightmare proportions.

The third book

The inquest had not closed the door on the publicity problem, and Mother was already on her way back.

MOTHER OF 'BRAIN' EXPERT FLIES HOME
EVENING NEWS REPORTER

MRS. TURING, mother of Dr. Alan Mathison Turing, the mechanical brain expert, who was found dead in bed at his home in Adlington Road, Wilmslow, is believed to be flying back from Italy where she was spending a holiday.

An inquest was being held at Wilmslow to-day.

Dr. Turing, who was 41, was a reader in the theory of computing at Manchester University and was regarded as a brilliant mathematician. […] The 'brain' which he played such a big part in developing was capable of carrying out more calculations in a day than the average man can do in a lifetime.[5]

As usual there was a long report in the *Alderley, Knutsford and Wilmslow Advertiser*.[6]

SCIENTIST FOUND DEAD ON BED, HAD TAKEN CYANIDE
A FINDING that Dr. Alan Mathison Turing (41), of Hollymeade, Adlington Road, Wilmslow, committed suicide by taking poison while the balance of his mind was disturbed, was recorded at the Wilmslow inquest on Thursday, last week.

Dr. Turing, of Manchester University, was a reader in the theory of computing, and set the problems for the electronic brain.

Mrs Eliza Clayton, Mount Pleasant, Lacey Green, Wilmslow, a daily housekeeper, said she last saw Dr. Turing alive on June 3, when he appeared to be in his usual health. On Tuesday, she went to the house at about five o'clock in the afternoon and saw a light burning in the bedroom, which was unusual. She entered the house and found Dr. Turing lying dead on his bed. The clothes were pulled up to his face and there was froth over his mouth.

George Williamson Gibson said he saw the doctor either on Saturday evening or Sunday dressed in shirt sleeves and grey pullover – 'his usual untidy appearance.' He knew the doctor by sight but had not spoken to him beyond 'good morning.'

Sergeant L. Cottrell said that Dr. Turing was lying on the bed with the clothes pulled towards his chest. There was a white frothy liquid about the mouth with a faint smell of bitter almonds. On a table at the side of the bed was half an apple from the side of which several bites had been taken.

Dr. C. A. K. Bird, a Macclesfield pathologist, who had conducted a post mortem examination, said death was caused by asphyxia due to cyanide poisoning.

A man of Dr. Turing's knowledge could not have swallowed some of the contents without knowing what would happen. He did not think death could have been accidental, and thought the apple was used to take away some of the taste.

There were also reports in the *Daily Express* ('He fed the "brain"'), *Daily Dispatch* ('Did own cooking'), and a handful of other local papers, but mercifully none of the feared revelations. The *Daily Telegraph* carried a full report, describing the findings in Alan's home laboratory:[7]

WIRES FROM LIGHT

A small adjoining room had been used for electrical experiments. 'Connected with the light from the centre of the ceiling were two wires connected to a transformer, which was on the table,' [Police Sergeant Cottrell] said. 'On this table was a cooking pan with a double container in the centre. One contained a liquid and the centre container a black substance.

'Two electrical wires led to the pan, one connected with the handle and the other with the black substance,' he said. 'The contents of the pan were bubbling and there was a strong smell of bitter almonds.'

In a jam jar he found a liquid which also smelt strongly of bitter almonds. In another room he found a small bottle labelled 'Poison: Potassium Cyanide.'

Dr. C. A. K. Bird, pathologist, of Macclesfield, said the jar contained cyanide solution. Referring to the electrical apparatus, he said: 'I did not quite understand what it was for. There was some electrolysis going on.'

POISON DISSOLVED

Replying to the Coroner, he said he thought Dr Turing had dissolved the poison in water, possibly for the purpose of more easily ingesting it.

The Coroner: You are satisfied that this was not an accidental inhalation of cyanide fumes? – Yes, it must have been swallowed.

Dr. Bird added that he thought it probable the apple was to take away the taste.

John was searching for explanations as well. He was less worried about the amateur chemistry than what Mother would find out on her return:

In those unhappy days in Manchester I visited Alan's psychiatrist who told me a great deal about Alan that I did not know before – among other things that he loathed his mother. I refused to believe it. He then handed me two exercise books in which Alan had entered such matters as psychiatrists require of their patients, including their dreams. 'You had better take them away and read them,' he said, adding that there was a third book, probably in Alan's house.

[handwritten at top] Alan Turing was out walking on Monday, June 7 & spoke to a neighbour on his walk. This woman was employed by Mr Scott, The Croft, Dean Row, Wilmslow. E.S. Turing

POST MORTEM EXAMINATION REPORT

Name of deceased:	Alan Matheson TURING
Observers present at examination:	Chief Inspector Hudson, Sergeant Cottrell, no. 128
Date and Time:	8 p.m. Tuesday 8th. June 1954 (See back)
Place where performed:	The Public Mortuary, Wilmslow.
Estimated time of death:	More than 24 hours previously, in my opinion/during the night of 6th to 7th. June 1954. There was slight residual warmth of abdomen.

EXTERNAL EXAMINATION Apparent age: 40 Height: 5 ft. 10 ins.

Rigor Mortis: Very strong spasm of all the muscles of the body, the left arm was flexed at 90 degrees across the body, the right was extended, the body lying to the left, but also he was on his back.

Nourishment: Good

Marks of violence or identification marks, tattoo marks, etc.: There was gross cyanosis of the body which was red cyanosis, not blueness. There was slight frothing of the mouth and this froth smelled faintly of bitter almonds.

[handwritten] Charles Alan Kingsley Bird taken before me. Coroner.

INTERNAL EXAMINATION **CRANIAL CAVITY:**

Skull: Normal.

Brain: Congested, showed acute oedema and red cyanosis which on cutting was very obvious. The brain smelled of bitter almonds.

THORACIC CAVITY:

Mouth, Tongue, Larynx: Filled with froth, otherwise normal. The jaw was in powerful spasm.

Trachea, Lungs and Pleurae: Showed acute oedema, thin watery fluid filled the bronchi and the lungs and this smelled strongly of bitter almonds.

Pericardium, Heart, and Blood Vessels: Normal anatomically, but the blood of the whole body was red, and not blue and de-oxygenated. With the characteristic smell of bitter almonds this was typical of cyanide poisoning.

ABDOMINAL CAVITY:

Oesophagus: Contained froth.

Stomach and contents: Contained four ounces of fluid which smelled very strongly of bitter almonds, as does a solution of cyanide.

Peritoneum, Intestines and Mesenteric glands: Normal

Liver and Gall Bladder: Normal, but pale in colour as the blood in it was redder than normal.

Pancreas: Normal

Spleen: Again was red, and smelled of bitter almonds.

Kidneys and Ureters: Similar

Bladder and Urine: Normal

Generative Organs: Normal

Are all other organs healthy: Yes, with the exception of the colour of the organs, which were all redder than normal.

The cause of death as shown by the examination appears to be: Asphyxia, due to Cyanide poisoning. Death appeared to be due to violence.

Any further remarks: I was present at the house of the deceased when a solution of Cyanide (identified by characteristic smell) and a bottle of Potassium Cyanide in solid form were found. The smell of the solid was identical with the smell of the organs, and no other chemical smells the same.

Signature and Qualifications: *Dr Bird* L.R.C.P., M.R.C.S., D. Path.

Address: Scriven Lodge, Upton, Macclesfield, Cheshire.

The post-mortem report. (By kind permission of the Provost and Scholars of King's College, Cambridge)

I viewed the two books in my hotel with horror but I was still bent on proving the accident theory and decided I had better read them. I wish I had not. His comments on his mother were scarifying. I returned the books to the psychiatrist the following day.

There remained the problem of the third book for it was essential that it should be found so that it would not fall into my mother's hands.

There is little in the record to indicate the actual relationship between Alan and his mother after Julius Turing's death in 1947. Only two letters to Mother for this seven-year period were preserved. One is a typewritten letter (surely Sara would have disapproved of him using a typewriter; Alan's handwriting was no excuse for that kind of social lapse) of January 1952, in which Alan barely veils his exasperation with Mother's plans following a generous bequest when Aunt Sibyl had died. The other is from January 1954, about whether a Ministry of Supply document left by Alan at Mother's house was secret. There is nothing of a remotely private nature. It remains unknown to what extent Sara may have selected what should go into the archive. Her assertion, backed up by the forces marshalled by John to minimise her pain, was that all was sunny and open between them.

Now Sara Turing was heading for Manchester, in grief and shock, and in dismay at the perfunctory inquest. The evidence pointed one way, but the full facts could only make things worse for her. John put his energy into co-opting all those he could find, including Alan's own solicitors, into the cover story of an accident.[8]

CROFTON, CRAVEN & CO.
SOLICITORS.

17th June 1954

Dear Turing,

A.M. Turing Deceased.

Many thanks for your letter of the 15th instant. I obtained a key from the police yesterday and made a further search of the house and am quite satisfied that there are no documents left which may cause us any anxiety.

The mathematical books etc. are in a trunk in the lounge and Furbank and Gandy are going to the house this weekend when I expect they will arrange to remove it all. [...] There are a number of books on the shelf which were awarded to Alan as prizes which your mother may also like to have. I handed to Furbank the O.B.E. medal and a seal (which I think may be a family seal) and suggested that he should hand these over to Mrs. Turing. I cannot trace the 'third book' which you mention but I have not yet spoken to Dr. Greenbaum about it.

Yours sincerely,

W.N. Cookson

Confidential

21st June, 1954

Dear Cookson,

I am glad to be able to tell you that my mother had decided to prolong her stay with Mrs. Newman in Cambridge, and I understand that she will be going to stay with Dr. and Mrs. Greenbaum on Friday or Saturday of this week. I think by this means she should be spared most of the publicity which I understand is still active in the local papers circulating in Wilmslow.

I have the greatest confidence in Dr. Greenbaum, but I could wish that my mother had not decided to go and stay with him, as I feel certain that she will cross examine him very thoroughly and this will be of no advantage to anybody.

Shortly after my return home I spoke to Dr. Greenbaum on the telephone and I feel confident that I told him of the impressions that my mother had formed about the cause of my brother's death. I should, however, be obliged if you would speak privately to Dr. Greenbaum again on this subject stressing that my mother has persuaded herself that it was an accident.

Yours sincerely,

J.F. Turing

CLEGG (WILMSLOW) LTD.
Funeral Directors.

23 June 1954

Dear Mr Turing,

This morning I visited various newsagents, and have found the posters in question have been removed. I have also acquainted the Police with your desires, concerning your brother's death and I think I can count on their co-operation in this matter, should your dear mother call upon them. I have also spoken to the manager of our local paper requesting them to help to back up the theory of misadventure; so I trust no unfortunate conversation will reach the ears of Mrs Turing, whilst in Wilmslow and district.

Sincerely yours,

A J Killick

It wasn't just that the papers might harp on about the suicide verdict; the possibility of 'revelations' was still live. And there was still the problem of the missing exercise book in which Alan had exposed his soul.

CROFTON, CRAVEN & CO.
SOLICITORS.

June 1954

Dear Turing,

I have your letters of the 21st and 24th instant. I have been in touch with Dr. Greenbaum and have mentioned your mother's visit and he fully appreciates the position and I think we may rely upon his discretion in the matter. He referred to the paper in which the man Roy is mentioned and I have told him that I can show him the papers in my possession if he can arrange to call at the office. [...]

30th June 1954

Dear Turing,

<u>A.M. Turing Deceased.</u>

I to-day had a call from Mr. Gandy and you will be pleased to hear that he found the missing book which I have arranged for him to hand to Dr. Greenbaum. [...] I have looked up the file of papers again but the man there concerned was Arnold Murray. I have not come across the name 'Roy' but I am having a further search through the papers in readiness for Dr. Greenbaum's call.

Yours truly,

W.M. Cookson

The 'man Roy' remains a mystery. The efforts of Mr Killick to suppress the local papers in preparation for Sara Turing's visit seem to have succeeded. What Mr Cookson and Dr Greenbaum had discovered still remains unclear. Whether there is a clue here to the last days of Alan's life is difficult to say.

Unending inquiry

Much has been written on the difficult subject of Alan's death. Criticism has been levelled at the legal process, the unlikely speed with which the inquest was convened and concluded, and the thinness of the evidence heard by the coroner. Some have seen in all this an apparent readiness of John to exclude embarrassing evidence from the inquest, but there hadn't been time. Some of the other criticisms may be valid, and the actions to help Mother cloud the picture. The possibility that Alan did not commit suicide deserved full consideration, but it's unclear that a fuller examination would have helped anyone come to terms with what had happened.

First, there is a rather dotty theory that Alan was murdered. This seems to be based on a statement in the pathologist's report of the post-mortem examination. Completing the pre-printed form, the pathologist said:[9]

THE CAUSE OF DEATH AS SHOWN BY THE EXAMINATION APPEARS TO BE: Asphyxia, due to Cyanide poisoning. Death appeared to be due to violence.

Violence? One word is not enough to make a conspiracy. Cyanide can have neurotoxic effects, causing the victim to suffer tremors and convulsions. And Alan had had a large dose: the same pathologist's report indicates that there was cyanide in his brain, lungs, blood, stomach, spleen, kidneys and elsewhere, and that his blood was red yet deoxygenated. Moreover, 'the jaw was in powerful spasm'. It was not a comfortable death, but it was not a murder. What needs to be taken more seriously is the circumstantial evidence which people find hard to reconcile with a suicidal mind. That means it is right to reappraise the instinctive view originally held by John, that the whole business was a tragic accident. One example will suffice, though there are several similar accounts:[10]

> Professor James Lighthill worked closely with Alan Turing and was with him the night before he died. In fact he said he had never seemed more normal and had just bought two new pairs of socks which is the last thing he would have done if he intended to commit suicide. He describes the experiment he had been doing with cyanide just as Sara Turing describes. She had warned him not to get cyanide on his hands when she last saw him. 'Wash your hands Alan and keep your nails clean and do not put your fingers in your mouth' she had warned in vain.

That maxim from Mother has a ring of authenticity, but it cannot explain the fact that Alan died in his bed, when the laboratory was in the next-door room; nor does it explain the half-eaten apple at the bedside. In its report of the inquest, the *Manchester Guardian* had published the statement by Dr Bird, the pathologist, about the purpose of the apple. Sara objected strongly to the opinion expressed by Dr Bird in his evidence:[11]

The apple was certainly not to mitigate the taste. Alan used rashly to test his solutions with his finger: he may thus have transferred the cyanide to the apple which he customarily ate at bedtime. It is unlikely that in the state suggested he would have planned to lessen the taste – still less been able to go downstairs, fetch an apple & come up again & get into bed.

Sara firmly believed Alan's death to be an accident; as we have seen, everything was done to encourage her in that view. To support her theory, Sara left no stone unturned in her own examination of Alan's house. She found a teaspoon in his laboratory; knowing that potassium cyanide is used in some techniques for gold-plating, and that Alan had gold-plated another spoon, she concluded that this must show Alan's

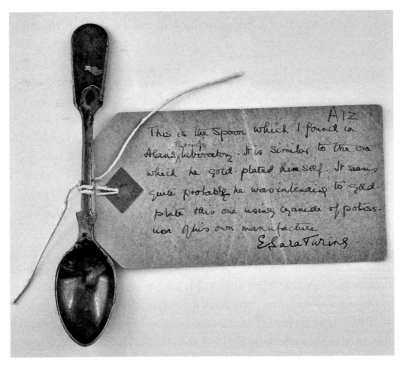

This labelled teaspoon, lodged by Sara Turing alongside more traditional materials in the King's College Archive, shows how she clung to the 'accident' theory of Alan Turing's death. (By kind permission of the Provost and Scholars of King's College, Cambridge)

handling of the cyanide to have been in the course of an experiment. She deposited the spoon in the King's College Archive along with her files, Alan's letters, and a collection of other written materials.

On 13 June 1954 Nick Furbank wrote to Robin Gandy:[12]

> I think I told you most of the things I had to tell you about Alan over the telephone. As I said, there appeared to be no messages. The brother was unsympathetic, I thought. He was desperately keen to keep any scandal out of the papers, and on the other hand, very anxious to have Alan's public distinction brought out in the obituaries. [Alan] had written but not posted an acceptance for some reception by the Royal Society, which perhaps argues against much premeditation. I don't know. The way he talked about suicide before, and his general way of doing things (plus the fact that he had rearranged his letters in labelled packets) still makes me think he could not have done it just on impulse.

To regard Alan's death as an accident may be unfair to him. Why assume, just because he was untidy and disorganised, that he did not know the risks of using notoriously poisonous chemicals? Why assume that he was not choosing cyanide to reassert control of his own destiny?

What troubles many, particularly those who were close to Alan at the time, is that it is not at all clear why Alan might have felt suicidal that terrible Whitsun weekend. How could it be that Alan felt such helplessness, inner loneliness or entrapment, and could see only one way out? It can be very difficult to accept that things could have been so badly wrong without anyone suspecting that it was so. The reaction described by Donald Bayley is how many people felt:

> My Dear Robin.
>
> There is probably no need to tell you how grieved and shocked I am about the Prof. When I first heard last Thursday, my immediate reaction was that it was half expected; it's only latterly that the full realisation of what it means is making itself felt.

Can you throw any light on why he did it? I thought at first he was in trouble again but there was no hint of it in the Press. Even if so he knew we would support him as we had before. It's a complete mystery to me because he did enjoy life so much – apart from that one aspect, and I thought he'd begun to have hope about that too.

Yet suicides do not follow a single pattern, and you do not have to look far to find troubles in Alan's life. Ultimately, all the speculation is pointless. Robin Gandy said – and he, as the closest of Alan's friends, knew best – 'Some things are too deep and private and should not be pried into'.[13] And I think we should now accept his advice.

Epilogue

ALAN TURING DECODED

Alan Turing's untimely death prompted a big postbag of letters of condolence and sympathy. Many summarise the writer's impressions of Alan; from the many I choose this, from Sir Geoffrey Jefferson to Sara Turing, written in October 1954:[1]

Dear Mrs Turing,

Late though the hour is I must thank you for your letter about your Alan in whom the lamp of genius burned so bright – too hot a flame perhaps it was for his endurance. He was so unversed in worldly ways, so childlike, it sometimes seemed to me, so unconventional so non-conformist to the general pattern. His genius flared because he had never quite grown up, he was I suppose a sort of scientific Shelley. I was early impressed by Professor Newman's care for him and his great opinion of him. He will miss him dreadfully. You yourself were Alan's great friend or so I gathered from him. I trust that I have said nothing to wound you. You said 'Don't answer' but I felt that I must. What happened in that last hour may well have been as you say: Alan was very absent minded. I only hope that he was not unhappy – or is not now.

Sincerely yours

Geoffrey Jefferson

He had real genius, it shone from him.

Impressions of Alan Turing are nowadays likely to be formed from the various portrayals of him in broadcast media. Notable and stirring performances by Derek Jacobi, Ed Stoppard and Benedict Cumberbatch stand out. There is of course a danger that Alan becomes defined by these interpretations; but there is more complexity to the man than any script or any actor can bring out without becoming tedious. Sometimes Alan was imperious, sometimes patient; invariably generous; often witty and sometimes biting; awkward in company not involving his peers. Contemporaries almost always mention his ability to connect with children. Mrs Webb, Alan Turing's next-door neighbour at Wilmslow, had a small boy called Rob:[2]

> Alan seemed to both of us to be so much better during the last few months. He was easier to talk to and much more friendly, and of course, always so nice with Rob. Rob loved to go and call on him and persuade him to come out for a game … the last time they were together I came upon them in the middle of a discussion as to whether God would catch cold if he sat on the wet grass!

His generosity was noted by everyone as well. John Turing remembered how different Alan was from the standard Turing model:[3]

> My father in retirement was always 'doing accounts' and insisted that my mother accounted for every penny of the housekeeping money in detail and when I had an allowance from him, before I was earning, I had to do the same. He made no secret of the fact that his own ambition was to be rid of the expense of his two sons! When he died he left my brother £400 more than myself because by some obscure calculations he reckoned that I had cost him that much more. My brother very sensibly and generously put this money straight into a trust for [a daughter of John's] who had been born too late for [Julius] to include in his will.

Harking back to the days at Baston Lodge, and one of the daughters of the house, John said:

Many years later, after her mother died, [Hazel Ward] achieved her life's ambition and became a missionary. It is very typical of my brother, who grudged every penny spent on himself, that he generously and of his own accord, financed Hazel in this. Quite unknown to me he had kept in touch with her for thirty years or more and they remained firm friends.

Contrary to John's own experience – unhappy and uprooted from his family and native environment – the Wards at Baston Lodge had provided a good family home for Alan's childhood years, even if they had provided no teddy bear. Alan was not a soldierly child and he was certainly unusual. You might expect that to be a recipe for disaster in a houseful of would-be Haigs, but Alan's achievements must be in part attributed to the nurture provided by a tolerant foster home and understanding schools. On the other hand, Alan's complex relationship with his parents may well have been coloured by their early distance and later proximity.

It has been a challenge for Alan Turing's biographers to describe his relationship with the family, and I have not found it easy either. Family relations are complicated. What is clear enough is that Alan's interests were quite different from those of his family. Alan's friends were not liked by the Turings, and the best thing back at home was Alan's ability to engage immediately with the children. Alan turned up dutifully for Christmases but not for other family occasions (for example, John turned out with Julius and Sara for Aunt Jean's funeral in December 1945, but Alan did not).

Late in life, Sara found an outlet for her energies in putting together a well-researched and well-written biography of her lost son. It is clearly a hagiography, and John cautions us not to take it at face value when it comes to relationships. By his account Mother found Alan exasperating, and he spent much of his adult life trying to swim against her stream of moral maxims. In his July 1953 letter to Nick Furbank, Alan reported: 'Mother has been staying here, and we seem to be getting on a good deal better. I have been subjecting her to a good deal of sexual enlightenment and she seems to have stood up to it very well.'[4] It must have been an ordeal for them both. It's very far from clear what Mother made of Alan's conviction for gross indecency. The family didn't discuss this, and the topic of Alan's death was equally avoided. What was talked about was his genius. People who had known Alan and worked with him were in awe of his unmatched intellect, so this was the first thing they would mention. Even to the obstinately non-technical Turings – those who did not know the existence of the *Entscheidungsproblem* and had never heard of phyllotaxis – it was apparent that Alan had something special which the rest of us do not. Sara's biography makes that light shine very brightly.

His achievements, as well as his insight, were massive. Alan Turing was not quite 42 years old when he died. In the course of his short life he had solved one of the great theoretical problems of mathematics; laid down the theory of multi-purpose programmable computing machines; designed a codebreaking machine which provided priceless intelligence to the Allied war effort; designed and written manuals for the first computers, and used them to explain patterns found in living things. By any reckoning this is an astonishing curriculum vitae. Yet Alan Turing's name was hardly known outside a small circle of mathematicians and computer scientists until the present century. Why is that?

Perhaps Alan is best known, now, outside that academic circle, for his work on the Enigma codes. Cue music. Specifically, Mussorgsky. *Pictures at an Exhibition* was the theme music for the BBC's series *The Secret War*, which was first broadcast in 1977. At home we had a small portable black-and-white television which, for family viewing, had to be placed on an unstable side table with spindly legs. The table was far too flimsy for the TV, but that's how it had to be set up so that the long retractable aerial would actually catch enough signal to enable viewing. (Other families had big colour TV sets connected to rooftop aerials, but not the Turings.) We huddled round the set to see Episode 6, entitled 'Still Secret', hoping to decipher from the snowstorm of portable-TV reception what had actually happened at Bletchley Park and Alan Turing's role in it.

Until very recently the activities of the GC&CS at Bletchley Park were a completely closed book. All participants were sworn to lifetime secrecy. In the mid-1970s only anecdotal and vague explanations could be given. None of the participants was permitted to explain; only one formal grainy photo of Alan Turing was shown in *The Secret War* and there was no real description of what he'd done. His was just another name in a roll call of clever and eccentric men of the professor type. After the series, life went back into the sharper focus of normal service, where few had heard of Alan Turing and absolutely nobody could spell the name correctly. And no one in the family was much the wiser about Bletchley Park or Alan Turing's role there.

THE UNIVERSITY OF NEWCASTLE UPON TYNE
COMPUTING LABORATORY

27th November, 1975

Dear Mrs. Turing,

I thought you would like to know that the Government have recently made an official release of information which contains an explicit recognition of the importance of your son's work to the development of the modern computer. They have admitted that there was a special purpose electronic computer developed for the Department of Communications at the Foreign Office in 1943. Their information release credited your son's work with having had a considerable influence on the design of this machine.

Further, a book has recently been published in the United States entitled 'Bodyguard of lies' which describes the work of the Allies during the war. This book credits your son as being the main person involved in the breaking of one of the most important German codes, the Enigma Code and thus implies that his work was of vital importance to the outcome of World War II. This latter information in the book 'Bodyguard of lies' is not, of course, official information but nevertheless it will, I believe, enable many people to obtain a yet fuller understanding of your son's genius. I am very pleased that this is now happening at last.

Yours sincerely,

Brian Randell

Sara Turing was 94 when she received this letter and living in a nursing home. She died the following March and I am unsure whether she ever had a proper opportunity to understand the true significance of her son's achievements. A facsimile of Professor Randell's letter is on display in the museum at Bletchley Park, next to a first-edition copy of Sara's 1959 biography of Alan.

The first English book on Bletchley Park, *The Ultra Secret* by F.W. Winterbotham, was published in 1974. It did not mention Alan Turing. The first significant description of his contribution was made by Gordon Welchman in *The Hut Six Story*, published in 1982 – a book which (in an unhappy parallel with Alan's own experience) led to Welchman losing his own security clearance and receiving a virulent letter of rebuke from the British government.

The treatment of Gordon Welchman was probably the high-water mark of official resistance to disclosures about Bletchley Park. By the 1980s the tide was changing. First, Andrew Hodges's masterly biography (and I have to acknowledge a huge debt to this work and his scholarship) explained to the world just how much there was to Alan Turing, and revealed in a majestic way the Shakespearian tragedy of Alan's hidden life and terrible end. Even so, it took a fuller revelation of the achievements of Bletchley Park to bring Alan Turing's story to a wider public. This has happened slowly as successive governments have felt able to release more material into the public domain; with that the role that Alan played has been put into sharper focus.

Bletchley Park itself has been the main player in a Shakespearian story of its own. After the war, the GC&CS (now rebranded as GCHQ) moved away from Bletchley, leaving the mansion, the wooden huts, and the sturdy if inelegant brick-built blocks to seek other tenants. Those tenants were varied and eclectic, but by 1991 the overall ugliness of the site, the decay of the wartime buildings, and the enthusiasm for town-perimeter supermarkets meant that regeneration was planned. 'Regeneration' would mean bulldozing the old buildings and putting in place something new and usable by a modern world. Only when a group of veterans assembled for a farewell party was a decision reached to save the site for posterity.

Imagination, determination and courage were needed in abundance to achieve that, and only recently has the majority of the Bletchley Park site been restored and reopened to visitors, who can now find out for themselves what actually happened there.

Alongside the rescue of Bletchley Park there has been spectacular growth of the market in personal computers. Before the 1990s it was rare to find that anyone had a computer in their home, and the uses to which it could be put were extremely limited. All that has changed, and with it has come curiosity as to the origins of computing and the inevitable question about 'who invented it'. Alan's involvement in the early days of computing became better known, not just as the person who wrote the paper on *Computable Numbers*, but as a designer of machinery at Bletchley and then later as a leading figure at the NPL and Manchester University.

What has remained more obscure is the work which Alan did towards the end of his life on animals and plants. The obscurity can only partly be explained by the incomplete nature of the work-in-progress on phyllotaxis. We need to look elsewhere to see why his ideas did not catch on. Perhaps it was because – as Alan foresaw – biologists have a tendency to be allergic to mathematics, or perhaps more accurately the time required to understand partial differential equations is a distraction from doing experiments, getting results, and finding funding for a research programme. However, I suspect there is more to it than that. Maybe it is because of an immense discovery in Cambridge towards the end of Alan's life: the famous paper by Watson and Crick on the double-helix structure of DNA was published in *Nature* on 25 April 1953. Their work was based on the reading, through computer-generated contour maps, of X-ray crystallographs, as described by Kendrew and Bennett in their lecture to the Manchester computer conference in July 1951.

The discovery of the structure of DNA created a new science, in the same way that Alan's pioneering work on computing machinery did. Molecular biology almost constituted a reverse takeover of the biological sciences, so that an air of invalidity or irrelevance hung over traditional methods of investigation, particularly as regards questions concerning development of organisms and evolution. Alan's ideas were theoretical, not experimental, did not depend on genetics, and were buried. Other theories concerning pattern formation came into the ascendant, notably the model advanced by Professor Lewis Wolpert that 'positional information' derived from a gradient of increasing concentration of a morphogen could explain a good deal about how developing organisms 'know' how to grow a limb in a particular place. However, experiments done in the last few years have pointed to weaknesses in the Wolpert model which can better be explained using Turing's model of reaction and diffusion. The story seems reminiscent of the debate on Bayesian statistics, used by Alan and I.J. Good in the attack on the U-boat codes, despite the use of such a technique being faintly subversive and at risk of being disparaged by the establishment. Biologists, dependent on peer-review for their publications, and needing to swim close to the mainstream to have their grant proposals accepted, cannot depart too radically from current orthodoxy. Nowadays, however, biologists are keen to have the authority of Alan Turing behind their plans and discoveries. Everyone wants to adopt Alan Turing now.

The more people found out about Alan, the more they became interested in his life story and the incredible – by the standards of the twenty-first century – official reaction to Alan's lifestyle. The mystery surrounding his final days has added to the piquancy of the tale. The British like their heroes to have had short, spicy lives, and a whiff of uncertainty adds intrigue to the recipe. Blue plaques and statues have sprung up everywhere. Ring roads have been named and documentaries made. Perhaps the most remarkable adoption has been by successive British governments of alternate political colours: first an apology under Gordon Brown's premiership, and later a (more controversial) Royal Pardon under David Cameron's. (The Pardon is very curious: one of the many reasons why one might find it questionable is to be found in that part of the Criminal Justice Act 1948 mentioned earlier, which said the conviction 'shall be deemed not to be a conviction' – so Alan Turing had no criminal record, and nothing remained for which he could actually be pardoned.) The

Brown government statement, which is far less odd than the Pardon, reads in part as follows:

> Thousands of people have come together to demand justice for Alan Turing and recognition of the appalling way he was treated. While Turing was dealt with under the law of the time, and we can't put the clock back, his treatment was of course utterly unfair, and I am pleased to have the chance to say how deeply sorry I and we all are for what happened to him. Alan and the many thousands of other gay men who were convicted, as he was convicted, under homophobic laws, were treated terribly. Over the years, millions more lived in fear [of] conviction.
>
> It is thanks to men and women who were totally committed to fighting fascism, people like Alan Turing, that the horrors of the Holocaust and of total war are part of Europe's history and not Europe's present. So on behalf of the British government, and all those who live freely thanks to Alan's work, I am very proud to say: we're sorry. You deserved so much better.
>
> Gordon Brown

This is, however, not the place to debate the relative merits of apologies and pardons. Perhaps we should remember that Alan Turing's life was not, except perhaps towards the end, governed by his sexuality. The dominant passions in his life were his ideas; it is those for which he should be remembered, and for them no apology is needed.

NOTES

References with AMT prefixes attributed to the King's College Archive and no further details are © the Estate of P.N. Furbank and reproduced by kind permission of Professor W.R. Owens and the Provost and Scholars of King's College, Cambridge. Visit www.turingarchive.org/browse.php.

References to TNA are to the UK National Archives (and should be assumed to be Crown copyright) and references to NARA are to the US National Archives Records Administration.

Chapter 1

1 F.W. Blagdon, *A Brief History of Ancient and Modern India*, Edward Orme (1805).
2 On Stoney Bowes, see Jesse Foot, *The Lives of Andrew Robinson Bowes, Esq. and the Countess of Strathmore, written from thirty-three years professional attendance, from letters, and other well authenticated documents*, Becket and Porter (*c.* 1815).
3 John Turing, 'The Half Was Not Told Me', unpublished autobiography (1967); other quotations of John Turing are also from this source.
4 Quoted by A.K. Clarke, *A History of the Cheltenham Ladies' College 1853–1953*, Faber & Faber (1953).

Chapter 2

1 Quotations of John Turing are from *op. cit.*, and other personal papers.
2 Maud Diver, *The Englishwoman in India*, Blackwood (1909).
3 See the splendid study of Raj families and their pressures by Elizabeth Buettner: *Empire Families*, Oxford University Press (2004).
4 Vyvyen Brendon, *Children of the Raj*, Weidenfeld & Nicolson (2005).
5 Quotations of Sara Turing are taken from her *Alan M. Turing*, W. Heffer & Sons (1959).
6 *Hazelhurst Gazette*, January 1921.
7 All Alan Turing's letters to his mother are in the King's College Alan Turing Archive, reference AMT/K/1. Visit www.turingarchive.org/browse.php.

Chapter 3

1 O'Hanlon (nickname 'Teacher') was Alan's housemaster. Supervised homework sessions, called 'prep' at most boarding schools, are called 'hall' at Sherborne. As to the jam, the words are interlineated above the crossed-out passage. The word shown by [??] is illegible. It's not surprising that Ethel was exasperated at Alan's untidy, blotted, unintelligible scrawl. Was she supposed to send rations or not? This and other quotations from Alan Turing's letters are from the King's College Alan Turing Archive, reference AMT/K/1.
2 See Elizabeth Buettner, *op. cit.*
3 Board of Education Report.
4 Head Master's Report to the Governors for 1909.
5 Sara Turing, *op. cit.* (1959).
6 Extracts from school reports are courtesy of Sherborne School Archive.
7 Quotations of John Turing are from 'My Brother Alan', in Sara Turing, *Alan M. Turing*, Centenary Edition, Cambridge University Press (2012).
8 O'Hanlon confounded everyone by getting married in 1933 at the age of 48 and producing a family of four children.
9 A.B. Gourlay, *A History of Sherborne School*, Warren & Son (1951).
10 Sara Turing, *op. cit.* (1959).

11 'Victor Cannon-Brookes, C.C.M.: A Memoir', unpublished; with thanks
to Christopher Morcom QC.

12 This and the following quotation from A.H. Trelawny-Ross, 'Christopher
Morcom', unpublished, Sherborne School Archive (*c.* 1930).

13 Alan Turing, 'Impressions of Chris', prepared for Mrs Morcom *c.* 1930;
with thanks to Christopher Morcom QC.

14 D.B. Eperson, 'Educating a Mathematical Genius', *The Shirburnian*, Trinity
(1993).

15 Transcript by Ethel Turing in Sherborne School Archive.

16 Sherborne School Archive; with much gratitude to Rachel Hassall.

Chapter 4

1 John Turing, *op. cit.*, and other personal papers.

2 Mary E. Swan and Kenneth R. Swan, *Sir Joseph Wilson Swan FRS*, Second
Edition, Oriel Press (1968).

3 Quotations from Mrs Morcom's diary, and Ethel Turing's and Alan
Turing's letters to Mrs Morcom by kind permission of the Morcom
family.

4 This and following quotation from the KCBC Captain's book, by kind
permission of the officers of the King's College Boat Club and the
Provost and Scholars of King's College, Cambridge.

5 Roughly taking the following form:

PROTAGONIST: His cigar is a sight and he stays up all night.

ASSEMBLY: Vive la compagnie!

PROTAGONIST: And his blood sweat and tears will give Hitler a fright.

ASSEMBLY: Vive la compagnie!

Vive-la, vive-la, vive la reine,

Vive-la, vive-la, vive le roi,

Vive-la, vive-la, vive l'esprit,

Vive la compagnie!

The Assembly then calls out their guess as to the subject of the Vive-la
(which ought to be obvious, though more acidic wit is expected than in
this feeble example). Other varieties of this traditional drinking (or boy
scout) song are less raucous.

6 Goldsworthy Lowes Dickinson, quoted by Patrick Wilkinson, *A Century of King's 1873–1972*, King's College, Cambridge (1980).

7 Julie Anne Tadeo, 'Plato's Apostles: Edwardian Cambridge and the "New Style of Love"', *Journal of the History of Sexuality*, Vol. 8, No. 2, pp. 196–228, University of Texas Press (October 1997).

8 King's encouraged students to return to college for a few weeks' informal study in a 'Long Vacation Term', which Alan means by the jargon 'the long'; the 'Mays' were second-year exams.

9 Wilkinson, *op. cit.*

10 John Turing, 'My Brother Alan', in Sara Turing, *op. cit.* (2012).

11 Wilkinson, *op. cit.*

12 The dissertation reports are from the King's College Archive KCAC/4/11/2, by kind permission of the Provost and Scholars of King's College, Cambridge.

Chapter 5

1 M.H.A. Newman, interview with Brian Randell (1975).

2 M.H.A. Newman, recorded interview, cassette No. 14, 'Pioneers of Computing' series, Science Museum Archive (1976).

3 This and other letters to Mother are in the King's College Archive, AMT/K/1.

4 A.M. Turing, 'On Computable Numbers, with an Application to the Entscheidungsproblem', *Proceedings of the London Mathematical Society*, Series 2, Vol. 42, pp. 230–65 (1937).

5 Alonzo Church papers, Princeton University Library RBSC, Box 20, Folder 6.

6 A.M. Turing, 'Solvable and Unsolvable Problems', *Science News*, Vol. 31, pp. 7–23 (1954).

7 Quotations from Mrs Morcom's diary by kind permission of the Morcom family.

8 'V' is Veronica Durrant, Isobel Morcom's assistant; 'Chris's window' refers to a memorial window installed in the local church by the Morcoms; 'Rupert' was Christopher's older brother.

9 Herbert B. Enderton, 'Alonzo Church: Life and Work', in *Collected Works of Alonzo Church*, MIT Press (online preprint available at UCLA).

10 Dean of Rochester, later Bishop of Bath and Wells, and an acquaintance of Ethel Turing.

11 *New Statesman and Nation*, 16 January 1937, p. 100.

12 Reproduced from S. Barry Cooper and Jan Van Leeuwen (eds), *Alan Turing: His Work and Impact*, Elsevier (2013).

13 Quoted in Andrew Hodges, *Alan Turing: The Enigma*, Burnett Books (1983).

14 'Princeton Mathematics Community in the 1930s', Transcript No. 5, Mudd Manuscript Library, Princeton University (1984).

15 King's Archive AMT/D/12. By kind permission of the Provost and Scholars of King's College, Cambridge.

16 King's Archive AMT/A/8. By kind permission of the Provost and Scholars of King's College, Cambridge.

17 Solomon Feferman, 'Turing's Thesis: Ordinal Logics and Oracle Computability', in S. Barry Cooper and Jan Van Leeuwen (eds), *op. cit.* (2013).

18 Patrick Wilkinson, 'Italian Naval Decrypts', Chapter 6 in F.H. Hinsley and Alan Stripp (eds), *Codebreakers: The Inside Story of Bletchley Park*, Oxford University Press (1993).

19 See Ludwig Wittgenstein, *Lectures on the Foundations of Mathematics*, ed. Cora Diamond, Harvester Press (1976).

20 A.M. Turing, Proposal for Royal Society grant, 24 March 1939.

21 Quoted in Brian Randell, 'On Alan Turing and the Origins of Digital Computers', in B. Meltzer and D. Michie (eds), *Machine Intelligence 7*, Edinburgh University Press (1972).

Chapter 6

1 This quotation and the longer passage below from TNA HW 62/21/7.

2 Landis Gores, *Ultra: I Was There*, Lulu Publishing Inc. (2008).

3 TNA FO 366/1059.

4 Quoted by Mavis Batey, *Dilly: The Man Who Broke Enigma*, Dialogue (2009). The capitalised terms (probably, and insofar as I can decode them) mean: Hutsix – Hut 6 at Bletchley was where German Army and Air Force Enigma messages were attacked; Wranglercoves – Cambridge mathematicians; Cyc – the cyclometer was a Polish device for identifying

rotor combinations which could produce 'females' (duplicated letters in
the message setting); Jeffreybrows, Babbage – J.R.F. Jeffreys and Dennis
Babbage, both Cambridge mathematicians; Netz – perforated cardboard
sheets; Umkehrwalze – reflector device in the Enigma machine;
Unconfirmed female – 'females' which might have arisen by chance,
rather than as part of the characteristic patterns driven by the choice
of rotors; Cottagecrowd – Knox's Enigma research section based in the
stable yard cottages at Bletchley Park; Registrators – the team who logged
and recorded intercepts; Cillis – instances where the ground and message
settings were chosen by the Enigma operator as a predictable sequence
or word, such as HIT and LER or ABC and DEF; Fosssheets – a 'paper'
version of Enigma wirings authored by Hugh Foss is at TNA HW 25/14;
Dillied – a self-deprecating reference to Knox's unorthodox behaviour;
Ringstellung – the position of the adjustable outer ring around each
Enigma rotor; Stecker – plugboard connection; Broke – found the
settings; Blue – a family of Enigma settings used by the Luftwaffe for
practice messages; Josh – J.E.S. Cooper, head of Bletchley's Air Section;
Luftgau – an administrative organisation in the Luftwaffe. The other terms
remain a mystery, to me at least.

5 C.H.O'D. Alexander, *Cryptographic History of Work on the German Naval Enigma*, TNA HW 25/1 (undated, probably 1945).
6 'Daughters of two members of [Denniston's] Ashtead golf club whom he knew well', recruited in August 1939.
7 Batey, *op. cit.* The description of Claire Harding and Elizabeth Grainger is from the same source.
8 Alan's letters to Mother are in the King's College Archive, AMT/K/1.
9 This and the first quotation in the bullets are from John Turing, 'My Brother Alan', in Sara Turing, *op. cit.* (2012).
10 Donald Michie joined Bletchley Park in 1942 and later became Professor of Machine Intelligence at Edinburgh University.
11 Sara Turing, *op. cit.* (1959).
12 Donald Michie, interview with Brian Randell (1975); I.J. Good, 'Pioneering Work on Computers at Bletchley', in N. Metropolis, J. Howlett and Gian-Carlo Rota (eds), *A History of Computing in the Twentieth Century*, Academic Press (1980).

13 I.J. Good, *op. cit.*

14 C.H.O'D. Alexander, *op. cit.*

15 TNA ADM 223/463.

16 *Ibid.*

17 Peter Twinn, the first mathematician hired by GC&CS, was Dilly Knox's chief assistant.

18 Joan Murray, 'Hut 8 and Naval Enigma, Part I', in F.H. Hinsley and Alan Stripp (eds), *op. cit.*

19 Joan Murray, interviewed in 1991 for BBC TV's *Horizon*: 'The Strange Life and Death of Dr Turing'.

20 John Turing, 'My Brother Alan', in Sara Turing, *op. cit.* (2012).

21 Patrick Beesly, *Very Special Intelligence: The Story of the Admiralty's Operational Intelligence Centre 1939–1945*, Hamish Hamilton (1977).

22 Gordon Welchman, *The Hut Six Story*, Allen Lane (1982).

23 The letter and Churchill's note are in TNA HW 1/155.

24 Joan Murray, *op. cit.*

25 Correspondence with Newman in the King's College Archive, AMT/D/2.

26 Donald Michie, interview with Brian Randell (1975).

27 T. Flowers, interview with Brian Randell (1975).

28 This and the following quotation from F.H. Hinsley *et al.*, *A History of British Intelligence in the Second World War*, HMSO (1981).

29 TNA HW 8/26, Memorandum for Commander Travis from Captain Holden, 2 October 1942.

30 NARA RG 38, HMS Entry A1-1030, Container 183. NARA Identifier 7525044.

Chapter 7

1 A.M. Turing, Report on Cryptographic Machinery available at Navy Department Washington, TNA HW 57/10 (1942).

2 This and following quotations of Alan Turing are from TNA HW 57/10.

3 The memo is undated and there is some possibility that it may have been written the year before his visit.

4 NARA RG 38, HMS Identifier AI-1030, Box 183, No 5750/441. NARA Identifier 7525044.

5   TNA CAB 120/767.

6   Dill–Marshall correspondence: TNA CAB 122/14.

7   M-228 quotations: NARA RG457, HMS Entry A1-9032, Container 948. NARA Identifier 2809364.

8   TNA HW 62/5.

9   This and following quotations relating to X-61753 from TNA CAB 120/768.

10 Donald Michie, interview with Brian Randell (1975).

11 F.H. Hinsley *et al.*, *A History of British Intelligence in the Second World War*, HMSO (1981).

12 TNA CAB 21/2522.

13 TNA HW 40/87, with thanks to the Director, GCHQ.

14 TNA HW 62/5.

15 Donald Bayley, interview with author (2014).

16 Donald Michie, interview with Brian Randell (1975).

17 TNA HW 62/5.

18 Robin Gandy, interviewed in 1991 for BBC TV's *Horizon*: 'The Strange Life and Death of Dr Turing'.

19 John Turing, 'My Brother Alan', in Sara Turing, *op. cit.* (2012).

20 Judges 16:xvi.

21 A.M. Turing and Lieutenant D. Bayley REME, Report on Speech Secrecy System Delilah, a Technical Description, TNA HW 25/36 (1945), also reproduced without diagrams in *Cryptologia*, Vol. 36, pp. 295–340 (2012).

22 TNA CAB 21/2522.

23 Adcock and de Grey letters to Newman: St John's College, Cambridge, and University of Portsmouth, Max Newman Digital Archive, www.cdpa.co.uk.

24 William Newman, 'Max Newman: Mathematician, Codebreaker and Computer Pioneer', in B. Jack Copeland *et al.*, *Colossus: The Secrets of Bletchley Park's Codebreaking Computers*, Oxford University Press (2006).

25 T. Flowers, interview with Brian Randell (1975).

26 The following two quotations are from Donald Michie, interview with Brian Randell (1975).

27 M.H.A. Newman, interview with Brian Randell (1975).

28 NSA TICOM Archive Vol. 8 www.nsa.gov/public_info/_files/european_
axis_sigint/Volume_8_miscellaneous.pdf.

29 Vierling file, by kind permission of the Director, GCHQ.

30 T. Flowers, interview with Brian Randell (1975).

31 Feuerstein materials located at NSA TICOM Archive, Vol. 8, Chapter VIII,
and Interim Report on Laboratorium Feuerstein, 2 August 1945. NARA
RG 457, HMS Entry P11, Container 45. NARA identifier 7240403.

32 Vierling file, by kind permission of the Director, GCHQ.

33 Friedman Report, 1 October 1945. NSA TICOM Ref ID A59501.

Chapter 8

1 Library of Congress, John von Neumann papers, LCCN mm82044180.

2 For sources and otherwise unattributed quotes relating to the NPL
period, see the wealth of material made available by Professors Copeland
and Proudfoot at www.alanturing.net/turing_archive/archive/index/
aceindex.html.

3 TNA DSIR 10/385.

4 Symposium on Large-Scale Digital Calculating Machinery, reissued by
MIT Press (1985).

5 Covering note by Professor Sir Maurice Wilkes on Professor Douglas
Hartree's notes on Turing's lectures, King's College Archive, AMT/B/2
(1976).

6 I.J. Good, interview with Brian Randell (1975).

7 Evans-Wilkinson interview: J.H. Wilkinson, recorded interview, cassette
No. 10, 'Pioneers of Computing' series, Science Museum Archive
(1976).

8 Two quotations from J.H. Wilkinson, 'Some Comments from a
Numerical Analyst, 1970 Turing Lecture', *Journal of the ACM*, Vol. 18,
No. 2, pp. 137–47 (1971).

9 Mike Woodger was also hired by the NPL to assist Turing.

10 M. Woodger, interview with Professor Jack Copeland, quoted in B. Jack
Copeland (ed.), *Alan Turing's Automatic Computing Engine*, Oxford
University Press (2005).

11 Copeland–Proudfoot collection.

12 A.M. Turing, lecture to the London Mathematical Society, King's College Archive AMT/B/1 (1947).

13 Remark reported by M. Woodger, quoted in B. Meltzer and D. Michie (eds), *Machine Intelligence 5*, Edinburgh University Press (1969).

14 King's College Archive, AMT/C/11; also www.npl.co.uk/about/history/notable-individuals/turing/intelligent-machinery.

15 King's College Archive, AMT/D/5.

16 Recollections of J.F. Harding, with thanks to Sue and Martin Gregory, Walton AC.

17 *Daily Telegraph* and *Morning Post*, 27 December 1946.

18 Alan's letters to Mother are in the King's College Archive, AMT/K/1.

19 John Turing, 'My Brother Alan', in Sara Turing, *op. cit.* (2012).

20 *The Times*, 25 August 1947.

21 Recollections of J.F. Harding, with thanks to Sue and Martin Gregory, Walton AC.

22 King's College Archive, AMT/D/5/14.

23 Stanley P. Frankel, quoted in Brian Randell, 'On Alan Turing and the Origins of Digital Computers', in D. Michie and B. Meltzer (eds), *Machine Intelligence 7* (1972).

24 Quoted in Norman Macrae, *John von Neumann*, Pantheon Books (1992).

25 John Todd, 'John von Neumann and the National Accounting Machine', *SIAM Review*, Vol. 16, No. 4, p. 526 (1974).

26 Library of Congress, John von Neumann papers, correspondence with Max H.A. Newman.

27 Copeland–Proudfoot collection.

28 TNA HW 64/59.

29 M.H.A. Newman, interview with Brian Randell (1975).

30 Copeland–Proudfoot collection.

31 F.C. Williams, 'Early Computers at Manchester University', *The Radio and Electronic Engineer*, Vol. 45, No. 7, pp. 327–31 (1975).

32 F.C. Williams, quoted in Brian Randell, 'On Alan Turing and the Origins of Digital Computers', in B. Meltzer and D. Michie (eds), *Machine Intelligence 7*, Edinburgh University Press (1972).

33 M.H.A. Newman, interview with Brian Randell (1975).

34 *The Times*, 11 June 1949.

35 Geoffrey Jefferson, 'The Mind of Mechanical Man', *BMJ*, Vol. 1, No. 4616, pp. 1105–10 (25 June 1949).

36 Letter from Lyn Newman to a friend, quoted in William Newman, 'Alan Turing Remembered', *Communications of the ACM*, Vol. 55, No. 12, pp. 39–40 (2012).

37 Newman and Trethowan letters: *The Times*, 14 June 1949.

38 This and the following quotation from Maurice Wilkes, *Memoirs of a Computer Pioneer*, MIT Press (1985).

39 'Computing Machinery and Intelligence', *Mind*, Vol. 59, pp. 433–60 (1950).

40 Robin Gandy, 'Human Versus Mechanical Intelligence', in Peter Millican and Andy Clark (eds), *Machines and Thought*, Oxford University Press (1996).

41 'Computing Machinery and Intelligence'.

42 King's College Archive, AMT/B/6.

Chapter 9

1 R.K. Livesey, *Minimum Weight Design: Memories of Alan Turing*, King's College Archive, AMT/C/33 (2001).

2 Christopher Strachey, 'The "Thinking" Machine', *Encounter*, Vol. 13, pp. 25–31 (1954).

3 Donald Michie, quoted by Sara Turing, *op. cit.* (1959).

4 Shaun Wylie was another codebreaker from Bletchley Park.

5 Good–Turing correspondence: King's College Archive, AMT/D/7.

6 David Champernowne, quoted by Sara Turing, *op. cit.* (1959).

7 Norbert Wiener, *Cybernetics or Control and Communication in the Animal and the Machine*, MIT Press (1948).

8 For quotations and references relating to the Ratio Club, see Phil Husbands and Owen Holland, 'The Ratio Club: A Hub of British Cybernetics', in P. Husbands, M. Wheeler and O. Holland, *The Mechanical Mind in History*, MIT Press (2008).

9 Young–Turing correspondence: King's College Archive, AMT/D/5 and AMT/K/1/78.

10 Science Museum Library, NPL Woodger Collection, file M15.

11 King's College Archive, AMT/A/30.

12 King's College Archive, AMT/D/13.

13 This and the following two quotations are from A.M. Turing, 'The Chemical Basis of Morphogenesis', *Philosophical Transactions of the Royal Society B*, Vol. 237, pp. 37–72 (1952).

14 King's College Archive, AMT/D/5.

15 Newman paper in Report of Manchester University Computer Inaugural Conference, Manchester University Archives, NAHC/MUC/2/D3.

Chapter 10

1 John Turing, 'My Brother Alan', in Sara Turing, *op. cit.* (2012).

2 *Alderley, Knutsford and Wilmslow Advertiser*, 29 February 1952.

3 Indictment of Harold Thacker, Chester Archives, Court records QJF 380/2.

4 *Alderley, Knutsford and Wilmslow Advertiser*, 29 February 1952.

5 Alan Turing letters to Norman Routledge: King's College Archive, AMT/D/14a.

6 King's College Archive, AMT/D/15.

7 L. Radzinowicz (ed.), *English Studies in Criminal Science*, Vol. IX, *Sexual Offences*, Macmillan (1957).

8 H. Montgomery Hyde, *The Other Love*, Heinemann (1970).

9 Hansard, HC Deb, 3 December 1953, Vol. 521, Cols 1295–9.

10 John Turing, 'My Brother Alan', in Sara Turing, *op. cit.* (2012).

11 Cheshire Archives Quarter Sessions Minute Book 1947–1955 (reference QJB 4/83). Further details of the Turing/Murray trial are in QJF 380/2.

12 *Alderley, Knutsford and Wilmslow Advertiser*, 4 April 1952.

13 Quarter Sessions Book for 31 March 1952, Cheshire Record Office, QJB 4/83.

14 Report of the Committee on Homosexual Offences and Prostitution, Cmnd 247 (1957) (the Wolfenden Report).

15 Criminal Justice Act 1948.

16 Desmond Curran and Denis Parr, 'Homosexuality: An Analysis of 100 Male Cases Seen in Private Practice', *BMJ*, Vol. 1, No. 5022, pp. 797–801 (1957).

17 F.H. Taylor, 'Homosexual Offences and Their Relation to Psychotherapy', *BMJ*, Vol. 2, No. 4526, pp. 525–9 (1947).

18 Cited in the Wolfenden Report, almost certainly a reference to Dr Woodward's study (infra).

19 Max Grünhut, *Probation and Mental Treatment*, Tavistock Publications (1963).

20 M.J. MacCulloch and M.P. Feldman, 'Aversion Therapy in Management of 43 Homosexuals', *BMJ*, Vol. 2, No. 5552, pp. 594–7 (1967).

21 Timothy F. Murphy, 'Redirecting Sexual Orientation: Techniques and Justifications', *Journal of Sex Research*, Vol. 29, No. 4, pp. 501–23 (1992).

22 F.L. Golla and R. Sessions Hodge, 'Hormone Treatment of the Sexual Offender', *The Lancet*, 11 June 1949, pp. 1006–7.

23 Mary Woodward, 'The Diagnosis and Treatment of Homosexual Offenders: A Clinical Survey', *British Journal of Delinquency*, Vol. 9, No. 1, pp. 44–59 (1958).

24 Quoted in Hyde, *op. cit.*

25 King's College Archive, AMT/D/13.

26 Letter of Alan Turing of 28 May 1953 quoted by H.S.M. Coxeter in 'The Role of Intermediate Convergents in Tait's Explanation for Phyllotaxis', *Journal of Algebra*, Vol. 20, pp. 167–75 (1972).

27 Alan Garner interview available at www.ttbook.org/listen/57686.

28 William Newman, *op. cit.*

29 William Newman's older brother.

30 William Newman, 'Alan Turing Remembered', *Communications of the ACM*, Vol. 55, No. 12, pp. 39–40 (2012).

31 Lyn Irvine (Mrs Newman), foreword to Sara Turing, *op. cit.* (1959).

32 King's College Archive, AMT/A/13. Much of the draft is heavily crossed out and some words are difficult to read. The (editorial) symbol ^ denotes a word or passage which Alan deleted and which might affect the sense. Andrew Hodges's transcript has some different readings.

33 Turing letters to Gandy: King's College Archive, AMT/D/4.

34 King's College Archive, AMT/D/14a.

35 *The Shirburnian*, Lent 1953.

36 Turing remarks to Lyn Newman: King's College Archive, AMT/A/13, and letter Sara Turing to Dr Greenbaum, dated 12 June 1954.

37 King's College Archive, AMT/D/4.
38 Sara Turing, *op. cit.* (1959).
39 Turing letters to Furbank: King's College Archive, AMT/F/1.

Chapter 11

1 'Report on the Scientific Results of the Voyage of H.M.S. Challenger during the years 1873–76', *Zoology*, Vol. XVIII: *First Part*, HMSO (1887).
2 Bernard Richards, 'Radiolaria: The Result of Morphogenesis', in S. Barry Cooper and Jan van Leeuwen (eds), *op. cit.*
3 Turing letters and postcards to Gandy: King's College Archive, AMT/D/4.
4 This and other quotations of John Turing from 'My Brother Alan', in Sara Turing, *op. cit.* (2012).
5 *Manchester Evening News*, 10 June 1954.
6 *Alderley, Knutsford and Wilmslow Advertiser*, 18 June 1954.
7 *Daily Telegraph*, 11 June 1954.
8 John Turing correspondence with Cookson and Killick: King's College Archive, AMT/A/47.
9 King's College Archive, AMT/K/6/1b.
10 Email from Mavis Batey to Dr Brian Oakley, 28 April 2012.
11 King's College Archive, AMT/A/11.
12 Letters to Gandy from Furbank and Bayley: King's College Archive, AMT/A/5.
13 Mike Yates, 'Obituary of Robin Gandy', *The Independent*, 24 November 1995.

Epilogue

1 King's College Archive, AMT/A/16.
2 King's College Archive, AMT/A/17.
3 This and subsequent quotation of John Turing from 'The Half Was Not Told Me', and other personal papers.
4 King's College Archive, AMT/F/1.

INDEX

Note: *italicised* page references indicate illustrations.